DESIGN
WITH NATURE

IAN L. McHARG

Published for The American Museum of Natural History
Doubleday/Natural History Press
Doubleday & Company, Inc.
Garden City, New York

This book was written under a grant from The Conservation Foundation of Washington, D.C. 1967.

Paperback edition: 1971

DESIGN WITH NATURE was originally published in a hardcover edition by the Natural History Press in 1969. That edition was printed by Eugene Feldman, The Falcon Press, Philadelphia, U.S.A.

9   8   7

A procession of great men have addressed my students and me during the past decade. It is their conceptions that constitute the theory of this book, but they are absolved from its errors. There are too many for all to be identified but certain names must be recorded—Marston Bates, Harold Blum, Jack Calhoun, Wing T'sit Chan, John Christian, Carleton Coon, F. Fraser Darling, Edward Deevey, Leonard Duhl, Barrows Dunham, Loren Eiseley, Jack Fogg, David Goddard, Luna Leopold, Lewis Mumford, Robert McArthur, Howard Nemerov, Ruth Patrick, A.M.M. Payne, Morse Peckham, William Protheroe, Paul Tillich, Anthony Wallace, Alan Watts, Edgar T. Wherry and Gordon Wolman.

A number of case studies published in this book are the product of the professional office initially named Wallace, McHarg Associates and subsequently Wallace, McHarg, Roberts and Todd. The study of the Green Spring and Worthington Valleys was undertaken by the former while the studies of Staten Island, Richmond Parkway, Washington and a portion of the Potomac Study were done by the latter firm. I wish to make clear that these were the product of a partnership and to establish my gratitude to my partners Dr. David A. Wallace, Mr. William H. Roberts and Mr. Thomas A. Todd, and to my associates and staff.

The research project on metropolitan open space was conducted under the aegis of the Institute for Urban Studies (now Institute for Environmental Studies) of the University of Pennsylvania. It engaged Dr. David A. Wallace, Mr. William H. Roberts, Mrs. Anne Louise Strong and Mr. William Grigsby, (all of whom participated in the Green Spring and Worthington Valleys Study,) and Drs. Anthony Tomazinas and Nohad Toulon.

Graduate students of the Department of Landscape Architecture and Regional Planning of the University of Pennsylvania have contributed their perceptions and skills to a number of studies—the New Jersey Shore, the Potomac River Basin, the Metropolitan Region of Washington and the study of health and pathology in Philadelphia.

Several of my colleagues at the University of Pennsylvania offered valuable advice and criticism, notably Dr. John V. Phillips, Dr. Jack McCormick, Dr. Nicholas Muhlenberg and Dr. Reginald Shagam.

Several clients permitted the reproduction of material developed in studies—Mr. August Heckscher of the New York City Department of Parks, Mrs. Elisabeth Rowe of the National Capital Planning Commission, Mr. William C. McDonnell of the Green Spring and Worthington Planning Council and the Department of Housing and Urban Development.

Mrs. Joan Dickinson provided editorial assistance during the writing of the book. Miss Thelma Imschweiler was responsible for the entire secretarial function, performed by Mrs. Nancy J. Chavis and Mrs. Eileen Altman. Ravindra Bhan made many of the drawings, Charles Meyers took many photographs, and they, with Derik Sutphin, drew most of the graphics, assisted by Messrs. Turnbull, Drummond, Dickert, Neville and Grey. Mr. Narendra Juneja supervised several of the studies published herein—Richmond Parkway, Staten Island and Washington—and shared with me the design and production of the book.

The printer, Mr. Eugene Feldman of The Falcon Press, Philadelphia, contributed not only invaluable services but also sterling advice. My wife, Pauline, acted as the business manager of this unlikely enterprise.

To all of these, I give full acknowledgment of my indebtedness and my heartfelt thanks.

DESIGN
WITH NATURE

This book is dedicated to

Pauline, Alistair and Malcolm

and to those who helped bring it into being—
Russell Train and The Conservation Foundation,
Lewis Mumford, Narendra Juneja and Eugene Feldman

Introduction

There is still only a small shelf of books that deals with man's relation to his environment as a whole: not only with the so-called physical universe of the planets and the stars, the rocks and the soil and the seas, but with the creatures that inhabit the earth—all the forces and animate beings that have helped to make man himself what he is. This part of man's knowledge of himself was slow to develop; for the early Greek thinkers tended either to examine man in isolation, or to examine nature without noting the presence of man: as if any part of it could be understood except through the instruments and symbols that the human mind provided, for purposes that in one way or another furthered man's own existence.

Design With Nature is a notable addition to the handful of important texts that begin, at least in Western tradition, with Hippocrates' famous medical work on Airs, Waters and Places: the first public recognition that man's life, in sickness and in health, is bound up with the forces of nature, and that nature, so far from being opposed and conquered, must rather be treated as an ally and friend, whose ways must be understood, and whose counsel must be respected. Parts of this tradition were kept alive later by the medical profession, if only because ignorant violations of nature are so quickly penalized by physical disorders; but though efforts to overcome infectious and contagious diseases sometimes resulted in small environmental improvements, these countermeasures did little to establish a healthy working relationship between man and his environment, which did justice to all the latent possibilities for maintaining and enhancing human life. Despite nature's many earlier warnings, the pollution and destruction of the natural environment has gone on, intensively and extensively, for the last three hundred years, without awakening a sufficient reaction; and while industrialization and urbanization have transformed the human habitat, it is only during the last half century that any systematic effort has been made to determine what constitutes a balanced and self-renewing environment, containing all the ingredients necessary for man's biological prosperity, social cooperation and spiritual stimulation.

The name of this effort, in so far as it draws upon science, is "ecology," a body of knowledge that brings together so many aspects of nature that it necessarily came late upon the scene. Ian McHarg, while trained professionally as a town planner and a landscape architect, might better be described as an inspired ecologist: his is a mind that not merely looks at all nature and human activity from the external vantage point of ecology, but who likewise sees this world from within, as a participant and an actor, bringing to the cold, dry, colorless world of science the special contribution that differentiates the higher mammals, above all human beings, from all other animate things: vivid color and passion, emotions, feelings, sensitivities, erotic and esthetic delights—all that makes the human mind at its fullest so immensely superior to a computer, or to under-dimensioned minds that have adapted themselves to a computer's limitations. Not the least merit of this book, for all its wealth of relevant scientific information, is that "he who touches it touches a man." And as an old friend and admiring colleague, I may even add: What a man!

As a competent ecological planner, McHarg is not only aware of the destructive role that man has often played—from the moment Peking man learned to use fire—in changing the face of the earth: he is equally aware, as many people are at last becoming aware, of the way in which modern technology, through its hasty and unthinking applications of scientific knowledge or of technical facility, has been defacing the environment and lowering its habitability. Necessarily he recapitulates, at one point or another, every part of this dreadful story: the murky torrent of pesticides, herbicides, detergents and other chemical pollutants, and radioactive wastes that now insidiously undermines not only man's life directly, but that of all the cooperating species with whose well-being his own existence is involved. If this book only recapitulated this information, in McHarg's inimitable way, it would be valuable; but it would be only reenforcing what a great many other contemporaries have been bringing out, both in individual books, like Rachel Carson's **Silent Spring,** and collective symposia, like **Future Environments of North America,** to which McHarg himself contributed.

Fortunately, since his is a planner's constructive mind, McHarg goes much farther: he demonstrates, by taking difficult concrete examples, how this new knowledge may and must be applied to actual environments, to caring for natural areas, like swamps, lakes and rivers, to choosing sites for further urban settlements, to re-establishing human norms and life-furthering objectives in metropolitan conurbations like the Philadelphia area he by now knows so well. It is in this mixture of scientific insight and constructive environmental design, that this book makes its unique contribution.

In establishing the necessity for conscious intention, for ethical evaluation, for orderly organization, for deliberate esthetic expression in handling every part of the environment, McHarg's emphasis is not on either design or nature by itself, but upon the preposition **with,** which implies human cooperation and biological partnership. He seeks, not arbitrarily to impose design, but to use to the fullest the potentialities—and with them, necessarily, the restrictive conditions—that nature offers. So, too, in embracing nature, he knows that man's own mind, which is part of nature, has something precious to add that is not to be found at such a high point of development in raw nature, untouched by man.

One cannot predict the fate of such a book as this. But on its intrinsic merits I would put it on the same shelf that contains as yet only a handful of works in a similar vein, beginning with Hippocrates, and including such essential classics as those of Henry Thoreau, George Perkins Marsh, Patrick Geddes, Carl Sauer, Benton MacKaye, and Rachel Carson. This is not a book to be hastily read and dropped; it is rather a book to live with, to absorb slowly, and to return to, as one's own experience and knowledge increases. Though it is a call to action, it is not for those who believe in "crash programs" or instant solutions: rather, it lays a fresh course of stones on a ground plan already in being. Here are the foundations for a civilization that will replace the polluted, bulldozed, machine-dominated, dehumanized, explosion-threatened world that is even now disintegrating and disappearing before our eyes. In presenting us with a vision of organic exuberance and human delight, which ecology and ecological design promise to open up for us, McHarg revives the hope for a better world. Without the passion and courage and confident skill of people like McHarg that hope might fade and disappear forever.

LEWIS MUMFORD

Contents

City and Countryside

The world is a glorious bounty. There is more food than can be eaten if we would limit our numbers to those who can be cherished, there are more beautiful girls than can be dreamed of, more children than we can love, more laughter than can be endured, more wisdom than can be absorbed. Canvas and pigments lie in wait, stone, wood and metal are ready for sculpture, random noise is latent for symphonies, sites are gravid for cities, institutions lie in the wings ready to solve our most intractable problems, parables of moving power remain unformulated and yet, the world is finally unknowable.

How can we reap this bounty? This book is a modest inquiry into this subject. It is my investigation into a design with nature: the place of nature in man's world, my search for a way of looking and a way of doing—a simple plan for man in nature. It submits the best evidence that I have been able to collect, but since evidence tends to be too cold I feel it more honest and revealing to speak first of those adventures which have left their mark and instigated this search.

I spent my childhood and adolescence squarely between two diametrically different environments, the poles of man and nature. Almost ten miles from my home lay the city of Glasgow, one of the most implacable test-aments to the city of toil in all of Christendom, a memorial to an inordinate capacity to create ugliness, a sandstone excretion cemented with smoke and grime. Each night its pall on the eastern horizon was lit by the flames of the blast furnaces, a Turner fantasy made real.

To the west the lovely Firth of Clyde widened down its estuary to the Atlantic Ocean and the distant Paps of Jura. Due south lay the nearest town, Clydebank, birthplace of the Cunarders, Empress of Britain and Queen Mary, the giants of the British Navy, Hood and King George V. It could be seen as a distant forest of derricks, the raised hulls of ships in the making, the separate plumes of factory chimneys silhouetted against the Renfrew Hills.

In the other direction, to the north, farmlands folded upward to the Old Kilpatrick Hills and beyond to the purple distance of the Campsies.

During all of my childhood and youth there were two clear paths from my home, the one penetrating further and further to the city and ending in Glasgow, the other moving deeper into the countryside to the final wilderness of the Western Highlands and Islands.

The road to Glasgow lay downhill, soon reaching the shipyards and the factories of the Clyde where men built their dreams and pride into ships. The road was an endless succession of four- and six-story tenements, once red, now black sandstone. From their roofs rose the gray green sulfur smoke of coal fires, little shops and corner pubs fronted the street for the full ten miles. Neither sunlight nor sociability ever redeemed this path. There was courage and kindliness enough but they were barely visible. Whatever pleasure might wait at the terminus, the route to Glasgow and much of the city was a no-place, despondent, dreary beyond description, grimy, gritty, squalid, enduringly ugly and dispiriting.

The other route was also learned incrementally; each year I walked out a few miles more. But the first adventures were near the doorstep. Heavy, fetlocked Clydesdales, brindled Ayrshire cows, wheat and barley fields which first flowered with crimson poppies or mustard, stables and byres, hawthorn hedges with brambles and wild roses.

The next realm was the Black Woods, not more than a mile away. Clay drumlins and small forests, meadows and marshes—the burn, never more than a foot deep, ten times as wide. Further yet was Craigallion Loch and the firepot where hikers and climbers met, the Devil's Pulpit and the Pots of Gartness where the salmon leapt, as far from my home as Glasgow was. Beyond lay Balmaha and Loch Lomond and then, much later in adolescence, Glencoe and Loch Rannoch, Lismore and Mull, Staffa and Iona, the Western Isles.

My experience of the city during this period was colored by the fact that the Depression of the thirties had made poverty pervasive and stripped the pride of many a man. But even in these sad times there were some splendid events, the circus in the Kelvin Hall, a procession of pipe bands, cheering a Scottish soccer victory with over a hundred thousand at Hampden and the great launches: the most memorable being the 534 that became the Queen Mary. As the ship slid down the stocks, the great chains raised a cloud of rust red smoke, became taut and whipped the anchoring tugs clear from the water and the leviathan slid into the Clyde. There were also theatres and dances, choir concerts, mornings spent drawing the sculpture in the Art Galleries, city lights reflected in wet pavements, departures from the great railway stations. But these, as I remember them, were interludes in a gray impression of gloom and dreary ugliness.

In contrast the other path was always exhilarating and joy could be found in quite small events, the certainty of a still trout seen in the shadow of a bridge, the salmon leaping or a stag glimpsed fleetingly, the lambing, climbing through the clouds to the sunlight above, a cap full of wild strawberries or blaeberries, men back from the Spanish Civil War at the firepot or a lift from an American tourist in a Packard convertible.

Now in spite of the excoriation of Glasgow this memoir is not the catalogue of an evolving prejudice in favor of the country and against cities. I knew Edinburgh well and was moved by both its medieval and 18th-century neighborhoods. No, this is a response to a simple choice between the environment of industrial toil which Glasgow represented and a beautiful countryside, both equally accessible. There are cities that produce more stimulus and delight than can be borne, but it is rare when they are products of the industrial revolution or its aftermath. I wish to bring alive the experiences which have nurtured my attitudes and bred my quest. It is certain that given my choices, I opted for the countryside, finding there more delight and challenge, meaning and rewards than I could elsewhere. Yet, I chose the city as my place of work, my professional challenge. If we can create the humane city, rather than the city of bondage to toil, then the choice of city or countryside will be between two excellences, each indispensable, each different, both complementary, both life-enhancing. Man in Nature.

When at the age of sixteen I found that there might be a possibility of spending a life giving to others the benison which nature gave to me, and that this was called landscape architecture, I accepted the opportunity with enthusiasm. Nobody needed this more than the inhabitants of the city of bondage to the machine. But the practice of this profession proved to be a thwarting experience. There were few who believed in the benison, few who believed in the importance of nature in man's world, few who would design with nature.

I have found that it has been my instincts that have directed my paths and that my reason is employed after the fact, to explain where I find myself. Hindsight discerns a common theme, astonishingly consistent.

I spent the autumn and winter of 1943 and the following spring as an officer with the 2nd Independent Parachute Brigade Group in Italy. The episode began badly with the sinking of the Abdiel, vanguard of the invasion at Taranto; this was followed by a period behind the lines as protector and repairer-in-chief of the great Acquedotto Pugliese and then declined into more normal patterns in the winter battle of the Fiume Sangro which culminated in the bloody battle of Cassino.

The heart of this grim episode was spent in the great valley which runs from the Monte Maiella and the Gran Sasso d'Italia to the Adriatic. It was here that the allied offensive was halted by snow and mud and the battle settled into a pattern of patrols and skirmishes. The villages of Lama del Peligni, Poggiofiorito, Crechio, Arielli were progressively reduced to rubble by bombardment from the towering German positions in Guardiagrele and Orsogna, perched on the commanding escarpment.

The days were hideous with shelling, bombing and nebelwerfers, patrolling was conducted by night in the desperate flares of Verey pistols, in the pervasive smell of dead mules, chloride of lime and high explosives. Life was an incessant succession of small engagements, dead and wounded, shells, mines, barbed wire and shrapnel, machine gun and mortar, rifle, carbine and grenades. Through it all ran the manic stuttering of the mg34 and 42 and the conservative hammering of the British Bren. The few Italian civilians cowered in rubble basements, the combatants were barely distinguishable in muddy greatcoats; heroism was commonplace, the greatest virtue was the ability to endure.

Day after week after month it continued, no sleep by day, engagements by night, cold, wet and muddy, living in one and then another hole; the attrition became serious, "bomb happy" was a normal malaise, the ranks thinned, the time would surely come, it was ridiculous to expect to survive. But, unimaginably came the reprieve of two weeks' leave. I chose to spend this, not in the established leave centers of Naples, Bari or Brindisi, but at the Albergo Palumbo in Ravello, high on the Sorrento Peninsula.

Here was peace absolute, the only noises were the sound of footsteps on the stone floors, the whispering of servants, the ringing of church bells, the calls of the street vendor. The smells were of baked bread, garlic and pasta. Near to the piazza was a garden. From this, perched on cliff edge, could be seen the glittering bay and Capri, the road snaking down the mountain to the coast, Amalfi and Positano, the Grotto Esmeralda. I sailed the bay in a Monotipo, long days tacking in the silence of small unthreatening noises, wind in the sails, waves on the hull.

This was the rural shires of Dunbarton and Argyll in Mediterranean guise. Here was equanimity and health.

After the war I spent four years at Harvard where I received assurances that I was a professional landscape architect and city planner. Immediately I returned to Scotland determined to practice my faith upon that environment of drudgery that is the Clyde-side. I returned to my home for the first unhurried, nostalgic rediscovery of this land in over a decade. Nearest were the Black Woods, only a few square miles in area but of great richness—some low hills covered by forest, the burn, marshes with a native orchid, fields of buttercups, rock outcrops, some gorse, broom and heather, Scots Pine and larch, copses of beech edged with rowan and birch, thorns and laburnum, chest-high bracken. The burn had familiar stepping stones, overhangs where small trout and red-breasted minnows lived, shaded by reeds, osiers and willows. Whitewashed stone farmhouses sat squarely with their outbuildings and old trees marking the ridges.

Larks nested in the meadow, curlew in the plough, weasels, stoats and badgers lived in the hedgerows; there were red foxes, red squirrels and hedgehogs, grouse flew from heather underfoot. It was a myriad place. Its gem was Peel Glen, for most of the year an unremarkable woodland, mainly beech, deep shadowed and silent, but in Spring it was transformed. As you entered its shade there was no quick surprise—only slowly did the radiance of light from the carpet of bluebells enter and suffuse the consciousness. Cyclists from Glasgow gathered armfuls of these, strapped them to their carriers and left a trail of wilting beauty back to the city.

I came expecting to see it shrunken, for this is the lot of the place revisited, but not to find it obliterated. Yet the City of Glasgow had annexed this land and made it its own. Each hill had been bulldozed to fill a valley, the burn was buried in culverts, trees had been felled, farmhouses and smithy were demolished, every tree, shrub, marsh, rock, fern and orchid, every single vestige of that which had been, was gone. In their stead were uniform four-story walkup apartments, seventy feet face to face, seventy feet back to back, fifteen feet from gable to gable. The fronts were divided by an asphalt street lined with gaunt sodium lamps, the backs were stamped soil defined by drunken chestnut paling; drying green poles supported the sodden laundry.

The smear of Glasgow had moved out—taking much and destroying everything, it had given nothing. This was public investment for a perfectly necessary public purpose, accomplished in the name of architecture and planning. The reasons for living in this place were manifest. It held much, offered variety and delight. It could well have been marvelous but the results were otherwise.

Lark and curlew, grouse and thrush had gone, the caged canary and the budgerigar their mere replacements. No more fox and badger, squirrel and stoat, weasel and hedgehog but now only cat and dog, rats and mice, lice and fleas. The trout and minnow, newts and tadpoles, caddis and dragonfly are replaced by the goldfish alone; the glory of beech, pine, and larch, the rowan and laburnum, the fields of poppies and buttercups, the suffusion of the bluebell woods are irreplaceable—in the gardens are some

3

desultory lobelia and alyssum and sad, brave privet shoots. The burn is buried and water now is the gutter trickle and spit.

Now housing was urgently required and this was a fine place to build; some small perception, a minimal intelligence, a leavening of art could have made it enchanting. The place was complex, but it was made uniform. It had contained many delights, but these were obliterated. It has represented much that people had come far to seek, but this satisfaction to the spirit was denied to those who needed it most.

I was too late. Memory that had been pleasure was now a goad.

I returned to Scotland with some dreams, some parchments, a wife, son, and pulmonary tuberculosis. The Southfield Colony for Consumptives on the outskirts of Edinburgh became my hospital. This had once been a private house; the ward where I spent six sweating months must have been the living room. It had seven windows in front of which were as many beds. These windows were always open even when this produced snow for pillows on the beds. Fresh air, no matter how cold or wet, was basic to the cure. The windows were filthy. Dirty words of earlier times had been overlaid with layers of newer blasphemies.

Ceilings are important to a prostrate patient: these were of Italian plaster work, deeply configured, and in their recesses were dark spider webs with collections of flies. The entertainment of the place was to watch the blue tits fly into the room and gorge on these insects. Each morning a jolly fat slut came into the ward, threw handfuls of wet tea leaves upon the floor and brushed the dust into the air. There was no heat, patients gave their hot water bottles to their brave visitors who were threatened not only with tuberculosis but with chilblains.

The spirit of the place was acrid; the doctors lived in mutual dislike under a despotic chief, the staff were sad emblems of the nursing profession, filled with sullen animosity. There were enough patients in the place who had been there for a decade or more to infuse the sick with a quiet resignation. The sun never shone, the food was tepid and tasteless, there was little laughter and less hope.

At the end of six months in this pitiful Colony, I was a miserable, thin, sweating rag, dressed in discarded ill-fitting pajamas of unlikely hues, my bottom punctured to a colander. I sustained a small pocket of air suppressing the lung, stilling it to heal but this was not enough. While I was no longer infectious, elaborate and crippling surgery was thought necessary to provide a "cure."

Purely by accident I learned that beds in a Swiss sanatorium were maintained for British Parachutists. I enquired and found that I was eligible. It was possible to escape, and this I must, if only to survive and have the Southfield Colony for Consumptives gutted, its staff expelled and a new institution created, less demeaning to the human spirit.

The day of my escape finally arrived and for the first time in six months I washed and shaved myself, stood erect, dressed with care, and when this was finished I scrutinized myself to see whether the stigma of consumption was visible. I could not see it but wondered if others could. I felt a small movement in that shriveled prune that was my spirit. My luggage was packed, loaded on to a cab, not least a file of X-rays and a most dismal diagnosis and prognosis. I was very weak indeed.

The journey to London was without incident except that it was a wonder of freedom. From London to Dover the sun shone, it was May and the apple orchards were luminous with blossom. The Channel ferry was French; I had a lunch that wakened a dormant palate. A man can walk the deck of a steamer holding the handrail without being too conspicuous, and this I did, marveling at the women.

As soon as the train left Calais dinner was served, and I decided to invest the larger part of that sum which British travelers were then permitted to take abroad in a sumptuous meal. It was magnificent and I exulted over every single course and slept thereafter as I had not for six months.

At Lausanne the train again added a restaurant car, and to this I went in the morning for breakfast to expend the rest of my substance. I ate leisurely, savoring the coffee, one cup and another and yet one more as we passed Lake Léman, Chinon, the Dents du Midi, white houses in the sun, geraniums in flower boxes, and there was Aigle, my station. But my well-being was too recent and precious to be dissipated in a scramble for luggage so I stayed watching the platform recede as the train moved through the vineyard landscape of the Rhône Valley.

The return journey to Aigle was short but it offered the possibility to test a returning confidence in some tentative conversations. The funicular awaited at Aigle, ready to climb back from Spring back up to Winter. We left the vivid flower boxes, moved into the young leaves of the terraced vineyards, higher into the spring-lit meadows and fields of flowers—soon the scant patches of snow began to coalesce and the distant peaks were brilliant white against a winter sky beyond the dreams of Scotland.

At the summit was Leysin and the Hotel Bélvèdere commanding the village below, steep alpine meadows, Yvorne and the folded hills containing Lac Léman. The Dents du Midi shone, their peaks supported on cloud. I was examined immediately—temperature, pulse, blood sedimentation rate, the sad lung peered at through the fluoroscope. But now the record was different! In a short time I was advised that no surgery was contemplated; there were no pleural effusions, blood and temperature were normal, my abandoned pneumothorax would be resuscitated, no confinement to bed was necessary. And so for six lovely months I walked and climbed, the Petite Tour, La Grande Crevasse, the Tour d'Aï, past the jangling cows to the summit, lying on shelves watching the eagles sail below, finding gentian and edelweiss, equanimity and health.

This is strong stuff—such an experience engraves the belief that sun and sea, orchards in bloom, mountains and snow, fields of flowers, speak to the spirit as well as the flesh, or at least they do to me. The instincts that had chosen the countryside over Glasgow and its entrails were only confirmed by this experience.

Every city has some testimony to perception, intelligence and art, there are oases of concern and creation. But that example which I cull from my experience is noteworthy because so much is accomplished by so little.

In Scotland when the temperature rises above 75 degrees there is talk of heat waves and the newspapers publish photographs of panting polar bear and disheveled penguins. Being of this lineage I found the American summer to be absolutely intolerable—yet it was on the hottest and most humid of days in 1949 that I found myself in New York examining at first hand those few emblems of a modern architecture which were thought in Cambridge at that time to be symbols of the salvation of the world.

My companions and I scrutinized the Museum of Modern Art garden, the United Nations and Lever House as well as other projects which almost acquired distinction and, by the end of the day we were footsore, tired, sweaty, grubby, crumpled and thirsty. We came to the last project, a brownstone

conversion by Philip Johnson. We passed through the bland facade into a small vestibule and immediately left both heat and glare behind. We moved into a large and handsome living room, the end wall of glass subtending a small court defined by a guest wing. This was dominated by a pool with three stepping stones, a small fountain, a single aralia tree and on the white painted brick walls, a tendril of ivy. We stood on a narrow terrace beside the pool, savoring the silence, then discovering below it the small noises of the trickling fountain, drips and splashes, the rustle of the delicate aralia leaves, seeing the reticulated patterns in the pool, the dappled light. Here were these selfsame precious things, but consciously selected and arrayed, sun and shade, trees and water, the small sounds under silence. What enormous power was exerted by these few elements in this tiny space. They were not antagonistic to the city or to man but indispensable ingredients of a humane environment. Equanimity, health and introspection could live here.

These experiences are personal but far from unique. There are many people who look to nature for meaning and order, peace and tranquillity, introspection and stimulus. Many more look to nature and activity in the outdoors as the road to restoration and health. The best symbol of peace might better be the garden than the dove. But there are multitudes alive today for whom the cherished scene of their forefathers or their childhood has been defiled or obliterated in the name of progress. There is a smaller contingent who have seen areas redeemed by conscience and art.

We need nature as much in the city as in the countryside. In order to endure we must maintain the bounty of that great cornucopia which is our inheritance. It is clear that we must look deep to the values which we hold. These must be transformed if we

are to reap the bounty and create that fine visage for the home of the brave and the land of the free. We need, not only a better view of man and nature, but a working method by which the least of us can ensure that the product of his works is not more despoilation.

It is not a choice of either the city or the countryside: both are essential, but today it is nature, beleaguered in the country, too scarce in the city which has become precious. I sit at home overlooking the lovely Cresheim Valley, the heart of the city only twenty minutes away, alert to see a deer, familiar with the red-tailed hawk who rules the scene, enamored of the red squirrels, the titmouse and chickadees, the purple finches, nuthatches and cardinals. Yet each year, responding to a deeper need, I leave this urban idyll for the remoter lands of lake and forest to be found in northern Canada or the other wilderness of the sea, rocks and beaches where the osprey patrols.

This book is a personal testament to the power and importance of sun, moon, and stars, the changing seasons, seedtime and harvest, clouds, rain and rivers, the oceans and the forests, the creatures and the herbs. They are with us now, co-tenants of the phenomenal universe, participating in that timeless yearning that is evolution, vivid expression of time past, essential partners in survival and with us now involved in the creation of the future.

Our eyes do not divide us from the world, but unite us with it. Let this be known to be true. Let us then abandon the simplicity of separation and give unity its due. Let us abandon the self-mutilation which has been our way and give expression to the potential harmony of man-nature. The world is abundant, we require only a deference born of understanding to fulfill man's promise. Man is that uniquely conscious creature who can perceive and express. He must become the steward of the biosphere. To do this he must design with nature.

Sea and Survival

Many of the problems that society confronts are of such inordinate complexity that it takes the greatest dedication and zeal to assemble the necessary data, analyze and prescribe. Happily there are other problems, where a very small perception can produce astonishing results. If one accepts the simple proposition that nature is the arena of life and that a modicum of knowledge of her processes is indispensable for survival and rather more for existence, health and delight, it is amazing how many apparently difficult problems present ready resolution.

Let us accept the proposition that nature is process, that it is interacting, that it responds to laws, representing values and opportunities for human use with certain limitations and even prohibitions to certain of these.

We can take this proposition to confront and resolve many problems. Let us first employ it in a study of the New Jersey Shore.

The people of the Netherlands have been engaged with the sea for these two millennia. In the uncertain balance of this state of dependence, love and fear, the defenses against the violent sea have always been known. Between the sea and man have stood two barriers, the one natural, the other its human surrogate: dune and dike. It is the grassy dune, backdrop to sand castles, ice cream carts, the splashing bathers, this most benign of features, which provides the defense of the country. Where there are no natural dunes, as in a stretch of North Holland, then Dutchmen have built as replacement their three lines of dikes: The first of these, facing the sea is the Guardian *(Waker)*, the second the Sleeper *(Slaper)*, and the last defense is the Dreamer *(Dromer)*. These are great efforts indeed to replicate the role of a simple dune. The entire panoply of organization that is the *Waterstaat*, empowered to defend Holland from the sea, its polders and pumps, locks and harbors, windmills and dikes, are all built upon the single basic foundation that is nature's gift, the dune.

Now dunes are only little sand hills, formed by waves and wind and, where unstabilized, extremely vulnerable to these selfsame forces. Yet there are grasses, sedges in Europe and marram in the United States, which are the pioneers of this environment. They are astonishingly tolerant to high salinity, extreme glare, soils lacking humus, an uncertain and oscillating supply of water. Indeed they thrive on these conditions, and as the sand piles around the neck of the plants the roots extend below ground and the stems and leaves rise from the sand. The product is a dense mat of roots, which stabilize the dune below and the leaves that entrap sand and anchor it above ground level.

In their long dialogue with the sea the Dutch have learned that it cannot be stopped but merely directed or tempered, and so they have always selected flexible construction. Their dikes are not made, as are our defenses, with reinforced concrete. Rather they are constructed with layers of fascines —bundles of twigs—laid on courses of sand and clay, the whole of which is then armored with masonry. The dunes, stabilized with grasses, provide an even greater flexibility than dikes, accepting the waves but reducing their velocity and absorbing the muted forces. In contrast concrete walls invite the full force of the waves and finally succumb to the undercutting of the insidious sea. The Dutch dikes are fitting.

In the Netherlands this information is the stuff of kindergarten classes, but in the United States, even in those areas where survival depends upon such knowledge, it does not even repose in the intelligentsia, far less the political process. It has made no impact on engineering manuals, where dependence upon rigid construction has assumed the aspect of a creed. Yet this simple information has the same relevance to survival by the sea in New Jersey as does the knowledge that plant photosynthesis is the source of all

Unobstructed wind carries sand inland.

Pioneer plant communities invade the bay side of the bar.

STAGE 1   A sandbar is created by deposition from large waves breaking offshore.

Wind deposits sand at thicket line.

Dune grass spreads along north-south line of sand accumulation.

STAGE 2   Dune formation begins at the thicket line with deposition of windblown sand.

As sand accumulates on the dune, wind removes sand in front of the dune.

Thicket and woodland plants invade the rising backdune sand under the protection of the growing secondary dune.

STAGE 3   Secondary dune formation begins as the dune-grass community is established. Sand is removed from front of the dune.

The established dune-grass community initiates primary dune formation.

Mesic conditions allow dune-grass communities to spread seaward.

Thicket and woodland communities advance north and south behind the secondary dune.

STAGE 4   The dune-grass community advances seaward to the high-tide line. Primary dune formation begins.

The secondary dune is stabilized. Dune grass is replaced by plants not requiring sand deposition.

Salt spray is reduced by the primary dune and ground level rises. Xeric thickets replace dune grass.

Woodland is established behind the stabilized du

STAGE 5   The primary dune is established and the secondary dune is stabilized.

food and atmospheric oxygen. This knowledge is linked to survival.

The dune grass, hero of Holland, is an astonishingly hardy plant, thriving in the most inhospitable of environments. Alas, it is incapable of surmounting the final crucial test of man. In the Netherlands, the vulnerability of dune grasses to trampling is so well understood, that dunes are denied to public access; only licensed naturalists are permitted to walk on them. Sedge and marram succumb to man and here then is the first lesson. If you would have dunes protect you, and the dunes are stabilized by grasses, and these cannot tolerate man, then survival and the public interest is well served by protecting the grasses. But in New Jersey they are totally unprotected. Indeed nowhere along our entire eastern seaboard are they even recognized as valuable!

The first facts about survival by the sea have been recounted. But perhaps we should begin earlier; there are other facts to be learned before we can formulate policies which can give some promise of survival by the sea and indeed permit us to delight in the special joys of the ocean's edge.

The precipitous faces of the Hudson and Hatteras Canyons and the Blake Escarpment rise from the abyssal oceanic plain of the Atlantic to the Continental Shelf; it is on this shelf (which extends from Massachusetts to Florida) that rests the archipelago of sandbars that forms the New Jersey Shore. While Cape Cod is essentially a terminal moraine with outwash plains, the residue from the Buzzards Bay and Cape Cod ice lobes of the last glaciation, and the Florida Keys are old coral reefs, the sandbars that parallel New Jersey and reach south of Cape Hatteras have more recent origins.

It seems that the processes that determine the creation of sandbars are under the control of waves and wind. Storm waves breaking in relatively deep water offshore dig a trough in the sand and cause the deposition of a low submarine bar near to the shore and parallel to it. When this continues to raise the bar above water level, a dune is formed that is immediately affected by the wind. An angle of between five and ten degrees on the ocean floor is associated with bar and subsequent dune formation. Isolated bars emerge, then coalesce as a continuous dune. The area of water between dune and shore becomes a shallow lagoon or bay.

Ensuing dune formation then occurs on the seaward side, where another offshore submarine bar is formed which subsequently rises above the sea. The intervening area between the two dunes is filled with sand by the wind, resulting in a typical cross section: Beginning with the ocean there is the intertidal zone, the beach and the primary dune (primary in defense, but secondary in time); behind this is a trough, which rises to the inland dune, which in turn falls from the backdune to the flat zone, terminating in the bayshore and the bay.

Waves usually approach the beach from an angle, the water runs over the sand and recedes at right angles to the shore. As a result the sand carried by the receding wave is transported downdrift of its origin. This is described as *littoral drift* and it is a major factor in determining beach configuration.

As a result of this, sand continues to be transported in one direction. It is southward in the case of the New Jersey Shore. Thus the northern tips of islands here tend to be eroded and will shrink unless replenished with sand, while the southernmost tips of islands are elongated. A historical examination of the shore shows that this indeed has happened.

Such a cross section reveals a number of environments, and their variations are vividly reflected in plant ecology. Perhaps the most stringent factor is salinity, particularly as contributed by salt spray. The lagoon is likely to be brackish and this too is an important limiting factor. As oil floats on

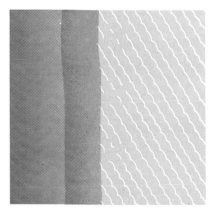

LITTORAL DRIFT

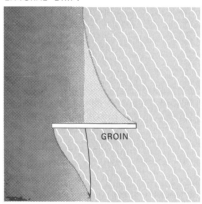

DEPOSITION AND EROSION FROM GROINS

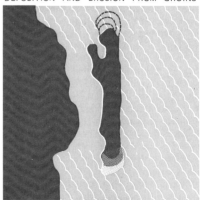

EROSION AND TRANSPORT

9

OCEAN   BEACH   PRIMARY DUNE

SAND MOVEMENT
SALT SPRAY

SOIL SALINITY
SOIL MOISTURE

LIMITING-FACTOR GRADIENTS

Dune grass

Low xeric thicket

COMMUNITY TYPES

water so does fresh water float on salt water. There is then a prism of fresh water within the dune, but it responds to tides and rises and falls twice each day. This falling of the water level will be more serious on the dunes than in the trough or the bayshore. The problem of onshore winds, combined with salt spray, is yet another environmental factor. As a consequence the foredune will be more exposed than the backdune, the sheltered trough and back of the inland dune will offer the most protected locations. In response to these variations of environment, plants occupy selected locations and create a mosaic of associations. But they are all responsive to the onshore wind with its attend-

ant sea spray and so the tips of the tallest plants conform to the profile of the wind initiated by the primary dune.

Salt spray and sand movement will present the greatest problem at the beach and reduce towards the bay; soil moisture and soil salinity are lowest at the beach and increase towards the bay.

As the dune begins to form, the marram grasses colonize it and enhance its growth by arresting grains of sand. From the bayshore the pioneer is reedgrass. Dune formation assumes the form of a continuous ridge on which the marrams spread. Sea myrtle arises

seaward of the reedgrass on the bayshore. A trough is formed in advance of the initial dune, which leads to the formation of the primary dune. This is colonized by dune grasses, which accelerate its formation and stabilize it. Beach heather ventures among the dune grass; bayberry and beach plum extend from the bayshore towards the backdune. As the primary dune grows, a dunegrass savanna develops in the trough, the marram and the beach heather consolidate the original dune, while woody plant material, notably red cedar, grows in the backdune and poison ivy joins the bayberries near the bayshore. In the final stage the beach remains devoid of vegetation, but the

**Drawing after William E. Martin, The Vegetation of Island Beach State Park, New Jersey. *Ecological Monographs, Vol. 29*, Jan. 1959, p. 43.

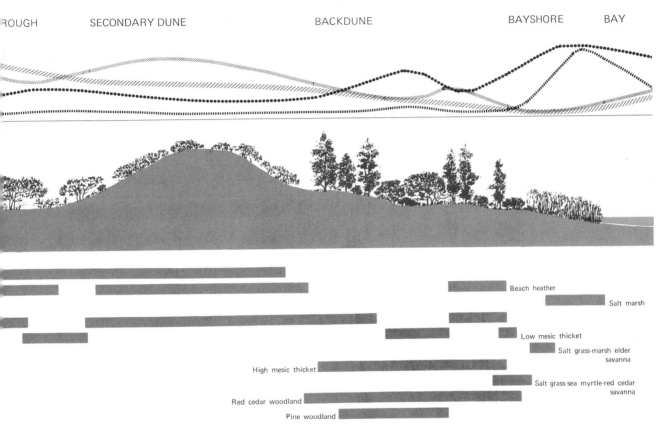

Beach heather

Salt marsh

Low mesic thicket

Salt grass-marsh elder savanna

High mesic thicket

Salt grass-sea myrtle-red cedar savanna

Red cedar woodland

Pine woodland

primary dune is a thick stand of dune grass while in the trough nestle low myrtle, beach plum and smilax thickets, which have replaced the grass. The face of the inland dune is covered by beach plum and parthenocissus, interspersed with grass, while in the backdune there is a red cedar-pine woodland, which graduates into a swampy red cedar woodland and thence to the reedgrass, thistles, and to the bay.

The ecologist describes these as plant associations. These include the dune grass association: dune grass-beach heather; low thicket of moderate moisture—"mesic" to the ecologist; fresh marsh; salt grass-myrtle; red cedar-pine woodlands; high mesic thicket-beach heather; salt marsh-marsh elder savanna, and the salt marsh.

While the distribution is likely to follow this sequence from ocean to bay, the pattern and distribution will be a mosaic rather than bands. These will reflect the variability of this environment in the most precise way.

We can draw some conclusions from this simple analysis. Unlike the Coastal Plain formed in Tertiary and in Cretaceous times or the Cambrian Piedmont, half a billion years old, the sand dune is a very recent formation. It will change its configuration in

response to autumn hurricanes and winter storms and will sometimes be breached—examination of old air photographs shows quite different water channels and land formations. During storms the bay is likely to fill and flood the bayshore and trough. In severe winter storms the sea may cross over the entire sandbar. The knowledge that the New Jersey Shore is not a certain land mass as is the Piedmont or Coastal Plain is of some importance. It is continuously involved in a contest with the sea; its shape is dynamic. Its relative stability is dependent upon the anchoring vegetation. This involves several convergent factors. The first of these is groundwater. If the use of shallow wells

11

DUNE GRASS

DUNE GRASS 6

BEACH HEATHER

GOLDENROD

8 VIRGINIA CREEPER 9

JUNIPER

HOLLY - RED CEDAR 12 MARSH CORD GRASS

lowers groundwater below a critical level, the stabilizing plants will die. On the other hand, if by the building of groins or any other tangential construction the littoral drift is arrested, the source of sand to supplement the dunes will be denied. The final point has already been mentioned—that this critical vegetation, the dune grass, is most vulnerable to trampling.

We now have a code of basic prohibitions for human use. Thou shalt not walk on the dune grasses. Thou shalt not lower groundwater below the critical level. Thou shalt not interrupt littoral drift. These proscriptions will merely ensure the perpetuation of a natural sandbar and its native vegetation and expression. This will merely sustain a public resource. We must now consider the matter of the people who would like to develop this resource. What can we say to them?

Perhaps the most reasonable approach would be to investigate the tolerance or intolerance of the various environments to human use in general and to some particular uses. The first zone is the beach and, fortunately for us all, it is astonishingly tolerant. It is cleaned by the tides twice a day of the debris that men leave, and even the most vulgar residues achieve a beauty when handled by the sea. The creatures that live in this area do so mostly in the sand and thus escape destruction from humans. So the beach is tolerant to all the happiest of uses—swimming and picnicking, the making of sand castles, fishing and sunbathing.

The next zone, the primary dune, is absolutely different: it is absolutely intolerant. It cannot stand any trampling. It must be prohibited to use. If it is to be crossed, and crossed it must be to reach the beach, then this must be accomplished by bridges. Moreover, if the dune is to offer defense against storms and floods, then it must not be breached. As a consequence no development should be permitted on the primary dune, no walking should be allowed and it should not be breached at any point.

The trough is much more tolerant; development can occur here. It is of course, more protected than the dune—from storm, wind and blowing sand. The problem here is groundwater. The vegetation that occupies this zone exists only because of the relative abundance of fresh water. Should this water level be lowered the plants would die. This could happen through withdrawals from wells, but it could also result from roofs and paving that divert runoff into drains and piped waste-water systems.

The inland dune is the second line of defense and is as vulnerable as the primary dune. It too is intolerant and should not be developed. The backdune, however, reveals a more permissive location and this is perhaps the most suitable environment on the sandbar for man. Normally this supports woody vegetation—red cedar and pine. The shade of these trees is a welcome relief from the blinding light, glare and heat that characterize the other zones. Fresh water is more abundant in this environment than any other—an important consideration for development.

The final zone is the bay. It is not well known that estuarine and bayshore environments are among the most productive in the world, exceeding those better-known examples of rice paddies and sugarcane farms. It is in these nutrient-rich locations that the infantile stage of most of the important fish takes place and where dwell the most valuable shellfish. They are the breeding grounds and homes of the most important wildfowl. In our society it would appear that there is an implicit law that enjoins all disposers of rubbish and garbage, all those who would gratify their heart's desire by filling land, to choose marshes and bayshores for their fulfillment. This reveals a profound ignorance of the values of nature; the marshes and bays are among the most productive areas that we have. Thou shalt not fill or dump here.

It takes only the shortest of reflection to realize that those environments which support aquatic and semi-aquatic vegetation are normally occupied by water or adjacent to it. Plants reveal variety in bands reflecting distance from the water's edge. Knowing this, it is not difficult to conclude which environment is owned by water and which is not. If, in disregard of this principle, the eelgrass flats on either side of the bayshore are filled, it is clear that the capacity of the bay to contain water will be reduced. We can assume that winter storms and hurricanes will continue with their normal frequency, but the water storage capacity of the lagoon will have been diminished. The water will then occupy that area which it requires, inevitably covering the prior area now occupied by building. Moreover, in the process of filling and building it is likely that erosion will tend to fill the lagoon, making it more shallow and reducing its storm-water capacity. This will lead to a larger area of the built-up land being inundated in any storm.

Thus we can say: if you wish to find a location that is likely to be flooded, then by all means fill in the marsh on either side of the bay and build there. If you wish to make a certainty of this eventuality, why, then fill the lagoon with sediments. In addition to these expectations you will also have the assurance of the least stable foundations possible. Consistency is not a very noble virtue, but it is the only one in this sad catalogue. Surely this is not the way to act. Let us rather say that marshes were not made to be filled, they constitute a present value and a real danger to human habitation.

Development should not occur on the narrowest sections of the sandbar, for that is where breaching is most likely, but in the search for a suitable environment for man we have disclosed a most fortunate situation. The width of a dune tends to be a function of its height and the angle of repose of stabilized sand; therefore the primary and secondary dunes do not occupy much space, but the flatter backdune area tends to be the widest of all the components of the sandbar

OCEAN	BEACH	PRIMARY DUNE
TOLERANT	TOLERANT	INTOLERANT
Intensive recreation	Intensive recreation	No passage, breaching or building
Subject to pollution controls	No building	

and it is here, propitiously, that the most delightful, diverse, safe and tolerant environment exists.

We could now consider positive recommendations for development of the shore based upon this little knowledge. The backdune's widest stretch would appear to offer the maximum opportunity for the concentration of facilities, be it a village, a group of houses or a recreational center—depending upon actual dimensions. There will of necessity be a highway. It will inevitably run parallel to the sea and the dunes and could well be located on the backdune. If sufficiently elevated, it could not only proffer splendid

views of the ocean and the beach, but it could provide a third dune, the equivalent of the Dutch Dreamer.

This backdune could offer protection from winter storms and could prevent the breaching of the sandbar from the bayshore as has happened in the past. In creating works like an artificial dune to support a highway, it is important that the sand be withdrawn from the ocean and not from the bay. The beach is not a very rich environment while the bay is the very richest. As Dr. Stanley Cain, the eminent ecologist, has revealed,* dredging of such rich environments can produce biological deserts.

Now if communities are established there arise the problems of water supply and sewage disposal. First let us consider the matter of water. There are resources of groundwater in the sandbars as we have seen, but the water level must not be lowered so far as will extinguish the stabilizing vegetation. This suggests that withdrawal be distributed among a number of wells. But water from this source will be a limiting factor to growth. Sewage presents another problem. The silts of the bayshore are unsuitable for septic tanks and, moreover, the employment of this technique is certain to pollute the groundwater supply. Both a sewer and a sewage treatment plant will be necessary before

*Stanley A. Cain, Letter to the Editor, *Landscape Architecture Quarterly*, Jan., 1967, Volume 57, page 103.

ROUGH   SECONDARY DUNE   BACKDUNE   BAYSHORE   BAY

ELATIVELY   INTOLERANT   TOLERANT   INTOLERANT   TOLERANT
    TOLERANT   No passage, breaching or building   Most suitable for development   No filling   Intensive
imited recreation   recreation
imited structures

development is permitted on the dune.

We now have the broad outlines of an eco-logical analysis and a planning prescription based upon this understanding. A spinal road could constitute a barrier dune and be located in the backdune area. It could contain all utilities, water, sewer, telephone and electricity and would be the guardian defense against backflooding. At the widest points of the backdune, settlement could be located in communities. Development would be excluded from the vulnerable, narrow sections of the sandbar. The bayshore would, in principle, be left inviolate. The beach would be available for the most inten-

sive recreational use, but without building. Approaches to it would be by bridges across the dunes, which would be prohibited to use. Limited development would be per-mitted in the trough, determined by ground-water withdrawals and the effect upon vegetation. A positive policy would suggest accelerating the stabilizing processes, both of dune formation and of vegetative growth. To do this the appropriate vegetation for the associations would be planted. Particular attention would be given to marram grasses on dunes and to planting red cedars and pines on the backdune.

In the Netherlands, confronted with a sim-

ilar situation, it became a matter of national resolve to reclaim land from the sea and a positive policy was developed towards that end. If this were applied to the New Jersey Shore it would involve the creation of continuous dikes and dunes facing the sea. There would be locks at these locations where the lagoon was connected to the ocean. Fresh-water flow from the land mass into the bay would be regulated as would incursions of salt water from the ocean. Con-straints would be exercised to maintain dunes and dikes, groundwater withdrawals and native vegetation.

Sadly, in New Jersey no such planning prin-

ciples have been developed. While all the principles are familiar to botanists and ecologists, this has no effect whatsoever upon the form of development. Houses are built upon dunes, grasses destroyed, dunes breached for beach access and housing; groundwater is withdrawn with little control, areas are paved, bayshore is filled and urbanized. Ignorance is compounded with anarchy and greed to make the raddled face of the Jersey Shore.

From the fifth to the eighth of March 1962, there came retribution. A violent storm lashed the entire northeast coast from Georgia to Long Island. For three days sixty-mile-an-hour winds whipped the high spring tides across a thousand miles of ocean. Forty-foot waves pounded the shore, breached the dunes and filled the bay, which spilled across the islands back to the ocean. When the storm subsided, the extent of the disaster was clear. Three days of storm had produced eighty million dollars worth of damage, twenty-four hundred houses destroyed or damaged beyond repair, eighty-three hundred houses partially damaged, several people killed and many injured in New Jersey alone. Fires subsequently added to this destruction; roads were destroyed, as were utilities.

There were, of course, other significant losses, not least the expectation of income from tourism, which is the major economic base of the New Jersey Shore. In addition, this place, thought to be a recreational resource for the region, looked a sorry sight. For the majority of people the damages were compounded because little was recoverable by insurance. Many, many people now make mortgage payments on houses that were bulldozed into the bay. Yet all of this disaster was caused by man through sins of commission and omission.

Immediately after the disaster, giant bulldozers pushed the wrecked houses into the

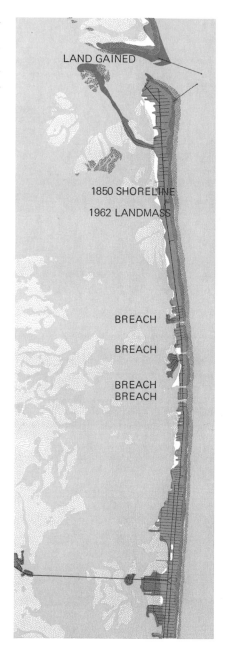

LAND GAINED

1850 SHORELINE
1962 LANDMASS

BREACH

BREACH

BREACH
BREACH

STORM DAMAGE - 1962

bay or burned them in great funeral pyres; sand dunes were re-formed, streets exhumed from under the overburden of sand and slowly houses reappeared to fill the selfsame sites of those that had been swept away. The commonest problem was the exposure of foundations; those houses that had sat high on the dune, commanding a view of the sea, found the sand swept from under them and there they stood, floors fifteen feet above the sand, grotesquely leaning, supported on their exposed telegraph pole foundations. But not all of them. In a remarkable example of wisdom and virtue rewarded, in those rare cases where the dune was stable and unbreached, clothed in grasses, the houses endured, suffering only broken windows and lost shingles.

The evidence is there to be read. The record of cause and effect constitutes the common knowledge of natural scientists. But the status quo ante is being reconstituted without direction or constraint. The future seems clear: the New Jersey Shore lies in the path of hurricanes. Winter storms are even more regular. Sandbars are recent and ephemeral, there is no assurance that they will endure. There is no reason to believe that the last storm was the worst. In the Netherlands it was a thousand-year storm, which took almost two thousand lives and caused untold damage, all but inundating this best prepared of people. What can the most unprepared people of New Jersey expect? We hope for the best, but it would be sanguine to expect anything less than disaster.

May it be that these simple ecological lessons will become known and incorporated into ordinance so that people can continue to enjoy the special delights of life by the sea.

The Case Study on the New Jersey Shore was undertaken by graduate students in Landscape Architecture of the University of Pennsylvania in the Spring of 1962 under the direction of the author. Technical advice was given to the students by Professor William Martin. The students participating were Roger D. Clemence, Ayre M. Dvir, Geoffrey A. Collens, Michael Laurie, William J. Oliphant and Peter Ker Walker.

The Plight

Thirty years ago the wilderness of Scotland looked inviolate to me and I would have been content to give my life to the creation of oases of delight in the heart of Glasgow or dream of a marriage of man and nature in new cities and towns. My boyhood sense of the rest of the world suggested that it was even wilder than Scotland. There were still explorers in those days and missionaries enough to build a stamp collection from their solicitations. The plight that moved me then was little enough compared to today. Then there was no threat of an atomic holocaust and no fear of radiation hazard. The population problem was one of declining birthrates and Mussolini exhorted and coerced Italian mothers to greater efforts while Presidents of France deplored an effete generation. DDT and Dieldrin were not yet festering thoughts; penicillin and streptomycin were not yet hopes. Man's inhumanity to man was commonplace in distant lands but had not achieved the pinnacle of depravity which at Belsen and Dachau a civilized nation was to achieve. Poverty and oppression were real and pervasive, and war was imminent enough so that I could conclude at seventeen that I had better be ready as a trained soldier by 1939.

Yet while the city was grim indeed, the countryside could be reached by foot, by bicycle or even for the few pennies that led to a tram terminus and the gateway to wild lands where no law of trespass constrained.

The country is not a remedy for the industrial city, but it does offer surcease and some balm to the spirit. Indeed, during the Depression there were many young men who would not submit to the indignity of the dole or its queues and who chose to live off the land, selling their strength where they could for food and poaching when they could not, sleeping in the bracken or a shepherd's bothy in good weather, living in hostels and public libraries in winter. They found independence, came to know the land and live from it, and sustained their spirit.

So, when first I encountered the problem of the place of nature in man's world it was not a beleaguered nature, but merely the local deprivation that was the industrial city. Scotland was wild enough, protected by those great conservators, poverty and inaccessibility. But this has changed dramatically in the intervening decades, so that today in Europe and the United States a great erosion has been accomplished which has diminished nature—not only in the countryside at large, but within the enlarging cities and, not least, in man as a natural being.

There are large numbers of urban poor for whom the countryside is known only as the backdrop to westerns or television advertisements. Paul Goodman speaks of poor children who would not eat carrots pulled from the ground because they were dirty, terror-stricken at the sight of a cow, who screamed in fear during a thunderstorm. The Army regularly absorbs young men who have not the faintest conception of living off the land, who know nothing of nature and its processes. In classical times the barbarians in fields and forest could only say "bar bar" like sheep; today their barbaric, sheepish descendants are asphalt men.

Clearly the problem of man and nature is not one of providing a decorative background for the human play, or even ameliorating the grim city: it is the necessity of sustaining nature as source of life, milieu, teacher, sanctum, challenge and, most of all, of rediscovering nature's corollary of the unknown in the self, the source of meaning.

There are still great realms of empty ocean, deserts reaching to the curvature of the earth, silent, ancient forests and rocky coasts, glaciers and volcanoes, but what will we do with them? There are rich contented farms, and idyllic villages, strong barns and white-steepled churches, tree-lined streets and covered bridges, but these are residues of another time. There are, too, the silhouettes of all the Manhattans, great and

small, the gleaming golden windows of corporate images—expressionless prisms suddenly menaced by another of our creations, the supersonic transport whose sonic boom may reduce this image to a sea of shattered glass.

But what do we say now, with our acts in city and countryside? While I first addressed this question to Scotland in my youth, today the world directs the same question to the United States. What is our performance and example? What are the visible testaments to the American mercantile creed—the hamburger stand, gas station, diner, the ubiquitous billboards, sagging wires, the parking lot, car cemetery and that most

complete conjunction of land rapacity and human disillusion, the subdivision. It is all but impossible to avoid the highway out of town, for here, arrayed in all its glory, is the quintessence of vulgarity, bedecked to give the maximum visibility to the least of our accomplishments.

And what of the cities? Think of the imprisoning gray areas that encircle the center. From here the sad suburb is an unrealizable dream. Call them no-place although they have many names. Race and hate, disease, poverty, rancor and despair, urine and spit live here in the shadows. United in poverty and ugliness, their symbol is the abandoned

carcasses of automobiles, broken glass, alleys of rubbish and garbage. Crime consorts with disease, group fights group, the only emancipation is the parked car.

What of the heart of the city, where the gleaming towers rise from the dirty skirts of poverty? Is it like midtown Manhattan where twenty per cent of the population was found to be indistinguishable from the patients in mental hospitals?* Both stimulus and stress live here with the bitch goddess success. As you look at the faceless prisms do you recognize the home of *anomie?*

Can you find the river that first made the

*Srole, Leo, *et al., Mental Health in the Metropolis: The Midtown Manhattan Study.* New York, McGraw-Hill, 1962.

28

29

city? Look behind the unkempt industry, cross the grassy railroad tracks and you will find the rotting piers and there is the great river, scummy and brown, wastes and sewage bobbing easily up and down with the tide, endlessly renewed.

If you fly to the city by day you will see it first as a smudge of smoke on the horizon. As you approach, the outlines of its towers will be revealed as soft silhouettes in the hazardous haze. Nearer you will perceive conspicuous plumes which, you learn, belong to the proudest names in industry. Our products are household words but it is clear that our industries are not yet housebroken.

Drive from the airport through the banks of gas storage tanks and the interminable refineries. Consider how dangerous they are, see their cynical spume, observe their ugliness. Refine they may, but refined they are not.

You will drive on an expressway, a clumsy concrete form, untouched by either humanity or art, testament to the sad illusion that there can be a solution for the unbridled automobile. It is ironic that this greatest public investment in cities has also financed their conquest. See the scars of the battle in the remorseless carving, the dismembered neighborhoods, the despoiled parks. Manufacturers are producing automobiles faster

than babies are being born. Think of the depredations yet to be accomplished by myopic highway builders to accommodate these toxic vehicles. You have plenty of time to consider in the long peak hour pauses of spasmodic driving in the blue gas corridors.

You leave the city and turn towards the countryside. But can you find it? To do so you will follow the paths of those who tried before you. Many stayed to build. But those who did so first are now deeply embedded in the fabric of the city. So as you go you transect the rings of the thwarted and disillusioned who are encapsulated in the city as nature endlessly eludes pursuit.

21

You can tell when you have reached the edge of the countryside for there are many emblems—the cadavers of old trees piled in untidy heaps at the edge of the razed deserts, the magnificent machines for land despoliation, for felling forests, filling marshes, culverting streams, and sterilizing farmland, making thick brown sediments of the creeks.

Is this the countryside, the green belt—or rather the greed belt, where the farmer sells land rather than crops, where the developer takes the public resource of the city's hinterland and subdivides to create a private profit and a public cost? Certainly here is the area where public powers are weakest—either absent or elastic—where the future costs of streets, sidewalks and sewers, schools, police and fire protection are unspoken. Here are the meek mulcted, the refugees thwarted.

Rural land persists around the metropolis, not because we have managed the land more wisely but because it is larger, more resistant to man's smear, more resilient. Nature regenerates faster in the country than in the city where the marks of men are well-nigh irreversible. But it still wears the imprint of man's toil. DDT is in the arctic ice, in the ocean deeps, in the rivers and on the land, atomic wastes rest on the Continental Shelf, many creatures are forever extinguished, the primeval forests have all but gone and only the uninitiated imagine that these third and fourth growth stands are more than shadows of their forebears. Although we can still see great fat farms, their once deep soils, a geological resource, are thinner now, and we might well know that farming is another kind of mining, dissipating the substance of aeons of summers and multitudes of life. The Mississippi is engorged with five cubic miles of soil each year, a mammoth prodigality in a starving world. Lake Erie is on the verge of becoming septic, New York City suffers from water shortages while the Hudson flows foully past, salt water encroaches in the Delaware, floods alternate with drought, the fruits of two centuries of

31

land mismanagement. Forest fires, mudslides and smog become a way of life in Los Angeles, and the San Andreas Fault rises in temperature to menace San Franciscans.

The maps all show the continent to be green wild landscapes save for the sepia cities huddled on lakes and seaboards, but look from a plane as it crosses the continent and makes an idiocy of distance, see the wild green sectioned as rigorously as the city. In the great plains nature persists only in the meandering stream and the flood plain forest, a meaningful geometry in the Mondriaan patterns of unknowing men.

It matters not if you choose to proceed to the next city or return to the first. You can confirm an urban destination from the increased shrillness of the neon shills, the diminished horizon, the loss of nature's companions until you are alone, with men, in the heart of the city, God's Junkyard—or should it be called Bedlam, for cacophony lives here. It is the expression of the inalienable right to create ugliness and disorder for private greed, the maximum expression of man's inhumanity to man. And so our cities grow, coalescing into a continental necklace of megalopoles, dead gray tissue encircling the nation.

Surely the indictment is too severe—there must be redeeming buildings, spaces, places, landscapes. Of course there are—random chance alone would have ensured some successful accidents. But there are also positive affirmations, yet it is important to recognize that many of these are bequests from earlier times. Independence, Carpenter and Faneuil Hall symbolize the small but precious heritage of the 18th century: the great State Houses, city halls, museums, concert halls, city universities and churches, the great urban park systems, were products of the last century. Here in these older areas you will find humane, generous suburbs where spacious men built their concern into houses and spaces so that dignity and peace, safety and quiet live there, shaded by old trees, warmed by neighborliness.

You may also see hints of a new vitality and new forms in the cities, promising resurgence. You may even have found, although I have not, an expressway that gives structure to a city, or, as I have, a parkway that both reveals and enhances the landscape. There are farmlands in good heart; there are landowners—few it is true—who have decided that growth is inevitable, but that it need not lead to despoliation but to enlargement. New towns are being constructed and concepts of regional planning are beginning to emerge. There is an increased awareness for the need to manage resources and even a title for this concern—The New Conservation. There is a widening certainty that the Gross National Product does not measure health or happiness, dignity, compassion, beauty or delight, and that these are, if not all inalienable rights, at least most worthy aspirations.

But these are rare among the countless city slums and scabrous towns, pathetic subdivisions, derelict industries, raped land, befouled rivers and filthy air.

At the time of the founding of the republic—and for millennia before—the city had been considered the inevitable residence for the urbane, civilized and polite. Indeed all of these names *say* city. It was as widely believed that rich countries and empires were inevitably built upon the wealth of the land. The original cities and towns of the American 18th century were admirable—Charleston and Savannah, Williamsburg, Boston, Philadelphia, New Orleans. The land was rich and beautiful, canons of taste espoused the 18th-century forms of architecture and town building, a wonder of humanity and elegance.

How then did our plight come to be and what can be done about it? It is a long story which must be told briefly and, for that reason, it is necessary to use a broad brush and paint with coarse strokes. This method

inevitably offends for it omits qualifying statements, employs broad generalities and often extrapolates from too slender evidence. Yet the basic question is so broad that one need not be concerned with niceties. The United States is the stage on which great populations have achieved emancipation from oppression, slavery, peonage and serfdom, where a heterogeneity of peoples has become one and where an unparalleled wealth has been widely distributed. These are the jewels of the American diadem. But the setting, the environment of this most successful social revolution, is a major indictment against the United States and a threat to her success and continued evolution.

Our failure is that of the Western World and lies in prevailing values. Show me a man-oriented society in which it is believed that reality exists only because man can perceive it, that the cosmos is a structure erected to support man on its pinnacle, that man exclusively is divine and given dominion over all things, indeed that God is made in the image of man, and I will predict the nature of its cities and their landscapes. I need not look far for we have seen them—the hot-dog stands, the neon shill, the ticky-tacky houses, dysgenic city and mined landscapes. This is the image of the anthropomorphic, anthropocentric man; he seeks not unity with nature but conquest. Yet unity he finally finds, but only when his arrogance and ignorance are stilled and he lies dead under the greensward. We need this unity to survive.

Among us it is widely believed that the world consists solely of a dialogue between men, or men and God, while nature is a faintly decorative backdrop to the human play. If nature receives attention, then it is only for the purpose of conquest, or even better, exploitation—for the latter not only accomplishes the first objective, but provides a financial reward for the conqueror.

We have but one explicit model of the world and that is built upon economics. The present face of the land of the free is its clearest testimony, even as the Gross National Product is the proof of its success. Money is our measure, convenience is its cohort, the short term is its span, and the devil may take the hindmost is the morality.

Perhaps there is a time and place for everything; and, with wars and revolutions, with the opening and development of continents, the major purposes of exploration and settlement override all lesser concerns and one concludes in favor of the enterprises while regretting the wastages and losses which are incurred in these extreme events. But if this was once acceptable as the inevitable way, that time has passed.

The pioneers, the builders of railroads and canals, the great industrialists who built the foundations for future growth were hard-driven, single-minded men. Like soldiers and revolutionaries, they destroyed much in disdain and in ignorance, but there are fruits from their energies and we share them today. Their successors, the merchants, are a different breed, more obsequious and insidious. The shock of the assassination of a President stilled for only one day their wheedling and coercive blandishments for our money. It is their ethos, with our consent, that sustains the slumlord and the land rapist, the polluters of rivers and atmosphere. In the name of profit they preempt the seashore and sterilize the landscape, fell the great forests, fill the protective marshes, build cynically in the flood plain. It is the claim of convenience for commerce—or its illusion—that drives the expressway through neighborhoods, homes and priceless parks, a taximeter of indifferent greed. Only the merchant's creed can justify the slum as a sound investment or offer tomato stakes as the highest utility for the priceless and irreplaceable redwoods.

The economists, with a few exceptions, are the merchants' minions and together they ask with the most barefaced effrontery that we accommodate our value system to theirs. Neither love nor compassion, health nor beauty, dignity nor freedom, grace nor delight are important unless they can be priced. If they are non-price benefits or costs they are relegated to inconsequence. The economic model proceeds inexorably towards its self-fulfillment of more and more despoliation, uglification and inhibition to life, all in the name of progress—yet, paradoxically, the components which the model excludes are the most important human ambitions and accomplishments and the requirements for survival.

The origins of societies and of exchange go back to an early world when man was a minor inconsequence in the face of an overwhelming nature. He bartered his surpluses of food and hides, cattle, sheep and goats and valued scarcities, gold and silver, myrrh and frankincense. But the indispensable elements of life and survival were beyond his ken and control: they could not and did not enter his value system save imperfectly, through religious views. Nor have they yet. But in the intervening millennia the valuations attributed to commodities have increased in range and precision and the understanding of the operation of the limited sphere of economics has increased dramatically. This imperfect view of the world as commodity fails to evaluate and incorporate physical and biological processes: we have lost the empirical knowledge of our ancestors. We are now unable to attribute value to indispensable natural processes, but we have developed an astonishing precision for ephemera.

It is obvious that such an institutionalized myopic prejudice will exclude the realities of the biophysical world. Its very man-centeredness ensures that those processes, essential to man's evolution and survival, will be excluded from consideration and from evaluation. We have no thought in the interminable dialogues among men for the sustaining sun, the moon and tides, the oceans and hydrologic cycle, the inclined axis of the earth and the seasons. As a society we neither know nor value the chemical elements and compounds that constitute life, and their cycles, the importance of the photosynthetic plant, the essential decomposers, the ecosystems, their constituent organisms, their roles and cooperative mechanisms, the prodigality of life forms, or even that greatest of values, the genetic pool with which we confront the future.

Yet we may soon learn. Consider the moon. It apparently lacks an atmosphere and oceans and the great inheritance of life forms which we enjoy. The costs of "terra-farming" this naked, hostile planet to that benign condition which can support life as abundantly as does the earth are considered of such a magnitude as to be inconceivable. Colonies on the moon will thus have to be small envelopes enclosing some of the essential commonplaces of earth transported as priceless and indispensable commodities. The man on the moon will know the value of these things.

But surely we need not await the confrontation with the inhospitable moon to learn a lesson so rudimentary, so well known to our ancient ancestors and as familiar to the simple societies of the world today.

Economic determinism as an imperfect evaluation of the biophysical world is only one of the consequences of our inheritance. An even more serious deficiency is the attitude towards nature and man which developed from the same source and of which our economic model is only one manifestation. The early men who were our ancestors wielded much the same scale of power over nature which Australian aboriginals do today. They were generally pantheists, animatists or animists. They tried to understand the phenomenal world and through behavior, placation and sacrifice, diminish adversity and increase beneficence. This early empiricism remains a *modus vivendi* for many tribal peoples, notably the American Indian—and conspicuously the Pueblo—today.

Whatever the earliest roots of the western attitude to nature it is clear that they were confirmed in Judaism. The emergence of monotheism had as its corollary the rejection of nature; the affirmation of Jehovah, the God in whose image man was made, was also a declaration of war on nature.

The great western religions born of monotheism have been the major source of our moral attitudes. It is from them that we have developed the preoccupation with the uniqueness of man, with justice and compassion. On the subject of man-nature, however, the Biblical creation story of the first chapter of Genesis, the source of the most generally accepted description of man's role and powers, not only fails to correspond to reality as we observe it, but in its insistence upon dominion and subjugation of nature, encourages the most exploitative and destructive instincts in man rather than those that are deferential and creative. Indeed, if one seeks license for those who would increase radioactivity, create canals and harbors with atomic bombs, employ poisons without constraint, or give consent to the bulldozer mentality, there could be no better injunction than this text. Here can be found the sanction and injunction to conquer nature—the enemy, the threat to Jehovah.

The creation story in Judaism was absorbed unchanged into Christianity. It emphasized the exclusive divinity of man, his God-given dominion over all things and licensed him to subdue the earth. While Abraham Heschel, Gustave Weigel, and Paul Tillich, speaking for Judaism and Christianity, reject the literality of this view and insist that it is an allegory, it is abundantly clear that it is the literal belief that has and does permeate the western view of nature and man. When this is understood, the conquest, the depredations and the despoliation are comprehensible, as is the imperfect value system.

From early, faintly ridiculous beginnings when a few inconsequential men proclaimed their absolute supremacy to an unhearing and uncaring world, this theme has grown. It had only a modest place in classical Greece, where it was tempered by a parallel pantheism. It enlarged during the Roman tenure but was also subject to the same constraints. When the Millennium passed without punishment it grew more confident. In the Humanism of the Renaissance it made a gigantic leap and it is somewhat poignant that the poverty of the Mediterranean today is a product of the land mismanagement that occurred during this great inflation of the human ego and the increase of man's powers over nature. The 18th century was a period of pause—the Naturalist view emerged—but it barely arrested the anthropomorphic, anthropocentric surge that swelled in the 19th century and is our full-blown inheritance today.

The Inquisition was so outraged by doubt cast upon the primacy of man and his planet that Galileo was required to rescind his certainty that the earth revolved around the sun. This same insistence upon human divinity takes hard the evidence of man's animal ancestry or indeed the history of evolution. It looks as if it will resist the evidence that man's pre-hominid ancestors might well have been feral killers whose evolutionary success can be attributed to this capacity.

If the highest values in a culture insist that man must subdue the earth and that this is his moral duty, it is certain that he will in time acquire the powers to accomplish that injunction. It is not that man has produced evidence for his exclusive divinity, but only that he has developed those powers that permit the fulfillment of his aggressive destructive dreams. He now can extirpate great realms of life: he is the single agent of evolutionary regression.

In times long past, when man represented no significant power to change nature, it mattered little to the world what views he held.

Today, when he has emerged as potentially the most destructive force in nature and its greatest exploiter, it matters very much indeed. One looks to see whether with the acquisition of knowledge and powers the western attitudes to nature and to man in nature have changed. But for all of modern science it is still pre-Copernican man whom we confront. He retains the same implicit view of exclusive divinity, man apart from nature, dominant, exhorted to subdue the earth—be he Jew, Christian or agnostic.

Yet surely this is an ancient deformity, an old bile of vengeance that we can no longer tolerate. This view neither approximates reality nor does it help us towards our objectives of survival and evolution. One longs for a world psychiatrist who could assure the patient that expressions of his cultural inferiority are no longer necessary or appropriate. Man is now emancipated, he can stand erect among the creatures. His ancient vengeance, a product of his resentment at an earlier insignificance, is obsolete. The exercise of his great destructive powers are less worthy of adulation than creative skills, but they are enough for the moment to assuage the yearnings for primacy so long denied. From his position of destructive eminence he can now look to his mute partners and determine who they are, what they are, what they do, and realistically appraise the system within which he lives—his role, his dependencies—and reconstitute a cosmography that better accords with the world he experiences and which sustains him.

For me the indictment of city, suburb, and countryside becomes comprehensible in terms of the attitudes to nature that society has and does espouse. These environmental degradations are the inevitable consequence of such views. It is not incongruous but inevitable that the most beautiful landscapes and the richest farmlands should be less highly valued than the most scabrous slum and loathsome roadside stand. Inevitably an anthropocentric society will choose tomato stakes as a higher utility than the priceless and irreplaceable redwoods they have supplanted.

Where you find a people who believe that man and nature are indivisible, and that survival and health are contingent upon an understanding of nature and her processes, these societies will be very different from ours, as will be their towns, cities and landscapes. The hydraulic civilizations, the good farmer through time, the vernacular city builders have all displayed this acuity. But it is in the traditional society of Japan that the full integration of this view is revealed. That people, as we know, has absorbed a little of the best of the West and much of the worst while relinquishing accomplishments that we have not yet attained and can only envy.

In that culture there was sustained an agriculture at once incredibly productive and beautiful, testimony to an astonishing acuity to nature. This perception is reflected in a language rich in descriptive power in which the nuances of natural processes, the tilth of the soil, the dryness of wind, the burgeoning seed, are all precisely describable. The poetry of this culture is rich and succinct, the graphic arts reveal the landscape as the icon. Architecture, village and town building use natural materials directly with stirring power, but it is garden making that is the unequaled art form of this society. The garden is the metaphysical symbol of society in Tao, Shinto and Zen—man in nature.

Yet this view is not enough: man has fared less well than nature here. The jewel of the western tradition is the insistence upon the uniqueness of the individual and the preoccupation with justice and compassion. The Japanese medieval feudal view has been casual to the individual human life and rights. The western assumption of superiority has been achieved at the expense of nature. The oriental harmony of man-nature has been achieved at the expense of the

33

27

IMPERIAL KATSURA PALACE GARDEN

THE ACROPOLIS

34

individuality of man. Surely a united duality can be achieved by accounting for man as a unique individual rather than as a species, man in nature.

Let us by all means honor the attribution of dignity, even divinity, to man. But do we need to destroy nature to justify man—or even to obtain God's undivided attention? We can only be enlarged by accepting the reality of history and seeing ourselves in a non-human past, our survival contingent upon non-human processes. The acceptance of this view is not only necessary for the emancipation of western man, it is essential for the survival of all men.

If the Orient is the storehouse of the art of naturalism, it is the West that is the repository of anthropocentric art. It is a great if narrow inheritance, a glorious wealth of music and painting, sculpture and architecture. The Acropolis and Saint Peter, Autun and Beauvais, Chartres and Chambord, Ely and Peterborough—all speak of the divinity of man. But when the same views are extended and used as the structure for urban form, their illusory basis is revealed. The cathedral as the stage for a dialogue between man and God is admirable as a metaphysical symbol. When the supremacy of man is expressed in the form of the city, one seeks the evidence to support this superiority and finds only an assertion. Moreover, the insistence upon the divinity of man over nature has as its companion the insistence in the divine supremacy of some man over all men. It requires a special innocence to delight in the monumental accomplishments of the Renaissance cities, notably Rome and Paris, without appreciating that the generating impulses were more authoritarian than humanitarian—authoritarian towards nature and man.

If we lower the eyes from the wonderful, strident but innocent assertions of man's supremacy, we can find another tradition, more pervasive than the island monuments, little responsive to the grand procession of architectural styles. This is the vernacular tradition. The empiricist may not know first principles, but he has observed relations between events—he is not a victim of dogma. The farmer is the prototype. He prospers only insofar as he understands the land and by his management maintains its bounty. So too with the man who builds. If he is perceptive to the processes of nature, to materials and to forms, his creations will be appropriate to the place; they will satisfy the needs of social process and shelter, be expressive and endure. As indeed they have, in the hill towns of Italy, the island architecture of Greece, the medieval communities of France and the Low Countries and, not least, the villages of England and New England.

Two widely divergent views have been discussed, the raucous anthropocentrism which insists upon the exclusive divinity of man, his role of dominion and subjugation on one hand, and the oriental view of man submerged in nature on the other. Each view has distinct advantages, both have adaptive value. Are the benefits of each mutually exclusive? I think not; but in order to achieve the best of both worlds it is necessary to retreat from polar extremes. There is indisputable evidence that man exists in nature; but it is important to recognize the uniqueness of the individual and thus his especial opportunities and responsibilities.

If the adaptation of the western view towards this more encompassing attitude required the West to accept Tao, Shinto or Zen, there would be little hope for any transformation. However, we have seen that the vernacular of the West has many similarities to the products of oriental pantheism. There is another great bridge, the 18th-century English landscape tradition. This movement originated in the poets and writers of the period, from whom developed the conception of a harmony of man and nature. The landscape image was derived from the painters of the Campagna—Claude Lorraine, Salvator Rosa and Poussin. It was confirmed in a new aesthetic by the discovery of the Orient and on these premises transformed England from a poverty-stricken and raddled land to that beautiful landscape that still is visible today. This is a valid western tradition, it presumes a unity of man and nature, it was developed empirically by a few landscape architects, it accomplished a most dramatic transformation, it has endured. Yet the precursory understanding of natural processes that underlay it was limited. A better source is that uniquely western preoccupation, science.

Surely the minimum requirement today for any attitude to man-nature is that it approximate reality. One could reasonably expect that if such a view prevailed, not only would it affect the value system, but also the expressions accomplished by society.

Where else can we turn for an accurate model of the world and ourselves but to science? We can accept that scientific knowledge is incomplete and will forever be so, but it is the best we have and it has that great merit, which religions lack, of being self-correcting. Moreover, if we wish to understand the phenomenal world, then we will reasonably direct our questions to those scientists who are concerned with this realm—the natural scientists. More precisely, when our preoccupation is with the interaction of organisms and environment—and I can think of no better description for our concern—then we must turn to ecologists, for that is their competence.

We will agree that science is not the only mode of perception—that the poet, painter, playwright and author can often reveal in metaphor that which science is unable to demonstrate. But, if we seek a workman's creed which approximates reality and can be used as a model of the world and ourselves, then science does provide the best evidence.

From the ecological view one can see that, since life is only transmitted by life, then, by living, each one of us is physically linked to the origins of life and thus—literally, not metaphorically—to all life. Moreover, since life originated from matter then, by living, man is physically united back through the evolution of matter to the primeval hydrogen. The planet Earth has been the one home for all of its processes and all of its myriad inhabitants since the beginning of time, from hydrogen to men. Only the bathing sunlight changes. Our phenomenal world contains our origins, our history, our milieu; it is our home. It is in this sense that ecology (derived from *oikos*) is the science of the home.

George Wald once wrote facetiously that "it would be a poor thing to be an atom in a Universe without physicists. And physicists are made of atoms. A physicist is the atom's way of knowing about atoms."[*] Who knows what atoms yearn to be, but we are their progeny. It would be just as sad to be an organism in a universe without ecologists, who are themselves organisms. May not the ecologist be the atom's way of learning about organisms—and ours?

The ecological view requires that we look upon the world, listen and learn. The place, creatures and men were, have been, are now and are in the process of becoming. We and they are here now, co-tenants of the phenomenal world, united in its origins and destiny.

As we contemplate the squalid city and the pathetic subdivision, suitcase agriculture and the cynical industrialist, the insidious merchant, and the product of all these in the necklace of megalopoles around the continent, their entrails coalescing, we fervently hope that there is another way. There is. The ecological view is the essential component in the search for the face of the land of the free and the home of the brave. This work seeks to persuade to that effect. It consists of borrowings from the thoughts and dreams of other men, forged into a workman's code—an ecological manual for the good steward who aspires to art.

*George Wald in *The Fitness of the Environment*, by Lawrence J. Henderson, Beacon Press, Boston, Massachusetts, 1958, p. xxiv.

A Step Forward

It took only the merest information to examine and prescribe for the Jersey Shore. Here the processes were simple as were their forms and the operative value was single and strident—survival by the sea. Yet can the values which nature represents be weighed and measured so that decent, prudent men can act in deference to them? Moreover—the example of the Jersey Shore involved such a dramatic threat—can the same ecological method be employed for more complex problems and less dramatic values?

The problem of a major highway presents an excellent opportunity to demonstrate that natural processes can be construed as values in such a way as to permit a rational response to a social value system. It is necessary only to abandon the economic model and the calloused indifference of anthropocentric man.

The highway is a particularly appropriate study. If one seeks a single example of an assertion of simple-minded single purpose, the analytical rather than the synthetic view and indifference to natural process—indeed an anti-ecological view—then the highway and its creators leap to mind. There are other aspirants who vie to deface shrines and desecrate sacred cows, but surely it is the highway commissioner and engineer who most passionately embrace insensitivity and

philistinism as way of life and profession.

In highway design, the problem is reduced to the simplest and most commonplace terms: traffic, volume, design speed, capacity, pavements, structures, horizontal and vertical alignment. These considerations are married to a thoroughly spurious cost-benefit formula and the consequences of this institutionalized myopia are seen in the scars upon the land and in the cities.

Who are as arrogant, as unmoved by public values and concerns as highway commissions and engineers? There they go, laden with money, offering the enormous bribe of ninety per cent of the cost of realizing their narrow purposes. Give us your beautiful rivers and valleys, and we will destroy them: Jones Falls in Baltimore, the Schuylkill River in Philadelphia, Rock Creek in Washington, the best beauty of Staten Island, the Stony Brook-Millstone Valley near Princeton. Give us your cities, their historic areas and buildings, their precious parks, cohesive neighborhoods, and we will rend them—in New Orleans and Boston, San Francisco and Memphis. Urban freeways cut white swaths through black neighborhoods but this is not discrimination, it matters little whether they are black or white, rich or poor—although black and poor is easier. Having scarred the cities, what next? Surely those areas

throughout the country that are particularly beautiful—these must be served by scenic highways. The accumulation of gasoline taxes in the Highway Fund must be expended, and the most powerful lobby in the United States is determined that it shall be so. Unmoved by the more pressing needs for humanizing cities, reducing poverty or improving education, four billion dollars will be expended on scenic highways. So those areas defined as beautiful must now be savaged. In the process scenic areas can only become less scenic.

Yet it was not always so and need not be today. The beginnings were more promising when the Bronx River Parkway was conceived, over forty years ago—the first example of a modern highway. The objective was not only to satisfy traffic requirements, but to use this investment of public funds to rehabilitate the foul river and its raddled landscape to create new public values. This it accomplished. The highway was used as an ameliorative device to improve the landscape and provide a satisfying visual experience for the driver, while meeting the clear needs of traffic. In areas where remedy was unnecessary and the scene was beautiful, the task of the highway was to intervene with the least possible damage, to exploit and reveal the visual qualities of the landscape while meeting traffic requirements. So that

31

in the Westchester County Parkway system conceived in the thirties, in the Palisades Parkway and, perhaps most clearly, in the Skyline Drive of the Blue Ridge Parkway, these objectives were accomplished. Now these were all designed by landscape architects: and it became clear that their effete concerns with such inconsequential considerations as natural beauty, historic buildings, reclamation of landscapes or even deference to topography were obstructions to the task of creating a highway system for an automotive America. So the task was given to those who, by instinct and training, were especially suited to gouge and scar landscape and city without remorse—the engineers. The landscape architects were then retained to apply balm to heal the scars and wounds inflicted on the landscape.

A plumber is a most important member of society—our civilization could not endure long without his services: but we do not ask plumbers to design cities or buildings. So too with highways: the engineer is most competent when considering the automobile as a projectile that responds to the laws of dynamics and statics. He understands structures and pavements very well indeed and his services are indispensable. But the matter of the man in the automobile as a creature with senses is outside his ken; the nature of the land as interacting biophysical processes is unknown to him. His competence is not the design of highways, merely of the structures that compose them—but only after they have been designed by persons more knowing of man and the land.

The method that has been used traditionally by the Bureau of Public Roads and State Highway Departments involves calculating the savings and costs derived from a proposed highway facility. Savings include savings in time, operating costs and reduction in accidents. Costs are those of construction and maintenance. It is necessary to obtain a minimum ratio of savings to costs of 1.2:1.0. Any qualitative factors are considered after the conclusion of the cost-benefit analysis, and then only descriptively.

The objective of an improved method should be to incorporate resource values, social values and aesthetic values in addition to the normal criteria of physiographic, traffic and engineering considerations. In short, the method should reveal the highway alignment having the maximum social benefit and the minimum social cost. This poses difficult problems. It is clear that new considerations must be interjected into the cost-benefit equation and that many of these are considered non-price factors. Yet the present method of highway cost-benefit analysis merely allocates approximate money values to convenience, a commodity as difficult to quantify as either health or beauty.

Interstate Highways should maximize public and private benefits:

1 by increasing the facility, convenience, pleasure and safety of traffic movement.

2 by safeguarding and enhancing land, water, air and biotic resources.

3 by contributing to public and private objectives of urban renewal, metropolitan and regional development, industry, commerce, residence, recreation, public health, conservation and beautification.

4 by generating new productive land uses and by sustaining or enhancing existing ones.

Such criteria include the orthodoxies of route selection, but place them in a larger context of social responsibility. The highway is no longer considered only in terms of automotive movement within its right of way, but in context of the physical, biological and social processes within its area of influence.

The highway is thus considered as a major public investment, which will affect the economy, the way of life, health and visual experience of the entire population within its sphere of influence. It is in relation to this expanded role that it should be located and designed.

It is clear that the highway route should be considered a multipurpose rather than a single-purpose facility. It is also clear that, when a highway route is so considered, there may be conflicting objectives. As in other multipurpose planning, the objective should be to maximize all potential complementary social benefits at the least social cost.

This means that the shortest distance between two points, meeting predetermined geometric standards, is not the best route. Nor is the shortest distance over the cheapest land. **The best route is the one that provides the maximum social benefit at the least social cost.**

The present method of cost-benefit analysis, as employed for route selection, has two major components: (i) the savings in time, operating costs and safety provided by the proposed facility and (ii) the sum of engineering, land and building purchase, financing, administrative, construction, operation and maintenance costs.

On the credit side it seems reasonable to allocate all economic benefits derived from the highway. These benefits accrue from the upgrading of land use, frequently from agricultural to industrial, commercial or residential uses. Great indeed are these values. In certain favored locations they may be multiples of the cost of the highway. But

highways do reduce economic values; they do constitute a health hazard, a nuisance and danger; they can destroy the integrity of communities, institutions, residential quality, scenic, historic and recreational value.

This being so, it appears necessary to represent the sum of effects attributable to a proposed highway alignment and to distinguish these as benefits, savings and costs. In certain cases these can be priced and can be designated price benefits, price savings, or price costs. In other cases, where valuation is difficult, certain factors can be identified as non-price benefits, savings or costs.

A balance sheet in which most of the com-

ponents of benefit and cost are shown should reveal the alignments of maximum social utility.

Considerations of traffic benefits as calculated by the Bureau of Public Roads can be computed for alternative alignments. The cost of alternative routes can be calculated. Areas in which increased land and building values may result can be located, if only tentatively, in relation to the highway and prospective intersections. Prospective depreciation of land and building value can also be approximately located. Increased convenience, safety and pleasure will presumably be provided within the highway right-of-way; inconvenience, danger and displeasure will parallel its path on both sides. The degree to which the highway sustains certain community values can be described as can the offense to health, community, scenery and other important resources.

The method proposed here is an attempt to remedy deficiencies in route-selection method. It consists, in essence, of identifying both social and natural processes as social values. We will agree that land and building values do reflect a price value system, we can also agree that for institutions that have no market value there is still a hierarchy in values—the Capitol is more valuable than an undifferentiated house in Washington, Independence Hall more precious than a house in Philadelphia's Society Hill or Central Park more valuable than any other in New York. So too with natural processes. It is not difficult to agree that different rocks have a variety of compressive strengths and thus offer both values and penalties for building; that some areas are subject to inundation during hurricanes and other areas are immune; that certain soils are more susceptible to erosion than others. Additionally, there are comparative measures of water quantity and quality, soil drainage characteristics. It is possible to rank forest or marsh quality, in terms of species, numbers, age and health in order of value. Wildlife habitats, scenic quality, the importance of

SUGGESTED CRITERIA FOR INTERSTATE HIGHWAY ROUTE SELECTION

BENEFITS AND SAVINGS	COSTS
Price Benefits	**Price Costs**
Reduced time distance	Survey
Reduced gasoline costs	Engineering
Reduced oil costs	Land and building acquisition
Reduced tire costs	Construction costs
Reduced vehicle depreciation	Financing costs
Increased traffic volume	Administrative costs, Operation and
	maintenance costs
Increase in Value (Land & Bldgs.):	Reduction in Value (Land & Bldgs.):
Industrial values	Industrial values
Commercial values	Commercial values
Residential values	Residential values
Recreational values	Recreational values
Institutional values	Institutional values
Agricultural land values	Agricultural land values
Non-price Benefits	**Non-price Costs**
Increased convenience	Reduced convenience to adjacent properties
Increased safety	Reduced safety to adjacent populations
Increased pleasure	Reduced pleasure to adjacent populations
	Health hazard and nuisance from toxic fumes,
	noise, glare, dust
Price Savings	**Price Costs**
Non-limiting topography	Difficult topography
Adequate foundation conditions present	Poor foundations
Adequate drainage conditions present	Poor drainage
Available sands, gravels, etc.	Absence of construction materials
Minimum bridge crossings, culverts,	Abundant structures required
and other structures required	
Non-price Savings	**Non-price Costs**
Community values maintained	Community values lost
Institutional values maintained	Institutional values lost
Residential quality maintained	Residential values lost
Scenic quality maintained	Scenic values lost
Historic values maintained	Historic values lost
Recreational values maintained	Recreational values lost
Surface water system unimpaired	Surface water resources impaired
Groundwater resources unimpaired	Groundwater resources impaired
Forest sources maintained	Forest resources impaired
Wildlife resources maintained	Wildlife resources impaired

historic buildings, recreational facilities can all be ranked.

If we can evaluate and rank aesthetic, natural-resource and social values, we can then proceed. Thus, if destruction or despoliation of existing social values were to be caused by proposed highway alignment, that alignment value would be decreased by the amount of the social costs. The physical costs of construction are social costs too. Therefore we can conclude that any alignment that transects areas of high social values and also incurs penalties in heightened construction costs will represent a maximum-social-cost solution. The alternative is always to be sought—an alignment that avoids areas of high social costs and incurs the least penalties in construction costs and creates new values. The basis of the method is constant for all case studies—that nature is interacting process, a seamless web, that it is responsive to laws, that it constitutes a value system with intrinsic opportunities and constraints to human use.

If we can accept the initial proposition we can advance to a second. That is, if physical, biological and social processes can be represented as values, then *any* proposals will affect these. One would ask that such changes be beneficial, that they add value. But changes to land use often incur costs. The best of all possible worlds would be a proposal that provided new values and incurred no costs. In the absence of this unlikely circumstance we might be satisfied if new values exceeded the costs incurred. Preferably these costs should not involve irreversible losses. The solution of maximum social benefit at least social cost might be the optimum. This could be called the solution of maximum social utility.

In essence, the method consists of identifying the area of concern as consisting of certain processes, in land, water and air—which represent values. These can be ranked—the most valuable land and the least, the most valuable water resources and the

least, the most and least productive agricultural land, the richest wildlife habitats and those of no value, the areas of great and little scenic beauty, historic buildings and their absence and so on. The interjection of a highway will transect this area; it will destroy certain values. Where will it destroy the least? Positively the highway requires certain conditions—propitious slopes, good foundation materials, rock, sand and gravel for its construction and other factors. Propitious circumstances represent savings, adverse factors are costs. Moreover, the highway can be consciously located to produce new values—more intense and productive land uses adjacent to intersections, a delightful experience for the motorist, an added convenience to the traveler. The method requires that we obtain the most benefit for the least cost but that we include as values social process, natural resources and beauty.

We can identify the critical factors affecting the physical construction of a highway and rank these from least to greatest cost. We can identify social values and rank them from high to low. Physiographic obstructions—the need for structures, poor foundations, etc.—will incur high social costs. We can represent these identically. For instance, let us map physiographic factors so that the darker the tone, the greater the cost. Let us similarly map social values so that the darker the tone, the higher the value. Let us make the maps transparent. When these are superimposed, the least-social-cost areas are revealed by the lightest tone.

However, there is one important qualification that must be recognized. While in every case there should be little doubt as to the ranking within a category, there is no possibility of ranking the categories themselves. For example, it is quite impossible to compare a unit of wildlife value with a unit of land value or to compare a unit of recreational value with one of hurricane danger. All that can be done is to identify natural and social processes and superimpose these. By so doing we can observe the maximum

concurrence of either high or low social values and seek that corridor which transects the areas of least social value in all categories. Exact resolution of this problem seems unrealizable. Economists have developed price values for many commodities but there seems no prospect that institutions, scenic quality, historic buildings, and those other social values considered, can be given exact price values.

It is immediately conceded that the parameters are not co-equal. In a given area, considered by itself, existing urbanization and residential quality are likely to be more important than scenic value or wildlife. Yet it is reasonable to presume that, where there is an overwhelming concentration of physiographic obstruction and social value, such areas should be excluded from consideration; where these factors are absent, there is a presumption that such areas justify consideration.

This is not yet a precise method for highway route selection; yet it has the merit of incorporating the parameters currently employed and adding new and important social considerations, revealing their locational characteristics, permitting comparison, disclosing aggregates of social values and costs. Whatever limitations of imprecision it may have, it does enlarge and improve existing method.

The preceding discussion has emphasized the identification of physiographic corridors containing the lowest social values as the preferred route for highways. In our discussion of cost-benefit analysis, we mentioned the role of the proposed highway in creating new values. This view deserves a greater emphasis. Within limits set by the points of origin and destination, responsive to physiographic obstructions and the pressure of social values, *the highway can be used as conscious public policy to create new and productive land uses at appropriate locations*. In any such analysis cost-benefit calculations would require that any depreciation of values would be discounted from value added. In addition, scenic value should be considered as possible added value. It is, of course, possible that a route could be physiographically satisfactory, avoid social costs, create new economic values at appropriate locations and also provide a satisfactory scenic experience.

The highway is likely to create new values whether or not this is an act of conscious policy. Without planning, new values may displace existing ones, but even if a net gain results there may well be considerable losses.

Some years ago I gave an address at Princeton on The Ecological View. I extolled the diagnostic and prescriptive powers of this integrative science. The following day I was asked to employ ecology in the selection of a thirty-mile route for I-95 between the Delaware and Raritan Rivers. The inhabitants of this bucolic region were threatened by an alignment that appeared to select almost all that was precious and beautiful—the maximum destruction to be accomplished with the least benefit at the greatest cost. The enraged citizenry constituted themselves into The Delaware-Raritan Committee on I-95. Faced with the problem, little time and less money, the method we have just outlined was developed and applied. Through the transparencies—like light shining through a stained glass window—was visible that alignment of least-social-cost. Its influence was felt and, one after another, through thirty-four alternative alignments, the proposed highway moved nearer and nearer to that ultimately proposed by the author.

To claim this as an ecological method is to flatter it. It is enough to say that it did use data reflecting social, resource and aesthetic values, but the data were hurriedly assembled and gross. Residential value was derived from land and building values that gave high social value to the wealthy and too little to the poor, urbanization was classed into a few gross categories, excluding the enormous variety of conditions within this description. Nonetheless, it offered a large measure of success. It provided a method whereby the values employed were explicit, where the selection method was explicit—where any man, assembling the same evidence, would come to the same conclusion. It introduced the least-social-cost/maximum-social-benefit solution, a relative-value system that could consider many nonprice benefits, savings and costs, and not least, the measure of scenic experience as a potential value.

Subsequently the method was employed in the Borough of Richmond in New York where, as is now commonplace, a treasured open space was threatened by highway destruction. Here the subject of traffic was not in dispute, no intersections were proposed for the controversial five-mile section of the Richmond Parkway, and social benefit was thus limited to the convenience of the trip and the scenic experience of the motorist. In this example the matter of reducing social costs to maintain social values was preponderant—but increasingly this is the overwhelming problem.

The issue was a simple one. Should the highway select the Greenbelt for its route in order to reveal it to the public or should it serve the Greenbelt, but avoid the destruction of transection? The character of the highway is not changed by entitling it a parkway but this title has been used to describe highways in areas of great natural beauty—the Blue Ridge and Palisades Parkways, for example. Here, where beautiful landscapes are abundant, there is little social loss and great social benefit. Where resources are as precious as the Greenbelt in Staten Island, this conception is not appropriate. Better, follow the example of the Bronx River Parkway and create new values while avoiding destruction of the few oases that remain for twelve million New Yorkers.

We can now apply the method to the Richmond Parkway. The first group of factors included some of those orthodox criteria normally employed by engineers—slope, bedrock geology, soil foundation conditions, soil drainage and susceptibility to erosion. The degree of opportunity or limitation they afford is reflected directly in the cost of highway construction. The next category concerns danger to life and property and includes areas vulnerable to flood inundation from hurricanes. The remaining categories are evaluations of natural and social processes including historic values, water values, forest values, wildlife values, scenic values, recreation values, residential values, institutional values and land values. Each factor, with its three grades of values, is photographed as a transparent print. The transparencies of the first group are superimposed upon one another and from this a summary map is produced that reveals the sum of physiographic factors influencing highway route alignment. Each subsequent parameter is then superimposed upon the preceding until all parameters are overlaid. The darkest tone then represents the sum of social values and physiographic obstructions to a highway corridor; the lightest tone reveals the areas of least social value representing the least direct cost for highway construction. The highway should be located in that corridor of least social value and cost, connecting points of origin and destination. Moreover, it should provide new values—not only of convenience, but also of scenic experience—as a product of public investment.

It is important to observe that the reader parallels the experience of the author at the beginning of the study. The method was known but the evidence was not. It was necessary to await its compilation, make the transparent maps, superimpose them over a light table and scrutinize them for their conclusion. One after another they were laid down, layer after layer of social values, an elaborate representation of the Island, like a complex X-ray photograph with dark and light tones. Yet in the increasing opacity there were always lighter areas and we can see their conclusion.

SLOPE

SURFACE DRAINAGE

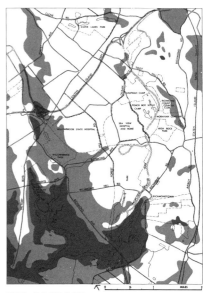

SOIL DRANAGE

BEDROCK FOUNDATION

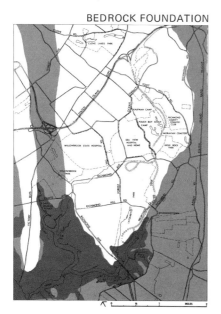

SOIL FOUNDATION

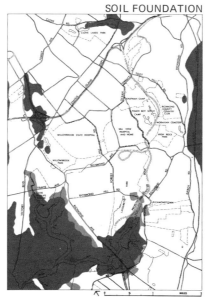

SUSCEPTIBILITY TO EROSION

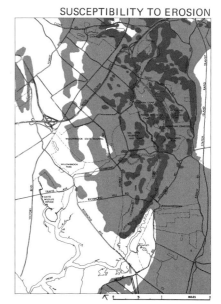

SLOPE

ZONE 1　Areas with slopes in excess of 10%.

ZONE 2　Areas with slopes less than 10% but in excess of 2½%.

ZONE 3　Areas with slopes less than 2½%.

SURFACE DRAINAGE

ZONE 1　Surface-water features—streams, lakes and ponds.

ZONE 2　Natural drainage channels and areas of constricted drainage.

ZONE 3　Absence of surface water or pronounced drainage channels.

SOIL DRAINAGE

ZONE 1　Salt marshes, brackish marshes, swamps, and other low-lying areas with poor drainage.

ZONE 2　Areas with high water table.

ZONE 3　Areas with good internal drainage.

BEDROCK FOUNDATION

ZONE 1　Areas identified as marshlands are the most obstructive to the highway; they have an extremely low compressive strength.

ZONE 2　The Cretaceous sediments: sands, clays, gravels; and shale.

ZONE 3　The most suitable foundation conditions are available on crystalline rocks: serpentine and diabase.

SOIL FOUNDATION

ZONE 1　Silts and clays are a major obstruction to the highway; they have poor stability and low compressive strength.

ZONE 2　Sandy loams and gravelly sandy to fine sandy loams.

ZONE 3　Gravelly sand or silt loams and gravelly to stony sandy loams.

SUSCEPTIBILITY TO EROSION

ZONE 1　All slopes in excess of 10% and gravelly sandy to fine sandy loam soils.

ZONE 2　Gravelly sand or silt loam soils and areas with slopes in excess of 2½% on gravelly to stony sandy loams.

ZONE 3　Other soils with finer texture and flat topography.

COMPOSITE: PHYSIOGRAPHIC OBSTRUCTIONS　　37

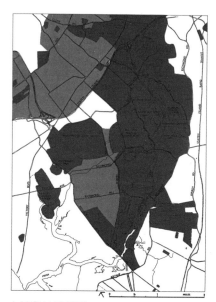

LAND VALUES

LAND VALUES

ZONE 1 $3.50 a square foot and over.
ZONE 2 $2.50-$3.50 a square foot.
ZONE 3   Less than $2.50 a square foot.

TIDAL INUNDATION

ZONE 1   Inundation during 1962 hurricane.
ZONE 2   Area of hurricane surge.
ZONE 3   Areas above flood line.

HISTORIC VALUES

ZONE 1   Richmondtown Historic Area.
ZONE 2   Historic landmarks.
ZONE 3   Absence of historic sites.

SCENIC VALUES

ZONE 1   Scenic elements.
ZONE 2   Open areas of high scenic value.
ZONE 3   Urbanized areas with low scenic value.

RECREATION VALUES

ZONE 1   Public open space and institutions.
ZONE 2   Non-urbanized areas with high potential.
ZONE 3   Area with low recreation potential.

WATER VALUES

ZONE 1   Lakes, ponds, streams and marshes.
ZONE 2   Major aquifer and watersheds of
             important streams.
ZONE 3   Secondary aquifers and urbanized
             streams.

FOREST VALUES

ZONE 1   Forests and marshes of high quality.
ZONE 2   All other existing forests and marshes.
ZONE 3   Unforested lands.

WILDLIFE VALUES

ZONE 1   Best quality habitats.
ZONE 2   Second quality habitats.
ZONE 3   Poor habitat areas.

RESIDENTIAL VALUES

ZONE 1   Market value over $50,000.
ZONE 2   Market value $25,000-$50,000.
ZONE 3   Market value less than $25,000.

INSTITUTIONAL VALUES

ZONE 1   Highest value.
ZONE 2   Intermediate value.
ZONE 3   Least value.

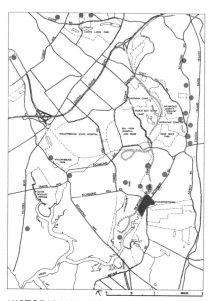

HISTORIC VALUES

TIDAL INUNDATION

WATER VALUES

38

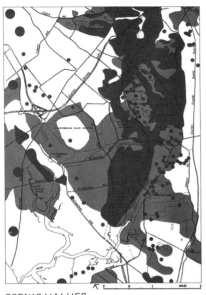

SCENIC VALUES

RECREATION VALUES

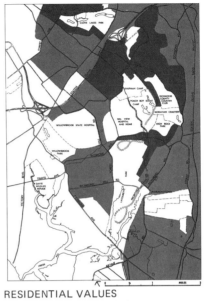

RESIDENTIAL VALUES

FOREST VALUES

WILDLIFE VALUES

INSTITUTIONAL VALUES

Each of the social values has now been superimposed. The first group of physiographic corridors is apparent. When the next factor of tidal inundation is examined it is seen to set western limits to the western corridor. Land values are highest in the Greenbelt but relatively low to the west save for the exception of a commercial area. Each subsequent superimposition of social values gives primacy to the Greenbelt until the final summation shows the highest concentration of social values and physiographic obstruction concentrated in the eastern sector. If the area of highest social value is clear, so too is that of the lowest value reflected in a broad band in the western physiographic corridor. The western limits of the zone of lowest social value are established by the Wildlife Refuge, the physiographic constraints offered by the sanitary landfill and marshes.

In sum, if the values identified and ranked are correct, the composite map on this page represents the sum of social values, physiographic opportunities and constraints. The darker the tone the greater the social cost of highway construction, the lighter the tone the less the social cost. The Greenbelt looms as the concentration of highest social value and physiographic obstruction; a path of least social cost is visible to the west.

The method is explicit in the identification and ranking of physiographic opportunities and limitations to a highway corridor. It is equally explicit as to social values. As can be seen clearly, the maximum concurrence of physiographic limitations and social values exists as a solid mass in the middle of the study area. This is the Staten Island Greenbelt. The presence and concurrence of these values is seen as a resistance to highway transection, their paucity as an opportunity. When the proposed alignments are examined from right to left, it is seen that the first would violate the highest social values and would incur the highest social costs. The second is as culpable, whereas the next two in large part conform to the corridor of least

COMPOSITE: ALL SOCIAL VALUES

0   ¼   1   MILES   2

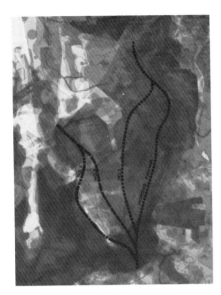

EVALUATION OF ALIGNMENTS

social cost. A propitious alignment can be found within the area defined by the two westward routes in their lower section, but to the north the least-social-cost corridor follows in a band to the west of the shared alignments.

The area free from tone on the adjacent map is the area of least social cost within which is revealed the least-social-cost corridor. Existing structures are superimposed on the map and the location of the two alternative minimum-social-cost alignments can be seen as a response to these local social values.

The Tri-State Transportation Commission reversed its decision to transect the Greenbelt with the Richmond Parkway and accepted the least-social-cost alignment developed in this study.

The Richmond Parkway Study was undertaken for the New York City Department of Parks by Wallace, McHarg, Roberts and Todd. The author was responsible for the project which was supervised by Mr. Narendra Juneja, assisted by Mr. Derik Sutphin and Mr. Charles Meyers.

RECOMMENDED MINIMUM-SOCIAL-COST ALIGNMENT

41

The Cast and the Capsule

Each year I confront a new generation of graduate students, secure in their excellence, incipient or confirmed professionals in one or another of the planning or design fields. My most important objectives in this first encounter are to challenge professional myopia, exclusively man-centered views, to initiate consideration of basic values and to focus particularly on the place of nature in man's world—the place of man in nature.

Over the years I have used two stories mercilessly in order to review accepted values.

The first is paraphrased from an image conceived by Loren Eiseley:*

*Lecture by Loren Eiseley in the series, *"The House We Live In,"* WCAU-TV, Feb. 5, 1961.

Man in space is enabled to look upon the distant earth, a celestial orb, a revolving sphere. He sees it to be green, from the verdure on the land, algae greening the oceans, a green celestial fruit. Looking closely at the earth, he perceives blotches, black, brown, gray and from these extend dynamic tentacles upon the green epidermis. These blemishes he recognizes as the cities and works of man and asks, "Is man but a planetary disease?"

The silence that follows provides the appropriate setting for the next story—my own, bred from introspection on the increase of nuclear power.

The atomic cataclysm has occurred. The earth is silent, covered by a gray pall. All life has been extinguished save in one deep leaden slit, where, long inured to radiation, persists a small colony of algae. They perceive that all life save theirs has been extinguished and that the entire task of evolution must begin again—some billions of years of life and death, mutation and adaptation, cooperation and competition, all to recover yesterday. They come to an immediate, spontaneous and unanimous conclusion: "Next time, no brains."

The audience, in common with western society at large, believes that the world, if not the universe, consists of a dialogue between men, or between men and an anthropomorphic God: the result of this view is that man, exclusively, is thought divine—given dominion over all life, enjoined among all creatures to subdue the earth. Nature is then an irrelevant backdrop to the human play called Progress, or Profit. If nature is brought to the foreground, it is only to be conquered—man versus nature.

In this context it is salutary to suggest that the path and direction of evolution may not be identical to human ideas of destiny; that man, while the current, latest dominant species, may not be an enduring climax; that brain may or may not be the culmination of biological evolution or it might in contrast be an aberration, a spinal tumor, and finally, although no man will hear it, the algae may laugh last. The burden of proof, then, lies with man and brain. He is required to demonstrate that he is capable of understanding and managing the world of life to ensure survival.

We can conclude that there are two extreme viewpoints of man-nature. In the first, anthropocentric man—ignorant of evolutionary history, innocent of man's dependence, his allies and cohorts, low-browed and brutish—destroys as he goes, while adulating man and his works. (Can we suggest that his aggression is only a cultural inferiority complex?) The opposing view is less certain of man's place. It reserves the right to justify man as not only a unique species, but one with the unequaled gift of consciousness. This man, aware of his past, his unity with all things and all life, proceeds with a deference born of understanding, seeking his creative role.

If we can abandon the sad arrogance of ignorance and introduce a mood of reasonable inquiry, then circumspection will temper our indictment and we can reinterpret the stories. If we assume that man is a beneficent and constructive agent in the world, we could imagine the green celestial

fruit as a great epidermis indeed, but we could consider the green film as cytoplasm and the black, brown, gray centers not as blemishes but as nuclei and plastids—directing, producing, storing and circulating material for the cytoplasm: the creative centers in the world life. But if we do offer this kinder interpretation, we must ask whether these centers do indeed perform the roles of nuclei and plastids for the biosphere. I think that in general the answer would have to be that they do not.

But the mood has at least changed; the cry is no longer the raucous crow of the cock on the dunghill. The question is asked, if man is not the apex of the universe and its total justification, then who are the principal actors? With whom does he share the stage?

Some years ago I spent a most instructive winter with the great architect Louis I. Kahn, searching for the appropriate elysian site for a prospective temple of science, the research arm of a large corporation. I learned much from my travels with this most perceptive of architects, but my knowledge was even more enlarged by an encounter with a member of the research organization. He was designing an experimental environment: his task was to find out how an astronaut might be sent to the moon with the least possible baggage to sustain him. This, of course, required a recirculating, which is to say, a biological system. The experiment design required a plywood capsule with a fluorescent tube representing the sun, a quantity of air, some water, some algae growing in water, some bacteria and a man. This is, you will agree, a modest hoard of groceries for so long a trip. In the hypothetical capsule the man breathes air, consumes oxygen and exhales carbon dioxide; the algae consume carbon dioxide and expel oxygen into the air which the man breathes, and so an oxygen-carbon dioxide cycle is ensured. The man thirsts, drinks some water, urinates, this passes into the water medium in which the algae and bacteria exist, the water is consumed by the algae, transpired, condensed,

ALGAE*

*Drawings by Harold J. Walter, *Algae in Water Supplies* by C. Mervin Palmer, Public Health Service Publication No. 657, U.S. Department of Health, Education and Welfare, Washington, D.C., 1962, Plates 1 & 2.

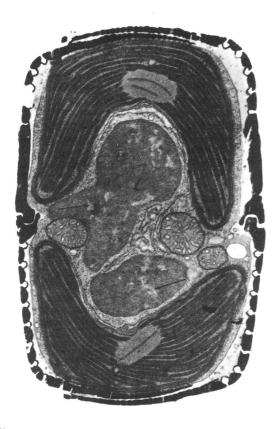

CHLOROPLAST*

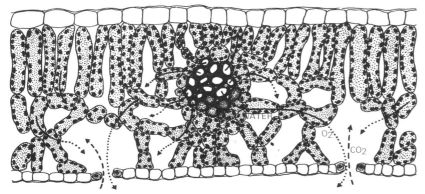

LEAF SECTION**

the man drinks the condensations and a closed cycle of water exists. When hungry, the man eats some algae, digests them, then defecates. Subsequently, the decomposers reduce the excrement into forms utilizable by the algae, which grow. The man eats more algae, and so a food chain has been created. The only import to the system is the light from the fluorescent tube—fossil sunlight; the only export from the system is heat.

Alas, experiments of this kind have not been sustained for more than twenty-four hours, a sad commentary on our understanding of man-nature. Nonetheless, they do contain splendid instructional material for the observer. The system depends first upon the sun, the net production of photosynthesis after respiration, upon the water and upon the cycling and recycling of the materials in the system by the decomposers. It is quite clear that the process requires that the substance or wastes, the output of one creature, are the imports or inputs to the others. The oxygen wastes of the plant were input to the man, the carbon dioxide of the man input to the plant; the substance of the plant input to the man, the wastes of the man input to the plant; the wastes of man and plant input to the decomposers, the wastes of these the input to the plant: and the water went round and round and round.

Is this indeed the way the world works? Yes, at least in essential terms. United we are as men, plant parasites, happily consuming the oxygen wastes of plant metabolism, rescued from encompassing ordure by both the decomposer and the plant, eating, burning and thus sustaining life from the energy of the sun, transmuted by photosynthesis. Now before we indulge in fulsome self-praise for our services to both plant and bacteria, let us stop to consider that they both existed before man and need him not at all. Our wastes are useful, but not necessary.

When I first pondered upon this experiment I found that I had to reformulate my view of

**After Sinott and Wilson, *Nature: Earth-Plants-Animals,* Doubleday & Company Inc., New York, 1960, p. 72.

*Photo micrograph, NAVICULA PELLICULOSA (Breb.) Hilse; 26,000:1, *Electron Microscopy of Diatom Cells* by R.W. Drum, H.S. Penkratz and E.F. Stoermer, J. Cramer, Lehre, 1966, plate 563.

man-nature. Instead of a paradise with Adam and Eve placed large in a garden graced by some benign, beautiful and useful plants and animals, the experiment showed that these myriad, beautiful creatures, thought to be a measure of grace added to life, were indeed indispensable, the source of life. Had the astronaut traveled to the moon with his companions, there is some doubt as to whether he would have found the algae and decomposers beautiful, but he would clearly have concluded that they were indispensable.

Moreover, whatever view our moon traveler had of man and environment as separate entities before his departure, it would surely have crossed his consciousness that, given enough time, the probability existed that all that had once been algae might well be man, all that had once been man, algae. The only difference between them, in terms of matter, lay in the templates of the genetic codes. What then is the environment? What then is man?

As I never obtained a college degree and entered graduate school without this dispensation, I never acquired the illusion of being educated which these diplomas often confer. Teaching is that device whereby I assemble a fragmentary, ragged and belated education. As it incurs no cost to the student and cannot be terminated with a degree, it clearly has certain advantages. But it does also have embarrassments, not least of which is the consternation of confronting the commonplace of knowledge as total novelty late in life. I well remember that occasion, when I first heard that all life, with minor exceptions, is now, and forever has been, entirely dependent upon photosynthesis and the plant. I recall looking around me, searching for other eyes equally overwhelmed by this revelatory statement. I found only the dead faces of those who had long since absorbed this information and for whom it had no moving power.

And that was not all. Not only is the chloro-

plast the overwhelmingly dominant mechanism whereby the light of the sun is transmuted into the substances supporting all life, the sugar and carbohydrates, but there are grounds for believing that it is from the exhalations of all plants in all time that an atmosphere with free oxygen has developed. Indeed, all food, all fossil fuels, fibres, all atmospheric oxygen, the stabilization of the earth's surface and its terrestrial water systems, the melioration of climate and microclimate have been accomplished by the plant: all animals and thus all men were plant parasites. It is the plant that colonized the land and thus permitted the evolution from the sea of amphibians, reptiles, mammals and man, and this dependence persists unchanged. Nor is this basic reliance negated by the fact that many animals perform essential services for plants.

This realization of dependence was a crushing blow to anthropocentrism. I looked around to see what effect this had had upon the class. Were they aware that, at least in thermodynamic terms, the world consisted of a working partnership between the sun and the leaf as man looked on—irrelevant, smiling benignly upon the scene, secure in the illusion of his primacy?

Suddenly I had an image of a green world, half turned towards the sun, leaves cupped to its light, encapsulating it through their templates, into their beings, this modified and ordered sunlight then transmuted by the inordinate variety of creatures and, through plants and animals, to man. Thus all life now, the residues of all life past, the transformations of all life in all time, all creatures and all men, are based upon the chloroplast, turned to the sun, arresting and ordering its energy as it passes to disorder. It is, as it were, as if the leaf said to the sun: "May I use some of your energy before it is degraded?" And the sun assented. So the leaf took the energy, ordered it into its being, sustained its growth and evolution, and those of all other creatures, before the energy, degraded, was yielded to disorder.

Consternation is an appropriate term to describe my continuing encounters with old but astonishing information. The second of these came, not from a lecture but from a book, *The Fitness of the Environment* by Lawrence Henderson. The most startling statement opens the preface:

Darwinian fitness is compounded of a mutual relationship between the organism and the environment. Of this, fitness of environment is quite as essential a component as the fitness which arises in the process of organic evolution; and in fundamental characteristics the actual environment is the fittest possible abode of life.

This conception then precedes the Darwinian theory in that it postulates evolution of matter to create the fitness of life and its evolution. It supplements natural selection, for not only is the successful organism adapted to the environment, but the environment is fit for the organism. "Fit" involves the assumption of the environment's provisions of opportunity for the organism, the latter is a response to this opportunity. Henderson supports his proposition by elaborating upon the characteristics of carbon, hydrogen and oxygen—to which George Wald would add nitrogen, including then those elements which constitute 99% of all organisms. But, of all matter which exhibits fitness, Henderson chooses the oceans and water:

The fitness of the environment results from characteristics which constitute a series of maxima—unique or nearly unique properties of water, carbonic acid, the compounds of carbon, hydrogen and oxygen and the ocean—so numerous, so varied, so nearly complete among all things which are concerned in the problem, that together they form certainly the greatest possible fitness. No other environment consisting of primary constituents, made up of other known elements, or lacking water and carbonic acid, could possess a like number of fit character-

istics, or in any manner such great fitness to promote complexity, durability, and the active metabolism in the organic mechanism we call life. *

The oceans, three-quarters of the earth's surface, are a great stable body with little variation in temperature and alkalinity and with both richness and constancy of chemical composition. It was here in this realm where sunlight penetrates, but beyond the range of toxic ultraviolet rays, that life could and did emerge. Here in this ancestral home life was created. The body fluids of simple marine organisms are all but identical with seawater. The blood of man is similar to the seas of earlier times. Loren Eiseley has said that the dimension of man's emancipation from the sea is the length of that cell which separates him from its source of blood, the ancient brine. All creatures are essentially aqueous solutions confined in membranes.

Ecologists describe the thin film of life covering the earth as the *biosphere,* the sum of all organisms and communities, acting as a single superorganism. Persuasive evidence for this derives from the oceans themselves—Henderson observed a marked correspondence between the regulatory mechanisms of the ocean and organisms, accomplished by temperature regulation through evaporation and regulation of alkalinity.

It is at least worthy of mention that the regulation of the ocean in general bears a striking resemblance to a physiological regulatory process, although such physiological processes are supposed to be the result of organic evolution alone. **

While the pyramid of life is dependent upon the sunlight captured by the chloroplast, the great work performed by the sun—a gigantic multiple of that employed in photosynthesis—is the evaporative phase of the hydrologic cycle in which water is transmuted into vapor, elevated and then precipitated as rain or snow, sustaining those

terrestrial creatures who have escaped from the sea but who are still dependent upon it.

Think then of the great work of the sun, distilling, raising and dropping the rain upon the waiting creatures on the land, who stand like dams across the water's implacable path, encapsulating it to form the larger part of their beings, ordering it with their unique templates—reservoirs of sea rain temporarily arrested on its inexorable gravitational path to the sea, but forever raised again and again to sustain and replenish those erstwhile sea creatures, membranes enclosing a briny solution.

The man who aspires to translate is limited not only by his knowledge of language but of substance. In wishing to bring a modicum of natural science to the planning process, I am, like most other planners, seriously hampered by ignorance of the subject. Yet, truly, who would expect to find that major world processes depend upon inconspicuous creatures called Foraminifera or Azotobacter. But indeed they do.

Four elements, abundant in the world—carbon, hydrogen, oxygen and nitrogen—constitute all but one per cent of living creatures. Their characteristics as well as their abundance constitute the best evidence of the fitness of the environment. These elements are indeed abundant: carbon as CO_2 in the atmosphere, in rocks, in the oceans and, above all, in the living; hydrogen and oxygen in the hydrosphere, oxygen 20% and nitrogen 78%, by volume, of the atmosphere.

Why should these four elements play such a central role in life? In his introduction to a new edition of Henderson's book, the biochemist George Wald answers this question—"I should say, because they are the smallest elements in the periodic system that achieve stable electronic configurations by gaining respectively 1, 2, 3 and 4 electrons. The special point of gaining electrons is that this is the mechanism by which chemical

*Lawrence J. Henderson, *The Fitness of the Environment,* The Macmillan Company, New York, 1913, page 272.

**The Fitness of the Environment, p. 188.

bonds, hence molecules, are formed. . . The point of these being the *smallest* such elements is that they tend to form the tightest and most stable bonds, and with few exceptions they alone form multiple . . . bonds. Why is that last thing important? Because, for example, in carbon dioxide the elements carbon and oxygen, by forming double bonds with one another, O=C=O, satisfy all their tendencies for chemical combination. As a result, independent molecules of carbon dioxide go off in the air as gas and dissolve in water; and from them plants can derive their substance, and animals by eating plants can derive theirs."[*]

Carbon, dominant in the chemistry of creatures, entered the primeval world in methane, but was oxidized to CO_2 and water. According to Hutchinson, "The resulting CO_2 could not accumulate on a wet planet . . . and so formed vast beds of limestone. The hypothetical pre-Cambrian limestone is to be regarded as the source of all CO_2 that has subsequently entered the atmosphere."[**]

In the modern earth carbon dioxide and thus carbon is found in the oceans, atmosphere and the rocky mantle and fixed in the biosphere. Carbon dioxide is involved in a great cycle, relatively imperfect. It begins with volcanic action releasing original and secondary sources of CO_2 that tend to concentrate in the oceanic depths. This material must be returned to the system by repeated volcanism if the cycle is to be completed. But it appears that more CO_2 is being fixed by the pelagic foraminifera in deep oceanic basins than is being returned to the system by volcanism—with a resulting net deficit. CO_2 is involved in smaller cycles—normally at the interfaces between the oceans, plants, soil and the atmosphere.

The oceans act as a major regulator in the system. CO_2 is fixed through plant photosynthesis; this is taken from the oceans, but equilibrium has been maintained with the

atmosphere during geologic time. In turn, respiration of plants and animals and decomposition add CO_2 to the ocean, which tends to come into equilibrium with the atmosphere.

Carbon is the fire at the heart of life. It has the unequaled ability to form complex compounds, exceeding in number all other chemical compounds, which it derives from its ability to form chains and rings of atoms.

It is this carbon—central to life, emerging from methane, fixed in beds of ancient limestone, released by volcanism and by solution as CO_2—which is used by plants again and again but is increasingly fixed in the oceanic foraminifera and lost to the system unless returned by volcanism. There is, however, a new element in the system—the enormous production of CO_2 as a byproduct of combustion—which has vastly increased the level of CO_2 with the result that ocean and atmosphere are not now in equilibrium.

It is the union of carbon and hydrogen that produces the hydrocarbons. Hydrogen, the first element, the primeval atom, is the basis of physical and thus biological evolution. It is as important as a constituent of water as it is a partner in the hydrocarbons. It is the hydrogen bond in the water molecule which provides the essential qualities of the latter, "its great surface tension, cohesiveness, high boiling point, high heat of vaporization."[***] And those are the attributes that Henderson used to identify water as the most fitting of the attributes of the environment.

Oxygen exists as 20% of the atmosphere. In the form of oxides it permeates the oceans, the lithosphere and life. It is the input in animal and plant respiration and decomposition, it is a net product of photosynthesis over time. It is the union of oxygen and hydrogen which constitutes water and gives it the essential attributes it exhibits; it is the union of oxygen and carbon which constitutes that most essential compound, carbon

41

dioxide. We need oxygen for survival.

While 78% of the atmosphere consists of nitrogen, it is in rocks that it is most abundant, constituting five-thousandths by weight. A considerable quantity of nitrogen is fixed from the atmosphere by organisms. According to Eugene Odum this may be as much as two hundred pounds per acre in cultivated areas, from one to six pounds per acre in the biosphere as a whole. Unlike the cycle of carbon dioxide and, as we shall see, phosphorus, the nitrogen cycle is relatively perfect. The major source of free nitrogen is the atmosphere. This is made available to

[*]George Wald in *The Fitness of the Environment* by Lawrence J. Henderson, Beacon Press, Boston, 1958, p. xx.

[**]G.E. Hutchinson, The Biochemistry of the Terrestrial Atmosphere, in *The Earth as a Planet,* edited by G.P. Kuiper, University of Chicago Press, Chicago, 1954, p. 388.

[***]George Wald, in Henderson, 1958, p. xxii.

plants by photochemical fixation, by nitrogen-fixing bacteria and algae, and, it is speculated, by lightning. As nitrates it is used in the protein synthesis of plants, animals and bacteria. The wastes of protein synthesis are reduced by decomposers to amino acids and organic residues. These are transformed by bacteria into ammonia, then to nitrites and finally to nitrates available once more for plant synthesis.

Nitrogen is added to the cycle from igneous rocks and is a product of volcanic action. There are losses to oceanic sediments, some of which are retrieved from marine birds and fishes.

In the cycles of oxygen, hydrogen and carbon, living organisms play an important part, but it is nonspecific—that is, all photosynthetic plants perform the same role in the oxygen-carbon dioxide cycle. But in the nitrogen cycle one finds unique groups of specialists who perform indispensable roles. Without them the cycle of nitrogen would be imperfect and the world of life would be limited to those creatures that could employ nitrogen in available non-organic form.

These indispensable creatures, performing their vital role in the nitrogen cycle, deserve to be household words, man's great heroes. Yet sadly those who named them had no thought of public honor and familiarity and called them Azotobacter and Clostridium, Rhizobium and Nostoc.

There remains an unidentified one per cent of matter constituted in organisms. Within this small proportion are many essential elements, including the trace metals, but one of these must be selected for particular attention because of the nature of its cycle. Phosphorus, essential for life, is involved in a system more simple, yet more critical, than nitrogen. The major reservoir is again in the rocks and deposits; it exists in the oceans and in organisms. Like nitrogen it is employed in protein synthesis of plants and

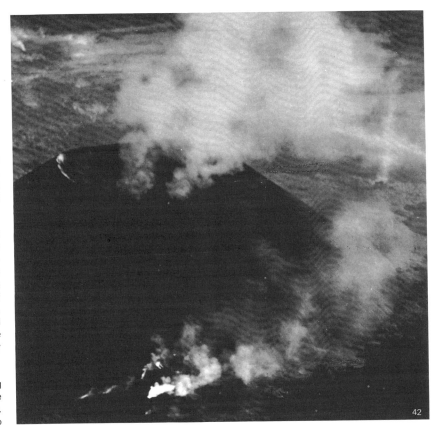

42

animals. The reservoir in the rocks is supplemented by volcanic apatite and from the excrement and residues of marine birds and fishes. As dissolved phosphate it is used by plants, animals and bacteria, and their excretions, bones and teeth are reduced by phosphatizing bacteria into a form again suitable for protein synthesis. In this cycle there is a continuous loss of phosphorus to the sea and to the oceanic depths where, unless returned by volcanism or upwelling by ocean currents, it is lost to the system. It appears that there is today an imperfection in the phosphorus cycle and that it is not being returned to the system as fast as it is being consumed.

Our understanding is growing: we have added the four major elements, carbon, hydrogen, oxygen and nitrogen and one important minor element, phosphorus, to our company; we have recognized the fundamental importance of some hitherto obscure and unknown algae and bacteria, Nostoc and Azotobacter; we have recognized that volcanic action and lightning are allies rather than enemies; we have learned to fear losses of carbon and phosphorus to the depths of the ocean and to respect water and the ocean as a primary component of the fitness of the environment.

Can we now see these elements, endlessly

recycled, the same finite source moving from the seas into the air, from rocks into solution, deposited and again raised by volcanism, passing through the streams of life, constituted into protoplasm, in the quick and the dead, mobilized in creatures from the beginning and forever? From the heart of volcanoes, from ancient beds of limestone, from high in the atmosphere or from deep in the seas this matter is endlessly recycled—sustaining life, fit for life.

Our identification, even of the major actors of the biosphere, is far from complete if we forget the encompassing envelope that is our milieu: the atmosphere—that membrane around the earth whose gases pervade the seas and the soil and permeate all living things.

> It would seem universally admitted that the earth's atmosphere is secondary, as is indicated by the extremely low content of the heavy rare gases . . . if by nothing else. It would also seem clear that the first atmosphere could not have contained much CO_2 . . . . It is also reasonably certain that, initially, it could not have contained free oxygen. The most likely constituents are ammonia, giving rise to nitrogen as hydrogen is lost, and methane, which would be fairly stable in the absence of oxygen. *

Such is G. Evelyn Hutchinson's description of the early atmosphere. It was in this situation, he hypothesizes, that "surface reactions on solids, [in shallow oceans] probably aluminosilicate clays . . . might provide further . . . opportunities not only for organic synthesis but also for incipient biological organization."**

There seems to be reason to believe that the original forms of life were anaerobic, existing without oxygen. There is indeed speculation that bioluminesence—which is most familiar today in the firefly—is a residue of this period when it was necessary for orga-

50

43

*G.E. Hutchinson in *The Earth as a Planet*, p. 422.

nisms to expel an oxygen that was toxic. There is a further and more entertaining speculation to the effect that this same primitive bioluminesence was a precursor of the evolution towards the nervous systems of animals and thus of the human brain, the great oxygen consumer. This suggests that the brain is the descendant of an early waste-disposal system.

There subsequently emerged the plant, consuming CO_2 and expelling oxygen. The product of this photosynthesis was an increase in free oxygen, first in the seas and subsequently in the atmosphere. It was this, with water vapor and CO_2, which reduced the toxicity of radiation and enlarged the arena in which life could exist. Thus it was life which modified the atmosphere; and the atmosphere in turn not only protected but encouraged and sustained life.

Let us think then of the atmosphere as the skin of the earth, the outer membrane of the biosphere. Let us think of the primeval earth when this thin film rose from the oceans, the exhalations of plants and animals, oxygen and carbon dioxide, which with water vapor, passed the life-giving light, but excluded the destroying rays. This bubble expands, rising from the sea to encompass the land and all the earth. This membrane is evolving, as truly as are the skins of creatures, elaborating to sustain more and more complex life. Now it covers us, raised high, this atmosphere of life, our outer membrane, the breaths of ancient lives, protecting and sustaining us, warming, shading, washing with rain, reverberating with thunderstorms charging the earth, modulating the light through days and changing seasons, source of climate and of weather, making the distant stars twinkle—this atmosphere which permeates us.

The chloroplast in the oceans and on land created that atmosphere which could sustain life. It is matter, water, the leaf, and the decomposers, which, with the sun, are the basis for all life now, all life past and the orderings accomplished by all life in all time. The creation of a life-sustaining atmosphere was one of the most important constituents of this evolutionary process.

Henderson observed that the regulatory powers exhibited by the ocean over temperature and alkalinity demonstrated a remarkable similarity to the homeostatic powers of an organism. In man, the maintenance of health permits only a very, very narrow deviation from a temperature of 98.6°F. The level of alkalinity in human blood, determined by CO_2 (as in the ocean) shows an equally small tolerance—forty-four parts per billion are associated with health, one tenth of a part per billion with coma and death.

The oceans maintain uniformity of alkalinity through the same action of CO_2, which tends towards equilibrium with the atmosphere. The temperature of the ocean maintains equilibrium from its mass, from the exceptionally high number of calories water requires to change temperature at all and by evaporation and convection. Both the organism and the oceans demonstrate similar mechanisms which maintain dynamic equilibrium. Does the atmosphere exhibit similar mechanisms? Is it also in some way organic and evolutionary?

Plants expel oxygen as a by-product of metabolism and consume it in respiration; animals consume oxygen and respire CO_2. Thus the availability of CO_2 limits plants; the availability of oxygen and plant protein limits animals and, when the available CO_2 reaches the lower limits, temperature regulation also inhibits plant growth. Here again is the same self-regulating mechanism as that exhibited by the oceans, described as "organic" by Henderson. The atmosphere, too, then must qualify for this description; it is organic and evolutionary.

As we absorb these fundamental truths, surely they change our image of the world and ourselves. When we see the atmosphere and the hydrosphere as evolutionary, exhibiting the characteristics of organisms, responsive, having self-regulating mechanisms, our conception of the biosphere must expand to include not only the film of living creatures on the earth, but the atmosphere above the extensive oceans as well. Water and air move through all life, the air surrounds and permeates us, the waters replenish that cistern which is ourselves. "The whole evolutionary process, both cosmic and organic, is one, and the biologist may now rightly regard the universe in its very essence as biocentric."* But not necessarily anthropocentric.

But life without death is unthinkable. Given sunlight, nutrients, water and suitable habitats, a colony of plants would so proliferate as to incorporate all available nutrients within itself. As life is defined not only by irritability or responsiveness but by growth, with no further nutrients available, no further life would be possible. Yet, non-growing organisms, encapsulating their own substances without release for use and re-use by the system would starve and die.

So death is necessary as is the decomposition of wastes and the matter of recent life. When the pathogens and the decomposers reduce the substances of living tissues and reconstitute them into forms usable by other organisms, these—with sunlight and water—make possible the creation of new life, which, by mutation and natural selection, ensures evolution.

The prospect of death begins with life, the span is written in the genetic code. In life the parasites, pathogens and age make incursions within their host while the environment and predators attack it from without. The agents of disease proceed towards death. This is not an instant but a process, in which the carrion eaters, scavengers, insects and their larvae, worms, fungi and bacteria reduce the matter into reusable forms.

Life continues, creatures live, propagate, die,

**Hutchinson, p. 424.

*Henderson, 1913, p. 312.

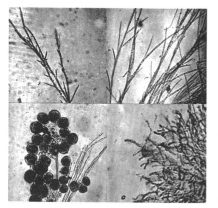

DECOMPOSERS*

*W. Irvine, Microphotographs of sewage fungus and other micro-organisms, *The Biology of Polluted Waters* by H.B.N. Hynes, Liverpool University Press, 1960, p. 96.

their progeny contain mutants and so evolution proceeds. The agents of disease are involved in their death and, with the decomposers, in their destruction and recycling in this return phase of matter to sustain life.

Here the eternal materials of the finite earth, increased by the residues of long dead encapsulations of ancient sunlit creatures, move again and again through plants, animals, wastes and the products of death, constantly recycled by the decomposers.

Decomposers have been described as the return stroke of matter in the cycles of life, some of them are illustrated—not with any hope of widespread public recognition but merely to give some shape and dimension to these indispensable organisms. Few indeed will wish to know their names but these do deserve our honor. The first is an alga—*Stigeoclonium tenue*—followed by *Fusarium aqueductum* and *Carchesium polypinum*. Next is *Zoogloea ramigera* alone and then mixed with *Sphaerotilus natans,* followed by *Beggiatoa alba* and *Apodya lactea*. A massive form of *Zoogloea* follows and in the next illustration is shown highly magnified. The penultimate example is *Leptothrix ochracea* while the last is *Gallionella ferruginea*.

Our list of characters, although still only partial, has become too large for the identification of its essential workmen. In the absence of specific recognition and salutation it might be well to extend a general air of appreciation and conciliation to all nature or even better, to begin to understand and act from understanding.

Darwin advanced the conception of biological evolution with natural selection as its primary mechanism. Henderson observed that the earth was peculiarly suited to the evolution of matter and of life, of creatures and of man. Both descriptions of fitness are necessary; they are complementary. Biological evolution still continues, but it does not respond easily to voluntary manipulation while the environment is in a constant flux, inevitably changed by the presence of organisms.

The environment—land, sea, air and creatures—does change; and so the question arises, can the environment be changed intentionally to make it more fit, to make it more fitting for man and the other creatures of the world? Yes, but to do this one must know the environment, its creatures and their interactions—which is to say ecology. This is the essential precondition for planning—the formulation of choices related to goals and the means for their realization.

In the long view one can see the great procession of the evolution of matter and of life, the history and direction of time and life forms. From the precision of evidence comes the poetic license which Wald invokes to speak of the yearnings of atoms as they evolved from hydrogen to the heaviest elements, the compounds as they evolved to the amino acids, unicellular creatures as they evolved to multifarious forms, the yearnings of the earliest tree shrews and their descendants that lead to man, and not least, the yearnings of man.

I can think of no better way of looking at the world and its processes than as if these were a timeless yearning, occurring in a milieu with a proclivity for evolution and for life, in which the environment is fit and may be made more fitting—in which the test is the capacity to adapt the environment and one's self.

There can be no present without a past, no future without both. That which is is only comprehensible in terms of what was. That which was may explain that which is, but cannot predict that which will be.

There is elaborate evidence of that which was in time past. To this we can attend. Much that has been has left evidence of its being. It is written in geomorphology, anatomy, physiology, morphology and cultural history, although some is too faint to be read. The place and the creature are textbook and teacher, they can speak to him who would and can read.

Perhaps the greatest conceptual contribution of the ecological view is the perception of the world and evolution as a creative process. This can be simply demonstrated by examining the difference between the early earth and the planet as we know it today. Take the mind back to the sterile orb, racked by volcanic action, still lacking oceans. Upon this the energy of the sun fell and an equal amount of energy was lost; this energy was degraded in the process.

Think now of the oceans which developed upon the earth. The sun's rays power both evaporation itself and the transport of the water vapor, which is precipitated upon the earth, moving from high to low elevation. In this process the same energy is employed as before, but work is being performed; the water at higher elevations has a greater potential energy than that in the oceans. Yet all water is proceeding towards its base level as surely as all energy is destined to be degraded. The water acts on land surfaces, and through erosion and sedimentation changes these surfaces towards equilibrium, a condition of repose in which matter moves from a condition of greater to lesser randomness. But, as Paul Sears notes, "while inorganic systems of matter and energy tend towards repose, those which involve life exhibit a countertendency so long as energy is available to keep them going."*

While entropy or degraded energy in any system must increase, in life systems and the orderings that they accomplish, there is evidence, not of degradation, but upgrading, the countertendency which Sears describes. "Energy impinging on living communities and stored in carbon compounds sustains a variety of forms of life, promoting their individual and group organization, enhancing the capacity of the habitat to sustain life, regulating the economy of water movement and chemical transformations—in short doing work."** In this energy is employed with matter through living processes. The energy is temporarily entrapped; it will inevitably be lost to entropy but it will also be replaced. Meanwhile the living creatures persist, evolve and in their beings and their modifications to the earth, act to raise matter to higher orders. This tendency, which is the sum of all life and all time, and the orderings which these have accomplished, is described as *negentropy*. Perhaps it can be given the more affirmative and colloquial title of *creation*—the world's creativity.

We can now see the earth as a process in which energy continuously falls, which inevitably will be degraded, but which through physical processes and life is arrested and entrapped in creatures, raising matter, as evolution proceeds, to higher and higher order. We can see the ordering of physical processes accomplished by precipitation, erosion and sedimentation, volcanism and uplifting, lightning and evaporation, all reducing the randomness of matter essential to this ordering: but overwhelmingly the plant is seen to be the basic agent which arrests and entraps sunlight, the basic agent for the ordering that is negentropy and creation.

Entropy is the rule, it demands its price; all energy is destined to be degraded but physical systems are becoming more ordered on earth, while life systems continue to evolve towards greater order, greater complexity, less randomness—towards negentropy. Abstract, absolute entropy would be that condition when all energy would be degraded, random, simple, uniform, disordered, unable to perform any further work. In contrast, idealized negentropy would exhibit high order, complexity, diversity, uniqueness, ability to perform work. Is this not a description of life and the direction of evolution—it is negentropic—creative.

Can one then imagine negentropy as a tide of ordering, moving deferentially against the force of entropy, paying its tithe, evolving from the order of the nonliving into life, from simple to complex life, from uniformity to diversity, from a small number to an infinitude of species, aspiring to dynamic equilibrium, always imperiled as evolution moves forward? Within this path the cycles of life, death and decay recycle the increasing storehouse of ordered matter, wrested from entropy, through the system. Within the biosphere the creatures in communities and their habitats increase in complexity, in the nature of their symbiotic relationships, in negentropy, evolving—as Teilhard de Chardin has suggested—towards increasing consciousness.

We may now be quite sure, that as men we depend upon the sun, the major elements and compounds, water, the chloroplast and the decomposers. With this new conviction we now turn to the sun and say, "Shine that we may live." We can contemplate matter and say, "From this is the universe, the world and life made." To the oceans we say, "Ancient home, nourish us with water." As the clouds rise from the sea, rains fall and rivers flow, we say, "Nourish us from the sea that we may live." Look to the plants, say, "Through you we breathe, through you we eat, through you we live." To the atmosphere we ask "Protect and sustain us." Hold in your hand some soil, know that the essential decomposers are there and say, "Be and work that we may be."

When we do these things, and say these things with understanding, we have crossed into another realm—leaving behind the simple innocence of ignorance. We can see the world more clearly now, our allies and ourselves. We have formulated a rudimentary value system and we are further on the path to the formulation of a workman's code, the view of the good steward.

53

*Paul B. Sears, *The Ecology of Man,* Condon Lectures, University of Oregon Press, 1957, p. 44.

**Sears, p. 45.

45

The discussion on matter and cycles may have appeared as an unnecessary excursion into biophysical science. Was it really necessary? Consider. The arguments that are normally mobilized in plaintive bleeding-heartism are clearly inadequate to arrest the spread of mindless destruction. Better arguments are necessary. The accumulation of some evidence of the ways of the working world produces an effective starting point. In the remarkably unsuccessful early years of my battles against the philistines I found that proffering my palpitating heart accomplished little remedy but that the diagnostic and prescriptive powers of a rudimentary ecology carried more weight, and had more value.

If we can assume that the reader has left the metaphorical space capsule with the same understanding of some basic physical and biological laws as the astronaut, we can assume that his interest in nature is not even remotely sentimental. We can now assume his solicitude for these indispensable processes as intelligent self-interest. We can also expect that the initial proposition now evokes a deeper understanding and acceptance—nature can be considered as interacting process, responsive to laws, constituting a value system, offering intrinsic opportunities and limitations to human uses. Now better armed, we can take our knowl-edge of nature as process and apply this to a problem—to discern the place of nature in a metropolitan region.

Some years ago I was asked to advise on which lands in the Philadelphia metropolitan region should be selected for open space. It became clear at the onset that the solution could only be obscured by limiting open space to the arena for organized sweating; it seemed more productive to consider the place of nature in the metropolis. In order to conclude on this place it appeared reasonable to suggest that nature performed work for man without his investment and that such work did represent a value. It also seemed reasonable to conclude that certain areas and natural processes were inhospitable to man—earthquake areas, hurricane paths, floodplains and the like—and that those should be prohibited or regulated to ensure public safety. This might seem a reasonable and prudent approach, but let us recognize that it is a rare one.

Consider that if you are required to design a flight of steps or a sidewalk there are clear and stringent regulations; there are constraints against the sale of cigarettes and alcohol to minors, society reacts sternly to the sale or use of narcotics and there are strong laws to deter assault, rape and murder. And we should be thankful indeed for these protections. But there is no comparable concern, reflected in law, that ensures that your house is not built on a floodplain, on unconsolidated sediments, in an earthquake zone, hurricane path, fire-prone forest, or in areas liable to subsidence or mudslides.

While great efforts are made to ensure that you do not break an ankle, there are few deterrents to arrest the dumping of poisons into the sources of public water supply or their injection into groundwater resources. You are clearly protected from assault by fist, knife or gun, but not from the equally dangerous threats of hydrocarbons, lead, nitrous oxides, ozone or carbon monoxide in the atmosphere. There is no protection from the assaults of noise, glare and stress. So while a handrail may be provided for your safety and convenience by a considerate government, you may drown in a floodplain, suffer loss of life and property from inundation of coastal areas, from an earthquake or hurricane; the damage or loss of life could be due to criminal negligence at worst and unpardonable ignorance at best, without the protection of governmental regulation or of laws.

It clearly should be otherwise; there is a need for simple regulations, which ensure that society protects the values of natural

55

processes and is itself protected. Conceivably such lands wherein exist these intrinsic values and constraints would provide the source of open space for metropolitan areas. If so, they would satisfy a double purpose: ensuring the operation of vital natural processes and employing lands unsuited to development in ways that would leave them unharmed by these often violent processes. Presumably, too, development would occur in areas that were intrinsically suitable, where dangers were absent and natural processes unharmed.

The formulation of these regulations requires no new science; we need move no nearer to the threshold of knowledge than the late 19th century. We can initially describe the major natural processes and their interactions and thereafter establish the degree to which these are permissive or prohibitive to certain land uses. This done, it will remain with the government and the courts to ensure our protection through the proper exercise of police power.

Before we move to this objective it is necessary to observe that there are two other views. They must be examined if only to be dismissed. The first is the economist's view of nature as a generally uniform commodity—appraised in terms of time distance, cost of land and development and allocated in terms of acres per unit of population. Nature, of course, is not uniform but varies as a function of historical geology, climate, physiography, soils, plants, animals and—consequently—intrinsic resources and land uses. Lakes, rivers, oceans and mountains are not where the economist might want them to be, but are where they are for clear and comprehensible reasons. Nature is *intrinsically* variable.

The geometric planner offers another alternative, that the city be ringed with a green circle in which green activities—agriculture, institutions and the like—are preserved or even introduced. Such greenbelts, where enforced by law, do ensure the perpetuation of open space and in the absence of an alternative they are successful—but it appears that nature outside the belt is no different from that within, that the greenbelt need not be the most suitable location for the green activities of agriculture or recreation. The ecological method would suggest that the lands reserved for open space in the metropolitan region be derived from natural-process lands, intrinsically suitable for "green" purposes: that is the place of nature in the metropolis.

A single drop of water in the uplands of a watershed may appear and reappear as cloud, precipitation, surface water in creek and river, lake and pond or groundwater; it can participate in plant and animal metabolism, transpiration, condensation, decomposition, combustion, respiration and evaporation. This same drop of water may appear in considerations of climate and microclimate, water supply, flood, drought and erosion control, industry, commerce, agriculture, forestry, recreation, scenic beauty, in cloud, snow, stream, river and sea. We conclude that nature is a single interacting system and that changes to any part will affect the operation of the whole.

If we use water as an indicator of the interaction of natural processes, we see that the forests felled in the uplands may have an identical effect upon the incidence of flood that is accomplished by filling estuarine marshes. Pollution of groundwater may affect surface water resources and vice versa; urbanization will affect the rate of runoff, erosion and sedimentation, causing water turbidity, diminution of aquatic organisms, and a reduction in natural water purification. These, in turn, will result in channel dredging costs, increased water treatment costs and, possibly, flood damages and drought costs.

So we can say that terrestrial processes require water and that freshwater processes are indissoluble from the land. It then follows that land management will affect water, water management will affect land processes. We cannot follow the path of every drop of water, but we can select certain identifiable aspects—precipitation and runoff, surface water in streams and rivers, marshes and floodplains, groundwater resources in aquifers and the most critical phase of these—aquifer recharge. We can now formulate some simple propositions. Simple they are indeed—almost to the point of idiocy—but they are novelties of high sophistication to the planning process and the bulk of local governmental agencies.

Water quality and quantity are related to both land and water management. Floods are natural phenomena and reveal cyclical frequencies; healthy water bodies reduce organic matter and this varies with seasons, turbidity, dissolved oxygen, alkalinity, temperature, and the biotic population; erosion and sedimentation are natural but are accelerated by almost all human adaptations—on a uniform soil, normally the greater the slope, the more the erosion. Groundwater and surface water are interacting—in periods of low precipitation the water in rivers and streams is usually groundwater; soils vary in their productivity for agriculture as a function of texture, organic matter, chemical composition, elevation, slope, and exposure. Marshes are flood storage areas, often aquifer recharges, the homes of wildfowl and both spawning and breeding grounds; the hinterland of a city is the source of the clean air that replaces the pollutants discharged by the city. The rural hinterland also contributes to a more temperate summer climate. Can we use this information to discriminate between lands that should remain in their natural condition, lands that are permissive to certain uses but not to others and those lands that are most tolerant to urbanization—free from danger, undamaging to other values?

But, first can we afford the indulgence of reserving natural-process lands and regulating development on them in order to capture their value? Indeed we can: land is abundant. According to the French urban geographer Jean Gottman, perhaps only 1.8% of the United States is urbanized today.* Even within metropolitan regions, there is plenty of land. In the Philadelphia Standard Metropolitan Statistical Area, 3,500 square miles—less than 20%—is urbanized today and even should the population increase to 6,000,000, there would remain at that time 70% or 2,300 square miles of open land.

If so, wherein lies the problem? Simply in the form of growth. Urbanization proceeds by increasing the density within and extending the periphery, always at the expense of open space. As a result—unlike other facilities—open space is most abundant where people are scarcest. This growth, we have seen, is totally unresponsive to natural processes and their values. Optimally, one would wish for two systems within the metropolitan region—one the pattern of natural processes preserved in open space, the other the pattern of urban development. If these were interfused, one could satisfy the provision of open space for the population. The present method of growth continuously preempts the edge, causing the open space to recede from the population center. Geometrically, a solution is not unthinkable. If the entire area of the Philadelphia region were represented in a circle it would have a radius of 33 miles. Present urbanization can be encircled by a 15-mile radius. If all the existing and proposed urbanization for a six-million population and one acre of open space for every thirty persons is encircled, then the radius is 20 miles—only five miles more than the present.

But rather than propose a blanket standard of open space, we wish to find discrete aspects of natural processes that carry their own values and prohibitions: it is from these that open space should be selected, it is these that should provide the pattern, not only of metropolitan open space, but also the positive pattern of development.

*Jean Gottman, *Megalopolis,* The Twentieth Century Fund, New York, 1961, p. 26.

EXISTING OPEN SPACE, PHILADELPHIA METROPOLIS

Later on we shall see that there are consistencies in land morphology, soils, stream patterns, plant association, wildlife habitats, and even land use, and that these can well be examined through the concept of the physiographic region. It is premature to employ this concept now. It is enough for the moment to insist that nature performs work for man—in many cases this is best done in a natural condition—further that certain areas are intrinsically suitable for certain uses while others are less so. We can begin with this simple proposition. Moreover, we can codify it. If we select eight dominant aspects of natural process and rank them in an order of both value and intolerance to human use and then reverse the order, it will be seen as a gross hierarchy of urban suitability.

Natural-process Value; Degree of Intolerance	Intrinsic Suitability for Urban Use
Surface water	Flat land
Marshes	Forest, woodlands
Floodplains	Steep slopes
Aquifer recharge areas	Aquifers
Aquifers	Aquifer recharge areas
Steep slopes	Floodplains
Forests, woodlands	Marshes
Flat land	Surface water

However, there is an obvious conflict in this hierarchy. The flat land, so often selected for urbanization, is often as suitable for agriculture: this category will have to be looked at more carefully. So prime agricultural land will be identified as intolerant to urbanization and constituting a high social value—all other flat land will be assumed to have a low value in the natural-process scale and a high value for urban suitability.

Within the metropolitan region natural features will vary, but it is possible to select certain of these that exist throughout and determine the degree to which they allow or discourage contemplated land uses. While these terms are relative, optimally development should occur on valuable or perilous natural-process land only when superior values are created or compensation can be awarded.

A complete study would involve identifying natural processes that performed work for man, those which offered protection or were hostile, those which were unique or especially precious and those values which were vulnerable. In the first category fall natural water purification, atmospheric pollution dispersal, climatic amelioration, water storage, flood, drought and erosion control, topsoil accumulation, forest and wildlife inventory increase. Areas that provided protection or were dangerous would include the estuarine marshes and the floodplains, among others. The important areas of geological, ecological and historic interest would represent the next category, while beach dunes, spawning and breeding grounds and water catchment areas would be included in the vulnerable areas.

No such elaborate examination has been attempted in this study. However, eight natural processes have been identified and these have been mapped and measured. Each one has been described with an eye to permissiveness and prohibition to certain land uses. It is from this analysis that the place of nature in the metropolis will be derived.

Surface Water (5,671 linear miles)

In principle, only land uses that are inseparable from waterfront locations should occupy them; and even these should be limited to those which do not diminish the present or prospective value of surface water for supply, recreation or amenity. Demands for industrial waterfront locations in the region are extravagantly predicted as 50 linear miles. Thus, even satisfying this demand, five thousand miles could remain in a natural condition.

Land uses consonant with this principle would include port and harbor facilities, marinas, water and sewage treatment plants, water-related and, in certain cases, water-using industries. In the category of land uses that would not damage these water resources fall agriculture, forestry, recreation, institutional and residential open space.

Marshes (173,984 acres; 8.09%)

In principle, land-use policy for marshes should reflect the roles of flood and water storage, wildlife habitat and fish spawning grounds. Land uses that do not diminish the operation of the primary roles include recreation, certain types of agriculture (notably cranberry bogs) and isolated urban development.

Floodplains (339,706 acres; 15.8%)

Increasingly, the 50-year, or 2%, probability floodplain is being accepted as that area from which all development should be excluded save for functions which are unharmed by flooding or for uses that are inseparable from floodplains.

In the former category fall agriculture, forestry, recreation, institutional open space and open space for housing. In the category of land uses inseparable from floodplains are ports and harbors, marinas, water-related

industry and—under certain circumstances—water-using industry.

Aquifers (181,792 acres; 8.3%)

An aquifer is a water-bearing stratum of rock, gravel or sand, a definition so general as to encompass enormous areas of land. In the region under study, the great deposits of porous material in the Coastal Plain are immediately distinguishable from all other aquifers in the region because of their extent and capacity. This may well be the single most important unexploited resource in the region. The aquifer parallel to Philadelphia in New Jersey has an estimated yield of one billion gallons per day. Clearly this valuable resource should not only be protected, but managed. Development that includes the disposal of toxic wastes, biological discharges or sewage should be prohibited. The use of injection wells, by which pollutants are disposed into aquifers, should be discontinued.

Development using sewers is clearly more satisfactory than septic tanks where aquifers can be contaminated, but it is well to recognize that even sewers leak significant quantities of material and are thus a hazard.

Land-use prescription is more difficult for aquifers than for any other category as these vary with respect to yield and quality, yet it is clear that agriculture, forestry, recreation and low-density development pose no danger to this resource while industry and urbanization in general do.

All prospective land uses should simply be examined against the degree to which they imperil the aquifer; those which do should be prohibited. It is important to recognize that aquifers may be managed effectively by the impoundment of rivers and streams that transect them.

Like many other cities, Philadelphia derives its water supply from major rivers which are

foul. This water is elaborately disinfected and is potable. In contrast to the prevailing view that one should select dirty water for human consumption and make it safe by superchlorination, it seems preferable to select pure water in the first place. Such water is abundant in the existing aquifers; it must be protected from the fate of the rivers.

Aquifer Recharge Areas (118,896 acres; 6%)

As the name implies, such areas are the points of interchange between surface water and aquifers. In any system there are likely to be critical interchanges. It is the movement of ground to surface water that contributes water to rivers and streams in periods of low flow. Obviously the point of interchange is also a location where the normally polluted rivers may contaminate the relatively clean—and in many cases, pure—water resources in aquifers. These points of interchange are then critical for the management and protection of groundwater resources.

In the Philadelphia region the interchange between the Delaware River and its tributaries with the adjacent aquifers is the location of greatest importance. The Delaware is foul—frequently it has been observed to lack any dissolved oxygen and was then septic. However, a thick layer of silt, almost thirty feet deep, acts as a gasket and reduces the passage of the polluted river to the adjacent aquifer. It is where an aquifer is overlaid with porous material that percolation from the ground surface will recharge it.

These two considerations, then, should regulate management of these areas. By the careful separation of polluted rivers from the aquifer and by the impoundment of clean streams that transect it, the aquifer can be managed and recharged. By regulating land uses on those permeable surfaces that contribute to aquifer recharge, normal percolation will be allowed to continue.

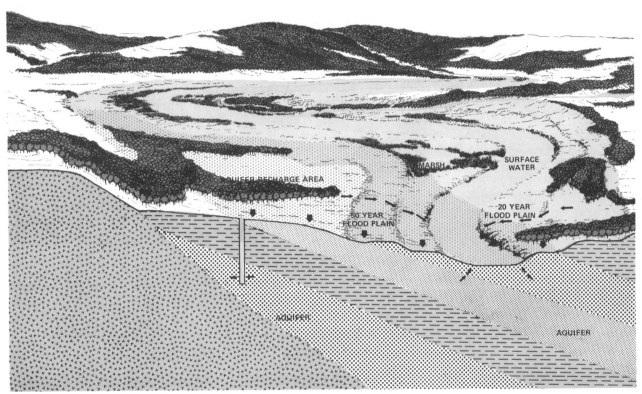

WATER FEATURES

SURFACE WATER

MARSHES

FLOODPLAINS

FOREST AND WOODLAND

STEEP LAND

PRIME AGRICULTURAL LAND

LAND FEATURES
Steep Lands

Steep lands, and the ridges which they constitute, are central to the problems of flood control and erosion. Slopes in excess of 12⁰ are not recommended for cultivation by the Soil Conservation Service. The same source suggests that, for reasons of erosion, these lands are unsuitable for development. The recommendations of the Soil Conservation Service are that steep slopes should be in forest and that their cultivation be abandoned.

The role of erosion control and diminution of the velocity of runoff is the principal problem here. Land uses compatible with this role would be mainly forestry and recreation, with low-density housing permitted on occasion.

Prime Agricultural Land (248,816 acres; 11.7%)
Prime agricultural soils represent the highest level of agricultural productivity; they are uniquely suitable for intensive cultivation with no conservation hazards. It is extremely difficult to defend agricultural lands when their cash value can be multiplied tenfold by employment for relatively cheap housing. Yet the farm is the basic factory—the farmer is the country's best landscape gardener and maintenance work force, the custodian of much scenic beauty. Mere market values of farmlands do not reflect the long-term value or the irreplaceable nature of these living soils. An omnibus protection of all farmland is difficult to defend; but protection of the best soils in a metropolitan area would appear not only defensible, but clearly desirable.

Jean Gottman has recommended that "the very good soils are not extensive enough in Megalopolis to be wastefully abandoned to non-agricultural uses."* The soils Gottman had in mind are identical to the Prime Agricultural Soils in the metropolitan area.

*Gottman, p. 95.

PRIME AGRICULTURAL LAND

STEEP LANDS

FORESTS AND WOODLANDS

The farmer, displaced from excellent soils by urbanization, often moves to another site on inferior soils. Excellent soils lost to agriculture for building can finally only be replaced by bringing inferior soils into production. This requires capital investment. "Land that is not considered cropland today will become cropland tomorrow, but at the price of much investment."*

In the Philadelphia Standard Metropolitan Statistical Area, by 1980 only 30% of the land area will be urbanized. 70% will remain open. Prime agricultural lands represent only 11.7% of the area. Therefore, given a choice, prime soils should not be developed.

*Edward Higbee, Chapter 6, in Gottman. *Megalopolis,* p. 326.

In principle, U.S.D.A. Category 1 soils should be exempted from development (save by those functions that do not diminish their productive potential). This would suggest retirement of prime soils into forest or their utilization as open space—for institutions, for recreation or in development for housing at densities no higher than one house per 25 acres.

Forests and Woodlands

The natural vegetative cover for most of this region is forest. Where present, it improves microclimate and it exercises a major balancing effect upon the water regimen—diminishing erosion, sedimentation, flood and drought. The scenic role of woodlands is apparent, as is their provision of a habitat for game; their recreational potential is among the highest of all categories. In addition, the forest is a low-maintenance, self-perpetuating landscape.

Forests can be employed for timber production, water management, wildlife habitats, as airsheds, recreation or for any combination of these uses. In addition, they can absorb development in concentrations to be determined by the demands of the natural process they are required to satisfy.

61

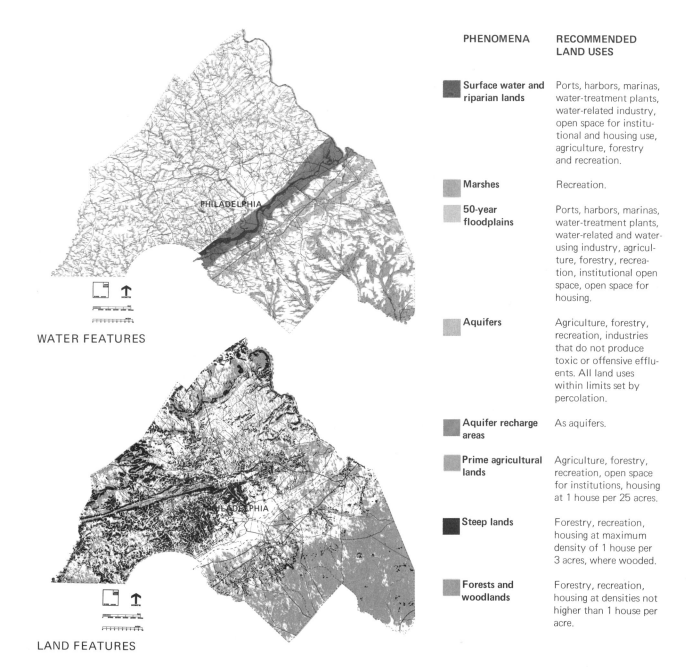

PHENOMENA RECOMMENDED LAND USES

Surface water and riparian lands   Ports, harbors, marinas, water-treatment plants, water-related industry, open space for institutional and housing use, agriculture, forestry and recreation.

Marshes   Recreation.

50-year floodplains   Ports, harbors, marinas, water-treatment plants, water-related and water-using industry, agriculture, forestry, recreation, institutional open space, open space for housing.

Aquifers   Agriculture, forestry, recreation, industries that do not produce toxic or offensive effluents. All land uses within limits set by percolation.

Aquifer recharge areas   As aquifers.

Prime agricultural lands   Agriculture, forestry, recreation, open space for institutions, housing at 1 house per 25 acres.

Steep lands   Forestry, recreation, housing at maximum density of 1 house per 3 acres, where wooded.

Forests and woodlands   Forestry, recreation, housing at densities not higher than 1 house per acre.

WATER FEATURES

LAND FEATURES

62

SUMMARY MAP OF WATER & LAND FEATURES FOR PART OF THE METROPOLITAN AREA

PHILADELPHIA

The resolution of atmospheric pollution depends mainly upon the reduction of pollution sources. While discussion of the subject increases in intensity, remedy shows no parallel acceleration, and it may be timely to consider one fact which, if recognized, can at least enhance the future possibility of solution. The city creates the filthy air. Clean air comes from the countryside. If we can identify the major wind directions, particularly those associated with inversion conditions, and ensure that pollution source industries are not located in these critical sectors of the urban hinterland, we will at least not exacerbate the situation.

The central phase of air pollution is linked to temperature inversion, during which the air near the ground does not rise to be replaced by in-moving air. Under inversion, characterized by clear nights with little wind, the earth is cooled by long-wave radiation and the air near the ground is cooled by the ground. During such temperature inversions with stable surface air layers, air movement is limited; in cities, pollution becomes increasingly concentrated. In Philadelphia "significant" inversions occur one night in three. Parallel and related to inversion is the incidence of high pollution levels, which occurred on twenty-four "episodes" from 2-5 days in duration between 1957 and 1959. Inversions then are common, as are "high" levels of pollution. The danger attends their conjunction and persistence. Relief, other than elimination of pollution sources, is a function of wind movement to disperse pollution over cities and, secondly, the necessity that in-moving air be cleaner than the air it replaces.

The concentration of pollution sources in Philadelphia covers an area fifteen miles by ten miles with the long axis running approximately northeast. Let us assume sulfur dioxide to be the indicator of pollution (830 tons per day produced), an air height of 500 feet as the effective dimension and an air volume of approximately 15 cubic miles to be replaced by a wind speed of 4 mph, selected as a critical speed. Then one cubic mile of ventilation is provided per mile of windspeed and it is seen to require 3¾ hours for wind movement to ventilate the long axis, 2½ hours to ventilate the cross axis. Thus, the tributary to ensure clean air on the long axis is 15 miles beyond the pollution area, 10 miles beyond for the cross axis. The wind rose for Philadelphia during inversions shows that wind movements are preponderantly northwest, west, and southwest, contributing 51.2% of wind movements; the other five cardinal and intercardinal points represent the remainder.

This very approximate examination suggests that airsheds should extend from 10 to 15 miles beyond the urban air pollution sources in those wind directions to be anticipated during inversion. The width of these belts should correspond to the dimension of the pollution core and, in very approximate terms, would probably be from three to five miles. *Such areas, described as airsheds, should be prohibited to pollution source industries.*

Under the heading of atmosphere the subject of climate and microclimate was raised. In the study area the major problem is summer heat and humidity. Relief of this condition responds to wind movements. Thus, a hinterland with more equable temperatures, particularly a lower summer temperature, is of importance to climate amelioration for the city. As we have seen, areas that are in vegetative cover, notably forests, are distinctly cooler than cities in summer—a margin of 10°F is not uncommon. Air movements over such areas moving into the city will bring cooler air. Relief from humidity also results mainly from air movements. These correspond to the directions important for relief of inversion. We can then say that the areas selected as urban airsheds are likely to be those selected as appropriate for amelioration of the urban microclimate. However, to clear air pollution by airsheds, it is important only that pollution sources be prohibited or limited. To relieve summer heat

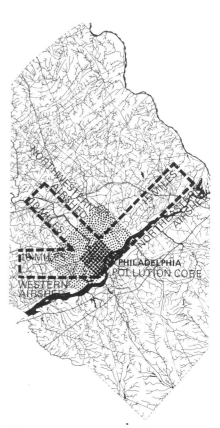

AIR SHEDS

and humidity, it is essential that these airsheds be substantially in vegetative cover, preferably forested.

The satisfaction of these two requirements, in the creation of urban airsheds as responses to atmospheric pollution control and microclimate control, would create fingers of open space penetrating from the rural hinterland, radially into the city. This is perhaps the broadest conception of natural process in metropolitan growth and metropolitan open-space distribution. Clearly, this proposal directs growth into the interstices between the airshed corridors and suggests that metropolitan open space exist within them.*

Human adaptations entail both benefits and costs, but natural processes are generally not attributed values; nor is there a generalized accounting system, reflecting total costs and benefits. Natural processes are unitary whereas human interventions tend to be fragmentary and incremental. The effect of filling the estuarine marshes or felling the upland forests is not perceived as related to the water regimen—to flood or drought—nor are both activities seen to be similar in their effect. The construction of outlying suburbs and siltation of river channels are not normally understood to be related—nor is waste disposal into rivers perceived to be connected with the pollution of distant wells.

Several factors can be observed. Normal urban growth tends to be incremental and unrelated to natural processes on the site. But the aggregate consequences of such development are not calculated nor are they allocated as costs to the individual developments. While benefits do accrue to certain developments that are deleterious to natural processes at large (for example, clear felling of forests or conversion of farmland into subdivisions), these benefits are *particular* (related, say, to that landowner who chooses to fell trees or sterilize soil), while the results and costs are general. Thus, costs and benefits are likely to be attributed to large numbers of different and unrelated persons, corporations and levels of government. It is unlikely that long-term benefits accrue from disdain of natural process; it is quite certain and provable that substantial costs *do* result from this disdain. Finally, in general, any benefits that do occur—usually economic—tend to accrue to the private sector, while remedies and long-range costs are usually the responsibility of the public domain.

The purpose of this exploration is to show that natural process, unitary in character, must be so considered in the planning process: that changes to parts of the system affect the entire system, that natural processes do represent values and that these values should be incorporated into a single accounting system. It is unfortunate that the information we have on cost-benefit ratios of specific interventions to natural process is inadequate. However, certain generalized relationships have been shown and presumptions advanced as the basis for judgment. It seems clear that laws pertaining to land use and development need to be elaborated to reflect the public costs and consequences of private action. Present land-use regulations neither recognize natural processes—the public good in terms of flood, drought, water quality, agriculture, amenity or recreational potential—nor allocate responsibility to the acts of landowner or developer.

We have seen that land is abundant, even within a metropolitan region confronting accelerated growth. There is, then, at least hypothetically, the opportunity for choice as to the location of development and open space.

The hypothesis, central to this study, is that the distribution of open space must respond to natural process. This conception should hold true for any metropolitan area, irrespective of location. In this particular case study, directed to the Philadelphia Metropolitan Region, an attempt has been made to focus on the fundamental natural processes that show the greatest relevance to the problem of determining the form of metropolitan growth and open space.

The problem lies not in absolute area but in distribution. We seek a concept that can provide an interfusion of open space and population. The low attributed value of open space ensures that it is transformed into urban use within the urban area and at the perimeter. Customary urbanization excludes interfusion and consumes peripheral open space.

Yet as the area of a circle grows with the square of the radius, large open-space increments can exist within the urban perimeter without major increase to the radius or to the time distance from city center to urban fringe.

This case study reveals the application of the ecological view to the problem of selecting open space in a metropolitan region. For the moment, it is enough to observe that this view could considerably enhance the present mode of planning, which disregards natural processes all but completely and which, in selecting open space, is motivated more by standards of acres per thousand for organized sweating than by a concern for the place and face of nature in the metropolis.

*Study on the Philadelphia airshed conducted under direction of the writer by Hideki Shimizu, Department of Landscape Architecture, University of Pennsylvania, 1963, unpublished.

This study was derived from Metropolitan Open Space from Natural Process, a research project supported by the Urban Renewal Administration, the States of Pennsylvania and New Jersey. The author was the principal investigator and the work published herein derives exclusively from his research. The initial project director was Dr. W. L. C. Wheaton. Subsequently this role was filled by Dr. David A. Wallace. Other investigators included Anne Louise Strong, Dr. William Grigsby, Dr. Anthony Tomazinas, Dr. Nohad Toulon and Mr. William H. Roberts. Research assistants, responsible for the mapping, were Mr. Donald Phimister and Mr. Frank Shaw.

On Values

Who can imagine that virgin continent of America accumulating in age and wealth, inordinately stable, rich beyond the dreams of avarice in everything that man could desire. Moreover, it was a new world, some ten thousand years ago, that land which we can never see again. Yet, the men who followed the trails of the huge herbivores during some interglacial period from Siberia across the land bridge to America, probably discerned little change; the new environment was much like the old. It could not have been until they made deep penetrations to the south that profound changes were discernible. Yet the passage of time must have been great and the memories of distant ice sheets would have been only tribal sagas, intermeshed with fancies and mythology.

The men who first entered this new world were another type of predator, in some ways little different from the sabertooth. Like any other predator, they were limited by the numbers of their prey—but man introduced a new and powerful tool which proved that he was no ordinary hunter.

The emergence of the seed in Jurassic times precipitated the explosion of the flower. The embryonic plant encapsulated in the seed was infinitely more enduring and mobile than the early naked seeds or the older spore. It was this new flowering plant with its fleshed embryo that colonized the world and made available a food source unknown in previous eras. Of all the repercussions of the angiosperm, none was more dramatic than the clothing of the prairies with grasses. It was these which sustained the enormous populations of large, fleet-footed, far-ranging creatures, in turn the prey of the predators, chief among which—one day—would be the human hunters. The grasses covered the prairies; the herbivores were sustained by them and proliferated. Onto this scene entered the new predator with a tool more powerful than required, beyond his power to control and of enormous consequence—a criticism as topical for atomic man.

This new and devastating tool was fire. It was no novelty in the prairie—lightning-caused fire was common and indeed the prairie climax was a response to it. But the induced fire of the hunter was more frequent than the natural occurrence. The prairies were burned to drive the bison and deer, the mammoth and mastodon into closed valleys or over precipices. This was a time of climatic adversity, threatening to the creatures as well as to men. It is thought that it was the combination of human hunters and a hostile climate that resulted in the extinction of this first great human inheritance in North America, the prairie herbivores. Firelike the grasses spread, firelike the herds of grazing animals swept to exploit the prairies—and it was the fire of the aboriginal hunter that hastened or accomplished their extinction. This was the first major impact of man on the continent during the aboriginal occupation.

In the subsequent millennia there were, as far as is known, no comparable depredations. If one can infer from the ways of the North American Indians, there evolved a most harmonious balance of man and nature. The gatherer and hunter learned to adapt his cropping to the capacity of the crop and prey. In this evolution there must have developed an understanding of creatures and their habits. Hunting must respond to the breeding seasons, be protective of pregnant females, cull the surplus males. This is a major step in human evolution. The first ancestral tree shrews were puny creatures among the gigantic, predatory dinosaurs. The fire-wielding human hunter was no longer puny—he had equaled the depredations of *Tyrannosaurus rex*—but the hunter who adapted his hunting practices to the habits and capacity of his prey was truly thinking man and this was the first testament to brains as a device to manage the biosphere. This is then no longer simply man, the speaking animal, the maker of stone tools or man, the agent of fire—it is man, the thinking hunter. Yet we must take care not to make too large a claim. Many other creatures, whose brains are less vaunted, have also been able to regulate their populations to available prey.

Considerations of "primitive" men have been obscured by the wide divergence of views that range between the idealized "noble savage" on one hand and the conception of aboriginal peoples being "missing links" on the other. It seems clear that simplicity neither ensures nor denies nobility, that the mental equipment of the primitive man is indistinguishable from that of his most sophisticated brethren. The supremacy of the latter, in his own terms, lies in the inheritance of the tools, information and powers from his predecessors. While there are a few exceptions, "wild nature" seldom provides an ideal environment and those men who live in primitive societies are susceptible to disease, suffer from a short lifespan and are vulnerable to extremes of heat and cold, drought, starvation and exposure. They often suffer from fears and superstitions, but they have frequently acquired an astonishing empirical knowledge of their environment, its creatures and their processes. This is absorbed into religion or superstitions. Indeed it might well be said that their success, their adaption, is precisely this understanding. Societies that sustained themselves for these many millennia are testimony to this understanding; it is indeed the best evidence in support of brain, the presumptive manager of the biosphere.

Paganism is an unnecessarily pejorative term; pantheism is a better word. Who knows God so well that he can reject other likenesses? With Voltaire one asks to see his credentials. Animism, which permeates pantheism, involves the theory of the existence of immaterial principle, inseparable from matter, to which all life and action are attributable. In the pantheist view the entire phenomenal world contains godlike attributes: the relations of man to this world are sacramental. It is believed that the actions of man in nature can affect his own fate, that these

actions are consequential, immediate and relevant to life. There is, in this relationship, no non-nature category—nor is there either romanticism or sentimentality.

The Iroquois view is typical of Indian pantheism. The Iroquois cosmography begins with a perfect sky world from which falls the earth mother, arrested by the birds, landing upon the back of a turtle, the earth. Her grandchildren are twins, one good and the other evil. All that is delightful and satisfactory derives from the first: twin streams that flow in both directions, fat corn, abundant game, soft stones and balmy climate. The evil twin is the source of bats and snakes, whirlpools and waterfalls, blighted corn, ice, age, disease and death. The opposition of these two forces is the arena of life; they can be affected by man's acts in the world of actuality. Consequently all acts—birth and growth, procreating, eating and evacuating, hunting and gathering, making voyages and journeys—are sacramental.

In a hunting society the attitude to the prey is of vital significance. Among the Iroquois the bear was highly esteemed. It provided not only an excellent hide and meat, but also oil that was used for cooking and could be stored. When the hunted bear was confronted, the kill was preceded by a long monologue in which the needs of the hunter were fully explained and assurances were given that the killing was motivated by need, not the wish to dishonor. Now if you would wish to develop an attitude to prey that would ensure stability in a hunting society, then such views are the guarantee. Like the crystal of potassium permanganate in a beaker of water, diffusing into equilibrium, in steady state, the hunter who believes that all matter and actions are sacramental and consequential will bring deference and understanding to his relations with the environment. He will achieve a steady state with this environment—he will live in harmony with nature and survive because of it.

It is deep in history that we abandoned such

a view. The conception of man—exclusively divine, given dominion over all life and non-life, enjoined to subdue the earth—contained in the creation story of Genesis represents the total antithesis of the pantheist view. While the Greeks conceived not only of man Gods, but nature Gods as well, this survived only marginally into the humanism of the Renaissance and pantheism has been lost to the western tradition; in Europe it persists only with the Lapps. Yet, as leading theologians retreat in consternation from the literality of Genesis—Buber and Heschel, Tillich and Weigel and even more Teilhard de Chardin, offended by its arrogant transcendence—the more quietly deferential view of the pantheists seems to present a better beginning, at least a working hypothesis. If divinity there is, then all is divine. If so, then the acts of man in nature are sacramental.

In Central and South America the aboriginal societies developed great cultures—Maya, Aztec, Tolmec, Toltec. In the north, there were no such products. Here, very simple hunting and gathering societies with a primitive agriculture evolved upon the land, thinking predators who managed to sustain equilibrium in the system for many thousands of years. They developed a great acuity to nature and its processes and institutionalized this in a variety of pantheist cosmologies. These may well be unacceptable to modern western man, but they were effective as a view of man-nature for these societies and their technology.

Generally the members of these aboriginal societies could promise their children the inheritance of a physical environment at least as good as had been inherited—a claim few of us can make today. They were, in the history of America, the first occupants and they could claim to have managed their resources well. Life and knowledge have become more complicated in the intervening centuries, but, whatever excuses we offer, it is clear that we cannot equal this claim.

It is quite impossible to recreate the awe-

some sense of discovery experienced by Columbus and Cortés, Cabot and Cartier, Frobisher and Drake. It is difficult to sense the wonder of the following thousands who too encountered lands and prospects as yet untouched, unseen by western man, they who came in search of refuge, land, gold, silver, furs or freedom and found, whether they knew it or not, the last great cornucopia of the world's bounty. Who again can experience with Balboa a new continent and a new ocean?

But still much remains untouched where men have only seen or left some footprints on the ground. Those great preservationists—inaccessibility and poverty—have ensured that there is still an image of an earlier time when the men of the west came to make this continent their own. Consider Mount McKinley and the Athabaska Glacier, the North Atlantic beating on the rocky coast of Maine, the Kilauea Volcano in Hawaii, the glory of Yosemite and the Tetons, the park landscape of Texas and Oklahoma, the extensive painted deserts of Arizona and New Mexico, the palmetto, the mangrove swamps, the sculpture of Zion and Bryce, the geological fantasy of the Grand Canyon, the sandbars of Hatteras, the Appalachian Plateau, heartland of the great eastern forest, the gigantic redwoods fringing the Pacific, the fogs that gather about them, Crater Lake, Nantucket, the Columbia, the Sangre di Cristo Mountains, the rain forest of the northwest, the rich beauty of the Adirondacks, the continent-draining Mississippi and its delta.

Sad losses there have been, but the grizzly is still with us as are the bison, elk, moose, caribou and antelope, the wild goat, mountain lion, cougar, lynx, bobcat, coyote, the bald eagle and osprey, the great heron, the whales breeding off Baja California, seals and sea lions, sharks, porpoise and dolphin, sailfish and tuna.

In Bandolier are the habitations of early Americans, at Mesa Verde the works of their

55

successors, while at Zuni, Taos and Acoma they live today. But of the jewels of this great inheritance, that which most of all justifies the title cornucopia, there remains only a whimpering trace. The fringe of the railroad and the uncultivated hedgerow are the descendants of those grasses which built the prairie sod, deep and fertile—a geological deposit of a richness exceeding all the dreams of gold and silver, coal and iron. Of the prairies there is hardly any trace and little more of the great beasts that once dominated them.

When Columbus, Ponce de León, Cortés, Cabrillo, and Coronado arrived in America, they brought with them the Iberian tradition. Cabot, Frobisher, Drake, Hudson and Baffin and their men transmitted the mores of England while Cartier, Marquette and Joliette were the vanguard for the culture of France. While these and their fellow nationals who followed were united in the zeal for exploration and conquest, there were important distinctions in the attitudes each brought to bear upon this primeval continent.

If one looks through that narrow aperture of history, at the attitudes to the land which these cultures brought, it is apparent that there are four distinct divisions and that each has national associations. The first explorations in the 16th century were reflections of the great release of Renaissance humanism. This originated in Italy and it was here that is to be found the humanist expression of man and nature.

This assumption of power by man, rejecting the cosmography of the Middle Ages, is seen in a procession of projects. The first of these are the villas and gardens of Florence, after which the epicenter of expression moved to Rome and Tivoli. Bramante, Ligorio, Raphael, Palladio and Vignola created the symbolic expression of humanism upon the land, to be seen in the Villa Medici, Poggio a Cajano, the Villa d'Este and the Villa Lante, the Villa Madama and the Boboli Gardens

MEDIEVAL GARDEN

VILLA D'ESTE

WALL OF FOUNTAINS-VILLA D'ESTE

70

58

PARTERRE DE BRODERIE

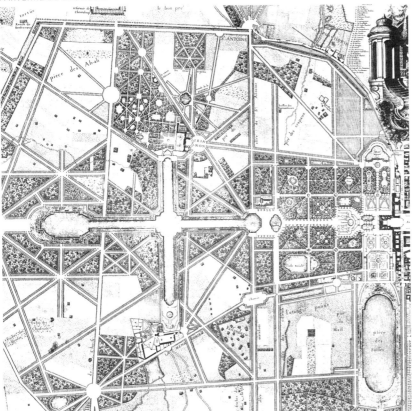
VERSAILLES

and, in the final phase, the Villa Aldobrandini and Mondragone. In these the authority of man was made visible by the imposition of a simple Euclidean geometry upon the landscape, and this is seen to increase within the period. Man imposes his simple, entertaining illusion of order, accomplished with great art, upon an unknowing and uncaring nature. The garden is offered as proof of man's superiority.

The second stage occurred a century later—at the time of the earliest colonial settlements—but the locus of power and expression had moved to France. Here the same anthropomorphic simplicity was applied at larger scale upon a flat and docile landscape. So at Vaux-le-Vicomte and Versailles one sees the French baroque expression through the works of André Le Nôtre, the zenith of Euclid upon the land. Louis XIV lay transected by the twin axes at Versailles, king by divine right, the ordered gardens below testimony to the divinity of man and his supremacy over a base and subject nature. Or so it seemed.

In the western tradition, with the single exception of the English 18th century and its extensions, landscape architecture has been identified with garden making—be it Alhambra, the Abbey of St. Gall, d'Este or Versailles. In this tradition, decorative and tractable plants are arranged in a simple geometry as a comprehensible metaphysical symbol of a submissive and orderly world, created by man.

Here the ornamental qualities of plants are paramount—no ecological concepts of community or association becloud the objective. Plants are analogous to domestic pets, dogs, cats, ponies, canaries and goldfish, tolerant to man and dependent upon him; lawn grasses, hedges, flowering shrubs and trees, tractable and benign, are thus man's companions, sharing his domestication.

This is the walled garden, separated from nature: a symbol of beneficence, island of

71

VAUX-LE-VICOMTE

the Orientalist Sir William Temple and, through the successive hands of William Kent, Humphrey Repton, Lancelot ("Capability") Brown, Uvedale Price, Payne Knight, and William Shenstone made over that raddled landscape of England into the fair image we can see today. Never has any society accomplished such a beneficent transformation of an entire landscape. It is the greatest creation of perception and art of the western world and it is a lesson still largely unlearned.

In the 18th century in England landscape architects "leaped the fence, and saw that all nature was a garden."* Beyond the fence "Men saw a new creation before their eyes." The leap did not occur until a new view of nature dispelled the old and a new aesthetic was developed consonant with the enlarged arena.

Starting with a denuded landscape, a backward agriculture and a medieval pattern of attenuated land holdings, this landscape tradition rehabilitated an entire countryside, allowing that fair image to persist to today. It is a testimony to the prescience of Kent, Brown, Repton and their followers that, lacking a science of ecology, they used native plant materials to create communities that so well reflected natural processes that their creations have endured and are self-perpetuating.

The functional objective was a productive, working landscape. Hilltops and hillsides were planted to forest, great meadows occupied the valley bottoms in which lakes were constructed and streams meandered. The product of this new landscape was the extensive meadow supporting cattle, horses and sheep. The forests provided valuable timber (the lack of which Evelyn had earlier deplored) and supported game, while freestanding copses in the meadows provided shade and shelter for grazing animals.

The planting reflected the necessities of shipbuilding. The preferred trees—oak and

delight, tranquility and introspection. It is quite consistent that the final symbol of this garden is the flower.

Not only is this a selected nature, decorative and tame, but the order of its array is, unlike the complexity of nature, reduced to a simple and comprehensible geometry. This is then a selected nature, simply ordered to create a symbolic reassurance of a benign and orderly world—an island within the world and separate from it. Yet the knowledge persists that nature reveals a different form and aspect beyond the wall. Loren Eiseley has said that "the unknown within the self is linked to the wild." The garden

symbolizes domesticated nature, the wild is beyond. It is indeed only the man who believes himself apart from nature who needs such a garden. For the pantheist nature itself best serves this role.

Each century saw a migration of power and in the 18th century it moved to England in the third phase, where there arose that unlikely efflorescence which is the beginning of a modern view. Believing that some unity of man-nature was possible and could not only be created but idealized, a handful of landscape architects took the dreams of writers and poets, images of painters of the period and the hints of a quite different order from

*Horace Walpole, *Anecdotes of Painting in England with some Account of the Principal Artists,* collected and digested by George Vertue, Henry G. Bohn, London, 1849, Vol. III, p. 801.

THE GLYME, BLENHEIM PALACE

beech—were climax species but they were planted *de novo.* On sites where these were inappropriate—northern slopes, thin soils, elevations—pine and birch were planted. Watercourses were graced with willows, alders and osiers, while the meadows supported grasses and meadow flowers.

The objective, however, was more complex than function alone. Paintings of the Roman Campagna by Claude Lorraine, Poussin and Salvator Rosa, a eulogy of nature, which obsessed poets and writers, had developed the concept of an ideal nature. Yet, it clearly had not existed in the medieval landscape. It had to be created. The ruling principle was

that "nature is the gardener's best designer" —an empirical ecology. Ornamental horticulture, which had obtained within garden walls, was disdained and a precursory ecology replaced it. The meadow was the single artifice—the remaining components were natural expressions, their dramatic and experiential qualities exploited, it is true, but deriving in the first place from that observed in nature.

Nature itself produced the aesthetic; the simple geometry—not simplicity but simple-mindedness—of the Renaissance was banished. "Nature abhors a straight line." The discovery of an established aesthetic in the

Orient based upon the occult balance of asymmetry confirmed this view. In the 18th century landscape began the revolution that banished the classical image and the imposition of its geometry as a symbol of man-nature.

This tradition is important in many respects. It founded applied ecology as the basis for function and aesthetics in the landscape. Indeed before the manifesto of modern architecture had been propounded—"form follows function"—it had been superseded by the 18th-century concept, in which form and process were indivisible aspects of a single phenomenon. It is important because of the scale of operation. One recalls that Capability Brown, when asked to undertake a project in Ireland, retorted "I have not finished England yet." Another reason for its importance lies in the fact that it was a creation. Here the landscape architect, like the empiricist doctor, found a land in ill health and brought it to good heart and to beauty. Man the artist, understanding nature's laws and forms, accelerated the process of regeneration so well indeed that who today can discern the artifice from the untouched? Nature completed man's works.

It is hard to find fault with this tradition: but one must observe that while the principles of ecology and its aesthetic are general, the realization of this movement was particular. It reflects an agricultural economy, principally based upon cattle, horses and sheep. It never confronted the city, which, in the 18th century, remains the Renaissance prototype. Only in the urban square, in parks, circles, and natural plantings is the 18th-century city distinguishable from its antecedents.

The rejection of nature as crude, vile—the lapsed paradise—and the recognition of the land as the milieu of life, which could be made rich and fair, is the great *volte face* of the western world. It did undoubtedly have some strange advocates; it encased the illusion of the noble savage and many other views, indeed it succumbed to an excess of romanticism—hired hermits standing picturesquely beside grottos and broken Greek urns—but it was a precursory ecology, its practitioners were more perceptive and capable than its theorist advocates. And it has endured.

Yet this entirely novel view, the best of all for those who would open a great natural treasure house, did not enter the American consciousness until the mid-19th century, when the gothic preoccupations attending its final phase were advocated by Andrew Jackson Downing. It was not until the end of the century that the English landscape

CENTRAL PARK, NEW YORK

tradition found a worthy advocate in Frederick Law Olmsted, but it was too late to affect the American ethos in any profound way; the west had been opened and the great depredations were not to be halted. Yet it was from this source that the National Park System, the parkway, the college campus and the humane suburb were all derived.

But only in the smallest part was the American style affected by the great 18th-century experiment. The dominant intention was to conquer nature and the resulting form is either the evidence of despoliation itself or, if it is symbolized, in the simple-mindedness of a Euclidean geometry. The 18th-century

landscape tradition exists in those reserves in which great natural beauty persists and in the small but precious oases that redeem the city.

Older than all of these—and, in a certain sense, a living tradition—is yet another quite different view: that derived from Islam and absorbed into the Spanish and the Hispano-American tradition. From the 9th to the 12th centuries the Moors civilized North Africa and the Iberian peninsula, offering testimonies of a culture undreamed of by their laggard European neighbors. They survived the uncultivated Crusaders, but in Spain succumbed to that great inconoclast

MYRTLE COURT, ALHAMBRA

Charles V, who relentlessly destroyed Muslim art and architecture to replace it with the parochial crudities of the Spanish Renaissance.

The attitude of Islam to nature derived from exactly the same source as the barbarism of Charles V. Both came from Genesis. The Moors emphasized the second chapter, with the injunction to dress the garden and keep it—man the steward—and developed the belief that man could make a garden of nature; paradise could be created by wise men and realized by artists. Moreover the paradise garden was an ingredient of urban form.

It would be charitable to suggest that this most benign, unchristian, Asian view permeated Spanish thought, but it does persist as a particularly felicitous adaptation to hot arid climates and provides a most direct and beautiful expression of which its Islamic prototypes, Alhambra and the Generalife, are the most brilliant testimonies. But the great Islamic tradition is all but dead, its present image composed of the decadent urban forms of the Ecole des Beaux Arts, with the new intrusions of an inappropriate International Style architecture.

The final phase includes the 19th and 20th centuries. In largest part it represents the age-old attitude of conquest, but now powered by larger and ever larger tools. Its great contribution is to the increasing concern for social justice—but as to the land, nothing has changed. We see the descendant of the small, cowering primitive animal, rather poorly endowed, omniverously eating carrion, roots, birds' eggs and the occasional kill, who has built a great cultural antagonism to a beneficent nature. The instincts that had sustained his ape ancestors and the empiric knowledge of his later human ancestors were lost and his brain was still inadequate to allow him to eat from the cornucopia: his hostility increased. Today he can savor the benison of the land, but his hos-

75

tility remains like a vestigial tail or appendix.

Our injunction is not ambiguous: man is exclusively divine, given dominion, enjoined to subdue the earth. Until Aaron David Gordon proposed, as a purpose of Zionism, that Jews return to the land to rediscover God, Judaism showed no contrary views. The medieval Christian Church introduced otherworldliness, which only exacerbated the consequence of the injunctions of the old law. Life on earth was seen as a probation for the life hereafter. The earth and nature were carnal, they constituted temptations of the devil. It was a lapsed earth, fallen from Eden—nature shared man's original sin: indeed it represented his temptation and the reason for his fall from grace. There were contrary views: Duns Scotus and Erigena sought to show nature to be a manifestation of God, while Francis of Assisi sought to love nature rather than to conquer it. But the view was not well received and on his death Francis received his reward—his Order was given to one of the most venal men in Christendom.

Within the Protestant movement there are two distinct variations. The Lutherans emphasized the here and now, the immanence of God, which required perception rather than action. In contrast, the Calvinists were determined to accomplish God's work on earth, to redeem nature through the works of godly man. Calvin believed that his role was to conquer carnal, bestial nature and make it subject to man, the servant of God.

In this perusal there are two clear paradoxes. The same Semitic people, living in the same arid and hostile environment, deriving their religious views from the same source in Genesis, developed two quite distinct views of man-nature. The first, represented in Islam, emphasized that man could make paradise on earth, make the desert bloom, that he was the creator and the steward. The Jews and the later Christians emphasized conquest.

The 18th century in England saw an astonishing efflorescence in which developed the view of all nature as a garden: man could make the earth at once rich and beautiful. Within a century this new view transformed the medieval face of an impoverished England, with the most backward agriculture in Europe, into its leader. Yet, this same England, with a mainly Anglican population—more akin in its views to Luther than to Calvin—was the cradle of the industrial revolution and became the leader in the conquest and despoilation of nature.

There remains that aberrant theme, the pagan view never completely suppressed, evident in classical Greece, widespread in Rome, vestigial in the Middle Ages—where its celebrations, incorporated into Christian festivals, retained some of their older connotations—and the naturalist theme in the 18th century. The neolithic memory persists perhaps most strongly today in that movement which is called Conservation. It seems clear that, whatever religion its adherents espouse, their devotion to nature and its cherishing and nurture derives little from either Judaism or Christianity.

The attitudes of Jews in the wilderness or in simple settlements had little immediate effect upon nature. The same attitudes in the medieval Christian Church were of as little consequence. Medieval cities huddled behind walls while nature surrounded them like a mighty ocean. Inside the city walls their paeans could rise in the high vaulted sublimity of Gothic architecture, but nature was unaffected. In the Renaissance the views of humanism produced many beautiful gardens based on a most inadequate view of man and nature, which (if not taken seriously as metaphysical symbols) can only delight. But in the French Renaissance, where the same theme was spoken with a louder voice, one begins to fear for the consequence of this great illusion. Its bearers are about to discover the ends of the earth and bring their conqueror's creed to other peoples and to all the waiting lands.

The 18th century produced the new view, the emancipated man: but while this transformation affected a nation, it did little or nothing to modify the attitudes of all of the *conquistadores* who spread to rape the earth. Indeed it was not sufficient to temper the next generation of Englishmen, who so eagerly espoused the industrial revolution. If Stowe and Woodstock, Rousham and Leasowes are the symbols of the 18th century, then the dark satanic mills, the Manchesters and Bradfords, are the symbols of its successor.

Such is our inheritance. A ragbag of ancient views, most of them breeding fear and hostility, based on ignorance, certain to destroy, incapable of creation. Show me the prototypical anthropocentric, anthropomorphizing man and you will see the destroyer, atomic demolition expert, clear feller of forests, careless miner, he who fouls the air and the water, destroys whole species of wildlife: the gratified driver of bulldozers, the uglifier.

The early colonists who came to this continent were truly pre-Copernican, their ignorance cannot be our excuse. Their rapacity was understandable if deplorable. Their whole inheritance had seemed a war against nature; they were determined to conquer this enemy. They were unaware that it had been the selfsame depredations, accomplished by the same ignorance, that had depleted their historic homelands. Yet this was their heritage and their view—nature bestial, savage, rude, the arena of the carnal, the temptation of the flesh, the antithesis of the aspiration to godliness. We might well ask whence came this astonishing illusion, this most destructive of all views, a testimony to a profound inferiority complex, reflected in aggression. The aboriginals whom they confronted bore no such resentment. They had other views of human destiny and fulfillment.

We have looked at the attitudes that our

ancestors of many races and creeds brought with them to this waiting continent. We can see today the consequences of these views—they are written on the land, our institutions and the cities. Much that can be seen is remarkable and the greatest of testimonies to this people. It is the arena of the only successful social revolution. Consider the disillusion of the justifiable Russian revolt, the tragedy of China embarking on a Russian adventure half a century later with nothing learned. The French Revolution was inconclusive and class conflict persists. The great glory of Madison and Hamilton, Jefferson and Washington was that they engineered the first successful social revolution. It is incomplete on several counts, but it remains the great example for the world to see.

Parallel to this great accomplishment runs a countertheme. During this same period when the streams of colonists and refugees exercised their industry and inventiveness, when the fruits of this labor were increasingly disbursed, there occurred the most wanton, prodigal despoliation of resources that the world has ever seen. More, the products of these efforts, made visible in cities and towns, increasingly preempted the exclusive title of the greatest uglification and vulgarity in world history. Much smaller nations—Switzerland and Sweden, Norway and the Netherlands—could offer to the world's view vastly superior evidence as land custodians and builders of cities.

The ransacking of the world's last great cornucopia has as its visible consequence the largest, most inhumane and ugliest cities ever made by man. This is the greatest indictment of the American experiment. Poverty can exercise a great constraint on vulgarity—and wealth is its fuel: but this alone cannot explain the American failure. It is clear that a profound ignorance, disdain and carelessness prevails. It is because of these that we are unable to create a handsome visage for the land of the free, the humane and life-enhancing forms for the cities and homes of the brave.

A Response to Values

So far, we have been concerned to establish that natural phenomena are dynamic interacting processes, responsive to laws, and that these proffer opportunities and limitations to human use. They can therefore be evaluated—each area of land or water has an intrinsic suitability for certain single or multiple land uses and a rank order within these use categories. But what of the land's capacity? Can this conception be tested using an existing site, with a predictable growth demand? Further, can the example be typical of a widespread social problem? Such is The Valleys. It is a case study of suburban growth in a metropolitan region—an area that usually becomes the victim of inchoate suburbanization. The problem then is to apply ecological planning principles and test them against the demands of metropolitan growth and the market mechanism.

The Grand National, My Lady's Manor and the Maryland Cup each year bring gentlemen jockeys and their splendid steeplechasers to the beautiful Green Spring and Worthington Valleys of Baltimore County, Maryland. Here in this spring landscape horses, Aberdeen Angus and Herefords graze in white-fenced fields as the meandering Jones Falls reveals its path from the bordering sycamores and willows. Plateaus rise from the valleys, thickly forested, transected by narrow roads that join at church or meeting

house. This landscape has been farmed and formed by families here for over two centuries and it is in good heart. For long it changed little as Baltimore grew, encompassing much else of the green surround; but with the construction of a radial expressway and the completion of a circumferential beltway, suddenly this bucolic enclave was brought into the orbit of the city. It was as if a new Homestead Act had been signed into law, as if every developer stood poised, his merchandise loaded on trucks—asphalt and concrete, lumber, bricks, steel and glass, pipes, coiled wire, diners, signs and, of course, billboards. There they were, each in wait, loans borrowed, deals made, contracts negotiated, all alert for the pistol shot that would permit inchoate growth to spread its relentless smear in the name of progress and profit, extinguishing the legacy of centuries of husbandry. Totally unprotected from despoliation by the existing powers of planning and zoning—in common with most of the remainder of the United States—a number of the landowners united in concern. With the encouragement of the County Administration, most particularly its office of Planning and Zoning, responsible citizens formed the Green Spring and Worthington Valley Planning Council, Inc., in 1962.

They found a consensus among the five thousand or so families in the area—unity in

the face of calamity—and concluded upon the necessity for a plan of action. They approached Dr. David A. Wallace, whose accomplishments in leading the renaissance of Baltimore with the plan for Charles Center had earned great confidence. He sought the assistance of the writer to contribute the ecological view and from this association was developed the Plan for the Valleys.*

The Council is a voluntary, nonprofit citizen group. It assumed the responsibility for preparing a plan to ensure preservation of the highest level of amenity with optimum development. It has as members a large, representative number of the residents and landowners in the Valleys.

The Valleys have the advantage of being defined by natural planning boundaries. The area of study extends from the Beltway to the northern slope of the Western Run, from Reisterstown Road and the Western Maryland Railroad to the Baltimore-Harrisburg Expressway. Its 70 square miles—almost 45,000 acres—contain great sweeping valleys, wooded ridges and plateaus, an intricate pattern of streams, farms, rural roads and copses of trees. It is a beautiful inheritance, a serious responsibility, an area threatened, a challenge and opportunity.

*Plan for the Valleys, Wallace-McHarg Associates, Philadelphia 1963.

The pressure of urbanization in the Valleys is perhaps more intensive than in any other area of the Baltimore Region. They are encroached on three sides by recent growth; highway construction has created great development potential; recent sewer studies indicate no permanent barriers to high-density development. If uncontrolled, this growth would surely wipe out the historic character and amenity of the area. Only responsible ownership and the concern of the County government has delayed calamity.

Good public policy would appear to coincide in this case with enlightened owner self-interest. Both recognize the need for retaining the natural beauty of the Valleys for private and public good. The objective of both is not to oppose inevitable change, but rather to prevent the rape of the countryside which unplanned, disorderly development would surely entail. This objective is not based on aesthetics or sentiment. Preliminary analysis clearly shows that early speculative development can have a devastating effect upon the realization of the full potential of the area. A few may make great profits at the expense of the many who will incur losses. The interests of residents and landowners coincide with the public objective of ensuring optimum development and equitable distribution of benefits.

The urban expansion that menaces the Green Spring and Worthington Valleys today is typical of a national problem. The normal expectation for this and other areas is that growth will be uncontrolled, sporadic, representing short-term values, with little taste or skill. Slowly nature will recede, to be replaced by growing islands of development. These will in time coalesce into a mass of low-grade urban tissue, having eliminated all natural beauty, diminished rare excellences, both historic and modern. The opportunity for realizing the American dream will recede again to a more distant area and a future generation. For this is the characteristic pattern by which those who escape to the country are encased within a faceless suburb, no-place, somewhere, U.S.A.

The evidence of this process is only too visible; the area abounds in examples; the process has an air of inevitability. Yet for the United States at large, for each metropolitan area in particular, for each specific landscape of great natural beauty and meaning, there is an urgent need to question this inevitability. Can we not create, from a beautiful natural landscape, an environment inhabited by man in which natural beauty is retained, man housed in community?

We must in faith believe this to be possible. The Green Spring and Worthington Valleys represent a unique opportunity to demonstrate the conjunction of private concern and action through civic and governmental process. Here is a small community, rich in intelligence, which has historically provided leadership. The problem is simplified by a single level of government and a harmony of private and public objectives. The process has begun most favorably with the creation of the Planning Council itself, the preparation of a plan and planning process. As will be seen, the problem can be solved, the prospective population can be accommodated without despolation. New communities may enhance the beauty of the area.

The United States awaits a large-scale demonstration of a beautiful landscape developed with wisdom, skill and taste—the evolution of a process that can produce a noble and ennobling physical environment: a step towards the American dream. No more propitious circumstances could exist than those in the Green Spring and Worthington Valleys today. The challenge is here and now.

The development of the plan for the Valleys contains some original contributions to planning theory and practice. The basic originality lies in the client and the problem—here landowners assumed the initiative and re-sponsibility for determining their destiny—a response at once unusual and commendable.

If planning requires the posing of alternatives with the costs and benefits of each, it is necessary to be able to demonstrate the physical and financial consequences of the *status quo* extended into the future. This is the second element in the study with some claim to wider relevance.

While it is an admirable device to be able to offer alternatives to society, it is also rather difficult to predict the future. In order to reveal the consequences of unplanned growth in the Valleys, David Wallace conceived the Uncontrolled Growth Model. In order to represent this it was necessary to specify the nature of the pressures and demands which would impinge on the area. This required population projection, which was undertaken by Mr. William C. McDonnell, the precise identification of property—its ownership, the nature of the owner—bona fide farmer, trust or speculator—land and building values. It involved familiarity with state and county proposals for highways, sewers and zoning. Dr. William Grigsby undertook a housing market analysis from which housing demand by type, price and location might be determined.

From this information Dr. Wallace simulated the pattern of growth that might occur in the absence of a plan or new powers. Subdivision after subdivision was laid down, irrespective of scenic beauty or physiographic phenomena, a wallpaper of development unrolled on the landscape. Each was designed with care yet the result was spontaneously described as The Specter.

Yet this melancholy process produces enormous profits in land sales and development. In the study area these could total $33,500,000 in development value by 1980. Consequently, any alternative method of development must accept this prospective development value. But when the nature of uncontrolled growth was represented in both

THE VALLEYS

LOCH RAVEN RESERVOIR

LIBERTY RESERVOIR

BALTIMORE

CHESAPEAKE BAY

BALTIMORE REGION

graphic and financial terms it was rejected as unacceptable by the residents of the region.

Given the anticipated population to be accommodated, and the development potential of the area, what principles can avert spoliation, ensure enhancement, and equal the development values of uncontrolled growth? The plan for the Valleys employed *physiographic determinism* to reveal the optimum pattern of development. This is the third original component. In short, physiographic determinism suggests that development should respond to the operation of natural processes. These processes will vary from region to region. The application of the concept in the study area is circumstantial, but the concept is general in its applicability.

The land was examined to reveal the intrinsic opportunities and constraints to urban development. Thereafter when permissive areas were tested against the housing market it was found that only a marginal increase in density was necessary to accomplish a fit.

When this proposal was examined in terms of the development value produced, it was seen to create an anticipated value of $7,000,000 in excess of the uncontrolled growth model.

Given a projection of population, the next question is how to carry out a development conception that satisfies both amenities and development values. The major innovation in this realm was the proposed real-estate syndicate. This device suggests that the landowners of the Valleys constitute themselves into a syndicate and acquire, among other powers, the development rights of the land for either cash or stock. The syndicate is seen as a private planning and/or development instrument supplementary to public planning processes.

The final aspect of the plan for the Valleys which may contain some wider relevance is the concept of an accumulation of powers. A sequence of both private and public ac-

81

tions, including the acquisition of new powers, is shown in a timed sequence.

The Proposition

The area is beautiful and vulnerable;

Development is inevitable and must be accommodated;

Uncontrolled growth is inevitably destructive;

Development must conform to regional goals;

Observance of conservation principles can avert destruction and ensure enhancement;

The area can absorb all prospective growth without despoliation;

Planned growth is more desirable than uncontrolled growth, and more profitable;

Public and private powers can be joined in partnership in a process to realize the plan.

The area is beautiful and vulnerable

Wherein lies its beauty, why is it vulnerable? What is the essential genius of this landscape? While there are many other areas of intimate beauty, the genius of the landscape resides in the great valleys—Green Spring, Caves, Worthington, and the wooded slopes that confine them. If the beauty and character of the landscape are to be sustained, then these great sweeping valleys, and the pastoral scene they contain, must be preserved unchanged.

These broad valleys are twice vulnerable. No landscape can be so quickly destroyed by small intrusions of development as can the broad valley in pasture. No sites are more attractive to the developers who can ruin them. Their character is as dependent upon their wooded walls as upon the valley floor. Should the woods be felled and replaced by development, the beauty and serenity of the scene will vanish. Only the absence of sewers in the valley has protected them from development and spoliation.

THE THREAT

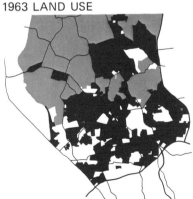

1963 LAND USE

RESIDENTIAL (ACRES PER DU)
UNIMPROVED
(ASSESSED RESIDENTIAL)
1 OR MORE (R 40)
0.5 TO 0.9 (R 20)
0.25 TO 0.49 (R 10)
0.24 AND LESS (R 6 GBA)
COMMERCIAL
INDUSTRIAL
PREDOMINANTLY OPEN LAND
(ASSESSED AGRICULTURAL)
INSTITUTIONAL

Development is inevitable and must be accommodated

Today the area is undeveloped, but high and rising land values are testimony to the imminence of development. Its advantages of amenity, the availability of developable land and accessibility, make inevitable a growing share of regional growth. The succeeding thirty years will see the population rise from 17,000 to 110,000; it may in fact rise as high as 150,000. This growth cannot be halted or diverted—it must be accommodated as an obligation of the area to the Baltimore Region.

Uncontrolled growth is inevitably destructive

Should no new powers be created, growth, of the magnitude described, would assume the same form in the area as it does elsewhere. Without new planning powers, there is no reason to believe that it would change its nature as it crossed Beltway and Expressway. Uncontrolled growth, occurring sporadically, spreading without discrimination, would slowly but surely obliterate the valleys, inexorably cover the landscape with its smear, irrevocably destroy all that is beautiful and memorable. No matter how well designed each individual subdivision might be, no matter if small parks were interfused with housing, the great landscape would be expunged.

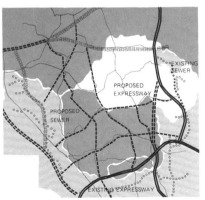

1963 UNIMPROVED LAND VALUE
IN FIVE VALUES, $1,000 to $7,000

CURRENT SUBDIVISION ACTIVITY

SEWERS AND HIGHWAYS

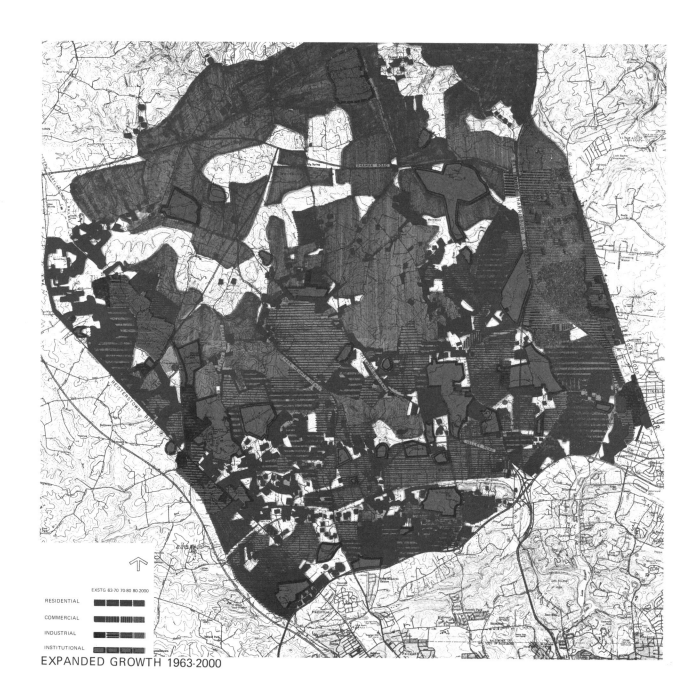

RESIDENTIAL

COMMERCIAL

INDUSTRIAL

INSTITUTIONAL

EXSTG 63-70 70-80 80-2000

EXPANDED GROWTH 1963-2000

84

SPECTER OF UNCONTROLLED GROWTH

Development must conform to regional goals

Regional growth to be accommodated by the study area has been identified. Regional and county planning agencies, deploring uncontrolled growth, have recommended four major concentrations bordering the study area: at Pikesville, Reisterstown, Towson and Hereford.

In this plan, the study area, which falls between these metrotowns, is proposed as regional open space with generally low-density development from which regional industry and commerce are excluded. The plan for the Valleys conforms to this objective. It is designed to accommodate the appropriate share of regional growth, in generally low-density development, but recommends minor nucleations in the interest of satisfying the regional open-space role. The plan thus conforms to regional goals.

ALTERNATE PATTERNS OF GROWTH

1 UNCONTROLLED

2 LINEAR ARTERIAL

3 PLAN FOR THE VALLEYS
  AND METROTOWNS

Observance of conservation principles can avert destruction and ensure enhancement

Consideration of the regional obligations of the Valleys indicates that the area must absorb 110,000 additional people in the next 40 years. While growth and development are thus inevitable, if controlled they need not be destructive. It is the purpose of this section to discuss those conservation principles that should be applied to avert destruction and ensure enhancement.

The natural processes examined included topography and subsurface geology, surface and groundwater, floodplains, soils (with particular reference to their permeability or imperviousness), steep slopes, forests and woodlands.

Each of these processes interacts with the others; each has implications for development. They have primary relevance in distinguishing the capacity of each area for development, the susceptibility to despoliation and the restraints and opportunities inherent in the landscape.

Physiographic principles for conservation and development

These principles indicate the types of development and densities appropriate to the various physiographic characteristics.

1 The valleys should be prohibited to development save by such land uses as are compatible with the present pastoral scene. These would include agriculture, large estates, low-intensity use, institutional open space, parks and recreation, public and private.

2 Development should be prohibited over all Cockeysville Marble aquifers.

3 50-year floodplains should be exempted from all development save agriculture, institutional open space and recreation.

4 Current state health regulations prohibiting development on all soils unsuitable for septic tanks should be rigidly enforced. On other soils, density of development using septic tanks should be regulated in relation to soil permeability and with reference to aquifers.

5 Surface watercourses should be retained in their natural condition to a width of not less than 200 feet on each side of the stream. In general, they should not be cultivated.

6 Dam sites and their impoundment areas should be prohibited to development as prospective water resources, artificial aquifer recharge and potential recreational areas.

7 All forests, woodlands, copses and freestanding trees above four-inch caliper should be surveyed and subject to preservation regulations.

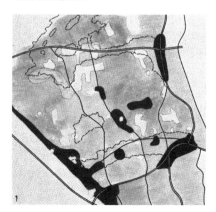

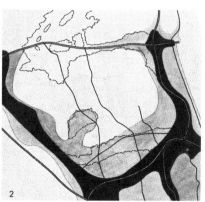

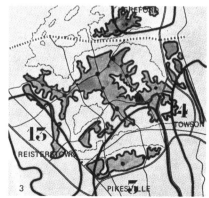

Development principles are as follows:

VALLEY WALLS WITHOUT FOREST COVER Such lands should be prohibited to development and should be planted to forest cover. When they are covered with the appropriate distribution of mixed hardwoods to an average height of 25 feet they may be considered as below.

VALLEY WALLS IN FOREST COVER These walls, exclusive of slopes of 25% or greater, should be developed in such a manner as to perpetuate their present wooded aspect. The maximum density permitted for development should be 1 house per 3 acres.

WALLS AND SLOPES OF 25% OR GREATER Valley walls, and all slopes of 25% or greater should be prohibited to development and should be planted to forest cover.

WOODED PLATEAU Forest and woodland sites on the plateau should not be developed at densities in excess of 1 house per acre.

PROMONTORY SITES On specific promontories, in wooded locations, the density limitations can be waived to permit tower apartment buildings with low coverage.

OPEN PLATEAU Development should be largely concentrated on the open plateau.

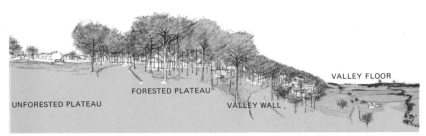

BASIC AMENITY

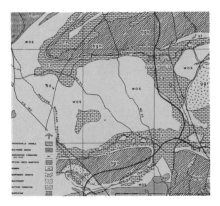

GEOLOGY

PHYSIOGRAPHIC SECTION

87

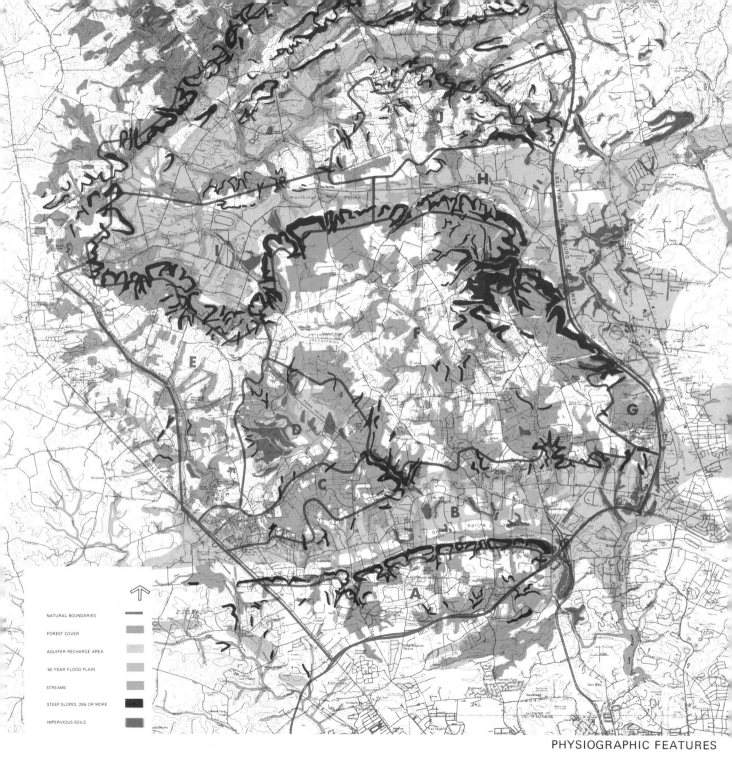

NATURAL BOUNDARIES

FOREST COVER

AQUIFER RECHARGE AREA

50 YEAR FLOOD PLAIN

STREAMS

STEEP SLOPES, 25% OR MORE

IMPERVIOUS SOILS

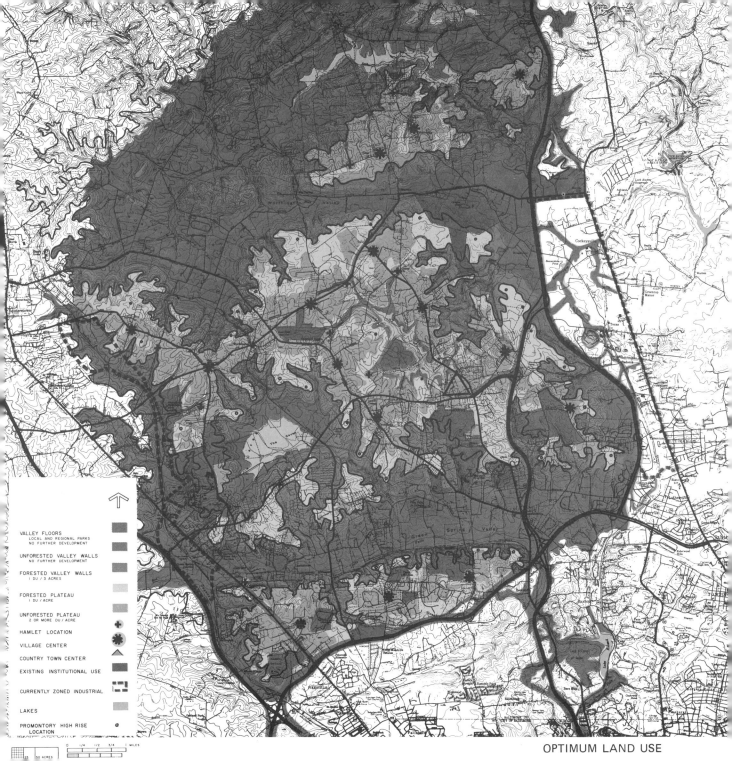

VALLEY FLOORS
LOCAL AND REGIONAL PARKS
NO FURTHER DEVELOPMENT

UNFORESTED VALLEY WALLS
NO FURTHER DEVELOPMENT

FORESTED VALLEY WALLS
1 DU / 3 ACRES

FORESTED PLATEAU
1 DU / ACRE

UNFORESTED PLATEAU
2 OR MORE DU / ACRE

HAMLET LOCATION

VILLAGE CENTER

COUNTRY TOWN CENTER

EXISTING INSTITUTIONAL USE

CURRENTLY ZONED INDUSTRIAL

LAKES

PROMONTORY HIGH RISE
LOCATION

0   1/4 1/2 3/4   1 MILES

50 ACRES

OPTIMUM LAND USE

UNFORESTED PLATEAU

FORESTED PLATEAU

FORESTED VALLEY WALL

TOWN CENTER

VILLAGE

HAMLET

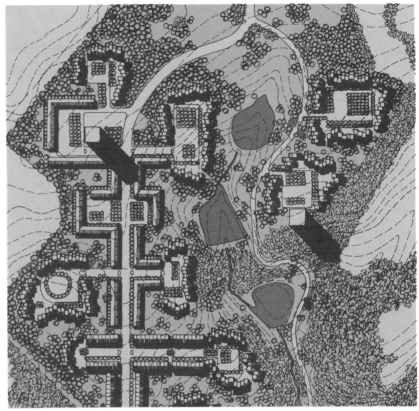

MAY'S CHAPEL VILLAGE

The area can absorb all prospective growth without despoliation

In fact there is not a scarcity of land but an abundance. The problem is one of diverting development to the plateau, which is capable of absorbing it, and deflecting it from the valleys where despoliation would result. Testing shows that the plateau will be able to absorb the prospective growth at densities consonant with housing market preferences. By developing as recommended, despoliation can be averted—it requires only a minor increase in average density for the prospective population to be accommodated on the areas indicated. This slight increase in average density is justified on two counts: first,

by the preservation of amenity and the open space thereby provided, secondly by the advantage of relative concentration in country town, villages and hamlets. Prospective growth can be absorbed in the plateau without transgressing the valleys or destroying their wooded slopes, at densities corresponding to market preferences.

When the physiographic guidelines were applied to the site it was apparent that propitious locations fell mainly on the plateaus. When these were examined in turn to reveal steep slopes and woodlands, streams and valleys and coherent areas suitable for development, it was found that many sites

91

BIRD'S-EYE VIEW

presented themselves. The variations suggested a variety of communities that ranged in size from a new country town with a prospective population of 20,000 to villages of some 5,000 population, and hamlets only one tenth that size. The housing market could be met with a single country town, more than a dozen villages and as many hamlets. This hierarchy of settlements would emphasize community rather than suburb. Housing would be nucleated around community facilities, their low-density edges consisting of one-acre clusters in adjacent woodlands or one house per three acres in the wooded slopes. The conception consists of an open-space system within which the communities are located, their internal open space continuous with the major system.

Planned growth is more desirable and as profitable as unplanned growth

The first part of this proposition is incontrovertible. Most cities and towns that we admire are as excellent as their planning is excellent. The matter of profit is more difficult to demonstrate only because we have not yet learned how to attribute value to the beauty and humanity of environments. If one excludes these vital factors and considers only the profits from land sales as between uncontrolled and planned growth

for the study area, the latter is seen to develop $7,000,000 in excess of uncontrolled growth. As the realization of the plan depends upon the exemption of development from the valleys, it would be desirable if payments were made to valley landowners deprived of the right to develop. The excess value of $7,000,000 over uncontrolled growth is sufficient to reimburse such landowners for rights to the 3,000 acres prohibited to development by 1980 at an average price of $2,300 per acre. Thus it is possible to claim conservatively that planned growth is at least as profitable as uncontrolled growth—and is definitely more desirable.

Public and private powers can be joined in partnership to realize the plan

A proposed land-use map is not a plan. It is an expression of physical, social and economic goals. It is the combination of these goals and the public and private powers to realize them that justifies the term "plan." Powers must be accumulated as part of a continuous process of guidance, control and implementation.

In the private domain the single most important recommendation is that landowners and residents constitute themselves into a Real Estate Syndicate and assume a major responsibility for realizing the plan. The Syndicate can both develop land and preserve open space. It may acquire either development rights, options, first refusals or title to land as a method of ensuring that development be in accord with the plan. For these rights it pays either in stock or in cash, in full or by installments. It may also be the agent through which bilateral or multilateral agreements between landowners are negotiated in conformity with the plan. It may thereafter sell title or rights or lease land for development according to the plan or may act as developer itself—either singly or in cooperation with other agents. The profits from these land transactions and development will be used for compensation of landowners whose property is not planned for development, for financing of additional purchases of rights or title, for outright development or for disbursement of profits to members of the Syndicate.

The basis for this proposal lies in the expectation that planned growth is likely to develop $7,000,000 more land value by 1980 than uncontrolled growth, that land values will appreciate over time—particularly on the plateau—and that a Real Estate Syndicate can utilize this increasing value as the basis of its operation.

It was also recommended that a Conservation Trust be created to receive gifts of land or money to purchase land for open space and that the Trust maintain such lands.

The public powers necessary to realize the plan extend from the vigorous enforcement of present powers to entirely new controls requiring State legislation. It was a primary objective to obtain public acceptance of the plan in principle, reflected in directives to various agencies of County government. A most important defense of the area still lies in the County intention to sewer the plateau but not the valleys. In the absence of sewers, the recent State health regulations prohibiting development on the 50-year floodplains, impervious soils and steep slopes are of vital importance. These regulations should be rigorously enforced. Sewer and highway policy can be used strategically to guide development to the plateau and divert it from the valleys.

In addition new public powers must be sought—mandatory cluster zoning, subsequently expanded to include deeding, minimum three-acre zoning, promontory zoning for highrise development, and 25-acre zoning are all advocated. Natural-resource zoning, including compensation where necessary, is recommended and would include floodplain zoning, forest and woodland zoning, steepslope zoning, and riparian zoning. Special Assessment Districts and Public Development Corporations are less immediate objectives.

The realization of the plan necessitates a process, public and private, wherein existing powers are supplemented by an increasing panoply of new controls over time. This requires tactics, recognition of immediate objectives and an intermediate- and long-range strategy. These powers can be accumulated.

Six years ago the Valleys confronted two extreme alternatives. The first was normal despoliation. The other depended upon the preparation of a plan linked to private and public powers. Only through private and governmental partnership and action, in con-tinuing process, has calamity been averted.

In the six years since the completion of the plan, no single development has been constructed in conflict with its proposals. The plan has been accepted by the County in principle, and its proposals have been accepted by various State departments. Developers sought to build in conflict with the plan. Their requests for zoning changes were denied and these decisions were upheld by the Courts. Subsequently the developers concluded in favor of realizing the plan. The principal development initiated is the planning and design of one of the proposed communities, May's Chapel Village. No single real estate syndicate has been formed but several are now in the process of forming. As a simpler response to the threat of development in unsuitable areas, the major landowners in the most threatened valley conjoined to write multilateral contracts binding themselves against sale or development of land not in conformity with the plan. The accumulation of powers, both public and private, that was recommended proceeds approximately on schedule with the single exception of the Real Estate Syndicate.

The plan and the action of the landowners and residents in the area did avert despoliation. So far development is occurring within the recommendations of the plan; public policies and actions are directed towards its realization. In this case, the people of an area sought to exercise some measure of control over their destiny and were, to an ususual degree, remarkably successful. The form of development derived directly from the ecological view.

This study was undertaken for the Green Spring and Worthington Valleys Planning Council by Wallace, McHarg Associates in 1963. It was published in full in that year under the title of *Plan for the Valleys*. Mrs. Anne Louise Strong, Mr. William Grigsby and Mr. William H. Roberts served as consultants while Mr. William C. McDonnell was resident planner.

The World is a Capsule

It is not a small accomplishment to challenge the Bureau of Public Roads, armed only with a little ecology and the ecological view; it is a matter of some small pride to take the same rudimentary knowledge and analyze and prescribe for the New Jersey Shore or a metropolitan open-space system or plan seventy miles of rural Baltimore County. If you are persuaded, as am I, that ecology and the view it provides can perform prodigies of work, then it becomes necessary to increase our knowledge of this illuminating field. We could then confront even larger and more intractable problems.

We can use the astronaut as our instructor: he too is pursuing the same quest. His aspiration is survival—but then, so is ours.

When the first capsule experiments began, our imaginary astronaut believed that physical fitness was one of the most important, if not the most important, of attributes. To maintain this, he pursued a regimen of great rigor. Each day he walked and ran several miles, much of this through a forest. At first, it was merely a measure of sweat. However, in time he came to welcome this green world and delighted in the dappled light that fell upon his path. He perceived the dark boles against the toplit canopy, the flash of the stream, the rump and tail of the deer. The

forest came to reveal some striking forms, the great gray beech, its taut hide inscribed with old loves, the luminous bloodroot in the rust leaves, the somber green of hemlocks, a great rock face, half-a-billion years old, mottled with mosses and lichens. He became more knowing—his colleagues taught him the names of some conspicuous creatures, the oak and tulip poplar, sycamore, ash and maple. As the seasons changed, different forms called for his attention: shadblow, dogwood, wild cherry, the rhododendrons and laurels, shading into the encompassing summer forest from which emerged the hints of autumn, the scarlet nyssa alone, then sassafras, the maples, the bitter yellow of the poplar, the bright fruits, the amber light, the sea of warm leaves and then again the skeletal forest.

The creatures, too, changed from unseen prints and noises to discrete records—the jay heard but not seen, deer prints by the water, traces of possum and raccoon; the clamor of crows bespoke an owl pursued, feathers and blood told of a hawk. But now the forest is anticipated—the swelling buds, those first inconspicuous maple flowers, spicebush yellow, the expectation of grossbeaks or a tumult of warblers, the file of young skunks, the unfurling fern, the first crimson leaf.

But the experiment in the capsule, which filled his working hours, had talked of sterner things: of biomass and energy systems, food pyramids, symbiosis—and always survival. It became clear in time that the forest was not, as he had thought, a group of benign and decorative creatures, orderly, tranquil, irrelevant, but rather the same kinds of living things and processes as the ones in the experiment, responding to the same laws: equally indispensable to his survival, but complex beyond his dreams. The astronaut learned that the external world could be viewed in the same way as in the capsule simulation but that one had to begin earlier and accept a wider stage and a larger cast of actors.

To learn of the evolution of physical and biological processes is an indispensable step towards the knowledge one needs before making changes to the land: but it is far from enough. It is as necessary to know how the world *works*. Who are the actors and how do they respond to the environment, to physical processes and to other creatures? The broadest outlines of this were discussed in the capsule experiment, but that was only a caricature. It is true, but simplified almost to the point of idiocy. Happily for the world, creatures and men are more complex than this. Can we proceed to add another layer of knowledge, to learn of the complexity of nature and its interactions? This we

need to know in order to be men and to act.

Yet, the step forward is a reluctant one. We look back enviously to those fewer, earlier men who, with smaller powers, built slowly, a little at a time, without harm and could change with less thought.

So let us return to an imagined capsule wherein an astronaut sits, lonely, the algae and bacteria present, but unseen—Nostoc, Azotobacter and the rest. In this vision the astronaut contemplates his algal broth without enthusiasm; he has little confidence in his companions; he is apprehensive about the experiment. And well he might be. The fruits of some billions of years of biological evolution are the complexity and diversity— the duplication, interlocking and overlapping of roles that best guarantee survival; and these are absent in the capsule. It has the simplicity of ignorance, of simple-mindedness. Happily for the astronaut, during the period of failure in creating a self-sustaining biological system, the parallel experiments in rocketry had advanced dramatically. We should not be surprised—after all, inert systems are by definition more simple than living ones. Nonetheless, it was the success in propulsion that made possible increase in the size of the capsule and thus elaboration of its biota.

It was, of course, always apparent that the peril of the adventure could be diminished by increasing the community of passengers. Clearly, in the early experiment, if either algae or decomposers died, so then did the man. Ignorance and vanity have no place here. The most anthropocentric man wishes better insurance than this on his moon flight.

In enlarging the capsule, the objectives remain unchanged: to create a self-sustaining ecosystem—whose only import is sunlight, whose only export is heat—sufficient to sustain a man for a certain period of time.

But now the rules are better known. Four

food-chain layers are better than three in terms of stability; so in the new experiment there shall be the plant producers, plant-eating consumers, carnivores or secondary consumers (man as the top carnivore) and finally the essential decomposers. These trophic layers must be in such numbers as will produce an energy pyramid. It is also known that the smaller the producer organism, the greater its production per unit of weight, so we will concentrate upon small producers. We also know that, with very few exceptions (among which rice and sugarcane are conspicuous), aquatic systems are much more productive than terrestrial ones. We will, therefore, concentrate upon aquatic environments.

The requirement for small, highly-productive photosynthetic agents causes us to turn unerringly to algae, those most ancient and enduring of plants—the filamentous algae, green algae, blue-green algae, and the diatoms. But, solicitude for the diet of the voyagers suggests we will also add watercress and wild rice. Upon this photosynthetic base we can superimpose the smallest consumers, the zooplankton—the astonishing propeller-driven rotifers, the darting copepods and Cladocera, all herbivores. The next group of plant eaters would include larger creatures— pond snails, crayfish, caddis fly larva and the mayfly nymph. Yet one other layer of herbivores, again increasing in size, would include frogs and their tadpoles, turtles, minnows and sunfish. The carnivores constitute, reasonably, a smaller group—diving beetles, water scorpion, damselfly and dragonfly nymphs, some bass, and, of course, the man. The decomposers will include not only the familiar bacteria and fungi but also bloodworms, "phantom larvae" and freshwater clams.

But now we have, in short, the major creatures in a pond ecosystem, derived from Eugene P. Odum.* But we have only the creatures in the food chains; what of the environments? As these creatures need environments as much as they need food, we add

*Eugene P. Odum, *Fundamentals of Ecology*, W.B. Saunders Company, Philadelphia, 1959.

cattails and bullrushes, arrowhead and water lily, pondweeds and muskgrass. These happen to accomplish photosynthesis, but their importance lies not in the food chain but as the elements of the environment, providing havens, homes, shelter and protection.

Now while we have accounted for the producers and the decomposers, we must still consider the nutrients. These must all exist and in the proper proportions. How best can this be accomplished? Perhaps if we could obtain healthy creatures from a healthy pond we could be assured of their presence in optimum quantities. So, indeed, this is what is done. First a control pond ecosystem is measured for the incidence of oxygen, carbon, nitrogen, hydrogen, the macronutrients (phosphorus, potassium, calcium, sulfur, magnesium) and the trace elements (iron and manganese, copper, zinc, boron, sodium, molybdenum, chlorine, vanadium, cobalt and iodine). These are measured in the air, the water, the mud, and in the man. A comparable pond ecosystem with its stock of nutrients is introduced into the capsule.

While the experimenters work on this, let us consider this rather provocative conclusion —that the best way of ensuring the appropriate distribution of the nutrients in an ecosystem is to ensure that the creatures that eat each other, their substances and their wastes, be healthy in the first instance. That is, in order for the members of the system to be healthy, if they live off each other, then all the members must be healthy. If they are healthy, then the nutrients in the system will exist in such proportions in this and that organism and in the environment, circulated through the system to ensure health. As men, however, we do not eat from an ecosystem, but take elements from many discrete, distant and different systems, and (most frequently) from crops that are not parts of natural systems. We know neither whether the plants are from ecosystems, nor, if they are, if the systems are healthy. In the capsule we must be sure; survival depends upon it.

Experiments now being conducted give presumptive evidence to support this conclusion. Health in a stable forest community, in its plants and animals appears to coexist with a certain constant distribution of trace metals that have long been circulated and recirculated through the system and are now in optimum quantities and distribution. In adjacent disturbed communities the level of health of the organisms is much lower and it has been found that trace minerals are more random in their distribution in the environment and in their incidence in the organisms.

By increasing the complexity of the experiment, a penalty has been incurred. When the food chain was simply man-algae, only 10% of the input to the algae was obtained by man. When the algae were eaten by the sunfish which was in turn eaten by the bass, before being eaten by the man, there were three transfers of energy, each only 10% of the preceding, so that one hundred times the plant production was required to produce the unit energy in bass that could be obtained less palatably from algae. But since light is not limiting in the experiment, and the creatures are not space-demanding, we can accept the penalty.

The system is tested. The oxygen-carbon dioxide cycle works very well. By regulating sunlight, photosynthesis or respiration can be varied to increase the oxygen or the carbon dioxide in the system. There has been a considerable improvement in the water cycle. It is found that the aquatic biota are, in fact, a water-purifying system and that the water is completely potable. We should not be surprised. It is the aquatic biota that ensure pure water. This waste-disposal system works very well indeed, not only through the action of the bacteria and fungi, but also by the actions of the snails, the clams and the bullrushes. But the greatest improvement is in our astronaut's diet—wild rice as the staple, watercress for salad, algal broth, snails, clams, frog's legs as appetizers, crayfish, turtle, panfish and bass as the main course: a great improvement

over algae alone, indeed, food for a gourmet.

The experiment proceeds most satisfactorily, day after day; but, as it moves into the second week, a certain erratic behavior might be observed. Certain organisms are flourishing, others declining dangerously. It is suspected that this is, in fact, being accomplished by the decomposers—these are known to release environmental hormones into systems that inhibit the growth of certain organisms and stimulate others. This mechanism is beyond the control of the researchers. They see the experiment disintegrate before their eyes, unresponsive to their best efforts. In what degree was the system inadequate, requiring remedy? None could say.

There was a postmortem, of course, and the first conclusion was that the second experiment had accomplished some limited successes. The state of the art had advanced, but it was regretted that science was still unable to comprehend all the roles played by the constituent organisms—obviously the most obdurate area of ignorance lay in the regulatory mechanisms in the system. It was concluded that research should be concentrated on these, but that, in the meantime, success was more likely to attend experiments that simulated to a greater degree larger natural environments, which had demonstrated stability over longer periods of time. In this conclusion the scientists had accepted that organisms can accomplish self-regulation and realize synthesis. Thus, the stability of a natural ecosystem was evidence enough—it was not required that all the constituent processes be fully understood. This is a conclusion of great importance: we can respond to nature's laws, even when these are imperfectly understood.

Now this conclusion had, of course, a most chastening effect upon those students who welcomed the concept of man omniscient, the controller of the nuclei and plastids in the world epidermis, the world life. In order to make such claims, one needs to demonstrate better success in the capsule. After all, the entire biota evolved quite independently of man. He exists as a creature for only a million years and he has been a puny inconsequence whose only power was the threat of power until the very recent past. Of course, his greatest strength—the ability to destroy—is a great power; but it contributes little to the capsule experiment. We need to demonstrate creative, rather than destructive skills, if we are to replicate nature or to manage it.

Let us imagine that space-exploration experiments moved forward—impelled by substantial appropriations—and that a new program has been formulated. A space buoy is envisaged to be located at a libration point—one of the five points in space where a body can remain relatively stationary with respect to the sun and the moon; where the gravitational pull of the earth, sun, and moon are so neatly balanced that little motion occurs. These locations, which are ideal for the examination of cosmic debris (which accumulates at these points) and solar "weather," are also "well suited for gravitational studies, redetermination of the gravitational constant, the nature of gravity and the study of biorhythms in the absence of a magnetic field."*

A program is designed. The theoretical space buoy must consist of a rotating sphere with an inclined axis, providing day and night and the changing seasons. A protective envelope will protect the inhabitants from toxic insolation, while transmitting the necessary spectrum. Within this envelope there must be an atmosphere of the necessary gases in the correct proportions at the appropriate pressure. A hydrosphere is required with an evaporation-condensation cycle, with storage and recirculating elements, all preferably operated by gravity. A lithosphere is necessary as a storehouse for matter—the base for living soils—and as an insulator. Temperature regulation is important: the hydrosphere, atmosphere and lithosphere must all be manipulated to provide an optimum range of temperature. It is the final component that is the most demanding: the creation of a biosphere—an energy pyramid, larger than before, with the trophic levels populated by complementary and supplementary creatures.

Now the disarray of the previous experiment was still a remembered humiliation. The intention to replicate a pond ecosystem had failed. It was found that the decomposers had released "environmental enzymes" that inhibited some organisms and stimulated others, resulting in a total collapse of the system. While research was proceeding towards an understanding of the role of these inhibitors and stimulants, the experiment could not wait: and so the scientists concluded that the wisest course was to replicate a system, adapted by man, able to sustain him, that had exhibited stability over a long period of time. The only examples of such adaptations are farms; it was decided to reproduce a miniature farm within the space buoy. Yet, farming has a short history—in only a few places has it endured for a thousand years. In most cases, it is far from self-sustaining, being entirely dependent upon fertilizers, irrigation and supplements of organic matter.

We think of farms as the source of cereals, root crops, beef, mutton, poultry and eggs: but, of course, farms do more than this. Consider a very large bell jar, some miles in diameter. Place it over an area of farmland. The consequences will be very small; the plants produce oxygen for the system and utilize carbon dioxide which they respire, and which is also obtained from decomposition. The numbers of animals and men in the system affect it little, nor does it limit them. Place the same bell jar over a city. If no gases can pass through the bell jar, then the inhabitants will shortly consume all of the oxygen and will asphyxiate. If they cannot dispose of human wastes, they will be encompassed in ordure. If they cannot provide food internally or import it, they will starve. The city is the source of water pollution—natural water purification occurs elsewhere. But, not so on the farmland, which is largely a self-sustaining system. So the farm can perform all the roles asked of the algae and decomposers in the first experiment, and of the modified pond ecosystem in the second; but it will be necessary to include all the creatures in the system—not only the large and conspicuous ones that seem superficially important to man.

And so the experiment proceeds, the selection of the chosen few, more elaborate than Noah ever dreamed, the identification of creatures, counted in number, added together in chains of dependencies, filaments of being interwoven into a single organic community. It is all exquisitely measured and observed: oxygen and carbon dioxide, the nutrients in proportion and distribution, temperature, photosynthesis and respiration, decomposition and recycling, soil, air and water, acidity and alkalinity, the provision for habitats and territories.

The principal actors of the previous experiment, while present in our new space-buoy model, are no longer conspicuous in this larger farm-like environment. The companions are more familiar to the astronaut and ourselves: there are the grains—wheat, corn, barley, hay; there is a large group of vegetables and some less familiar herbs; there are fruit trees and a farm woodlot. The animals are these ancient companions of man, long-serving and patient: cattle, sheep, pigs, hens, ducks, turkeys, pigeons, dogs, cats, and some rats and mice. There is a large community of birds and insects; the bacteria are in the air, the water, the soils, and in the creatures; the fungi and other decomposers are abundant in the soil, the mud of the farm pond and in living organisms.

The distribution of the essential nutrients is an important consideration, and lacking any better information, it is concluded that these will exist in the full range and appropriate distribution—provided the water, soil, and creatures of the ecosystem are healthy.

*Dr. I.M. Levitt, Director, Fels Planetarium, Philadelphia, in *The Philadelphia Inquirer,* Sunday, November 8, 1966.

Throughout the entire experiment, the major emphasis has been given to the creation of a regular energy pyramid of creatures in dynamic equilibrium. In this, the matter of population size, life-span, and replacement has been of consuming interest—but what of man? The system is designed to sustain several men; should they be individual males, a family, or a breeding population? The last must exist if, like the other creatures, man is to perpetuate himself.

If we can consider human reproduction in our ecosystem, then we must also consider death. This is a most important factor in the nonhuman biota. The predictable death of populations is essential for the operation of the ecosystem. So, if man in the system is to operate within the laws that obtain for all other components, then death and replacement must be included. How does one ensure the appropriate incidence of death in the system? This is normally a function of the pathogens. What are these? What incidence will produce immunity against epidemic, what level will sustain normal life-spans? This is not known and so we retreat to empiricism once more. We can assume that in the nonhuman biota, selected as healthy in the first place, the pathogens will be present and that life will run its course as it does outside of the experiment. For man, we can only assume that he is mortal and that he will die—presumably from agents within the simulated ecosystem, from the effects of aging, and the stresses of the environment.

We must now consider the persons who will man this experiment, not only in terms of their health, but for the skills they bring to the task. In the beginning of space exploration, coinciding with the first capsule experiment, the requirements were simple—experience as a test pilot, courage, and equanimity; these were the primary qualities. But, as the project moved into the second stage, it became clear that the astronaut who had perfunctorily learned some college chemistry and biology must need study these sciences more thoroughly. And so he did: physics and chemistry, botany and zoology, and, most important, ecology; so that as the experiment moved into the current stage, the astronaut was a natural scientist and an excellent research ecologist. Yet, the simulated farm ecosystem increasingly called for skills that emphasized green thumbs rather than abstruse knowledge; the major task was clearly not only understanding the system, but managing it. Indeed, while the astronaut had learned a great deal of indispensable science, his finest skill was that he could apply this in the management of the ecosystem. We could now call him an intelligent husbandman, a steward.

Now in the organization of this experiment some important conclusions were reached. Clearly, the level of radiation in the space buoy could not exceed the normal range of experience. Excessive radiation could kill critical species; lesser levels, while not toxic, could affect the rate of mutation; and the evolution of a mutant was an unpredictable exigency the scientists would rather avoid. It was also important that no organisms be extinguished, otherwise the experiment would fail. There was a premium on the survival of all of the members of the system, although a number of creatures found in the farm ecosystem had no roles that could be identified as critical. As all the creatures, their substances and their wastes passed through the entire system no poisons— herbicides or pesticides—could be employed. All wastes must be decomposed and regularly recycled. There could be no depletion of resources: so that losses which had occurred on the farm—of topsoil from erosion, of nutrients—could not be permitted in the capsule.

The author, like the reader, inherited the western anthropocentric view: but from a rudimentary ecology, his views have changed dramatically. Have the reader's attitudes changed as radically? Whether this has happened or not, we can assume that the astronaut is a man transformed. No one is more surprised than he for such had not been his expectation when first he volunteered for this assignment. At the onset he had been a simple and brave man of more than average intelligence. He was the product of our times and was viewed as a prideful symbol of its success. Although he might not have cared for the simile, he was a 20th-century conquistador. He was certain that his objectives were largely selfless; he sought to lead the conquest of nature by man into new realms, to enlarge the national pride by leaving a trail of human scent in some sparse, silent space never before haunted by man. His view of the world, when first he began, was simple and clear; man, the acme of creation, the lone architect of God, was destined to make the world into a human image.

Although in the course of his preparation he had learned of uncountable galaxies, careening from view at nearly the speed of light, and forever unknowable, this touched his assurance not one whit. He knew in the rational surface of the mind that it would require much of a man's life at all but the speed of light to reach the nearest stars, but this did not affect his innate sense of infinite superiority. His homocentric view was undeterred by inhabiting a minor galaxy, far from its center, sustained by a very ordinary star on an insignificant planet on which he was a most recent expression. Indeed, while his knowledge of these things was adequate, it had not in any way affected his profound attitudes to the universe or himself; he was, in fact, pre-Copernican in believing that man bestrode the earth around which the sun revolved, in turn the center of the surrounding cosmos, testifying to the primacy of man in whose image was God made.

As the experiments proceeded, he became absolutely transformed, unfamiliar to his friends, barely recognizable to himself. It was as if, long blind, he had been given the power of vision. He had learned that the universe was a great creative process that encompassed the sun and the earth. It had perhaps been necessary for a nova to explode to make the first evolutionary step from hydrogen to helium; it had been in the holocaust of a disintegrating supernova that all the elements had been formed. The stuff of these cosmic events provided the building blocks of the earth and of life, and pervaded them. This history was known to him, the evolution of matter and of creatures; he knew his ancestors, the living who were quick with him now, his kinship with them. The yearnings of all life in all time were his yearnings too. As he looked upon the world, he was aware of the myriad beings, their essential roles which sustained all life and its yearnings. He had the faintest glimmering of a uniquely human role.

The knowledge he had acquired he came to see as the essential evidence in the search for meaning and for purpose. It permitted him to see himself and his companions as the product of a great process, comprehensible through the past, with the future some unpredictable but amenable extension of past and present. The world was fit for life; life adapted to the world. The environment could be made more fitting: this appeared to be that role which man could uniquely fulfill.

In the course of the experiments, the astronaut had come to unite within himself the abstract knowledge of the natural sciences and of ecology with the reality of the visible world and its processes. He had emerged from this experience emancipated, a phenomenon in the phenomenal world. He had become in truth—although quite by accident—a true symbol of pride for a society that did not know it, and knew him not. He was now more than Copernican; he was a splendid testament to 20th-century man, freed from his cultural inferiority, secure in his history, conscious of his role in creation, aware of his consciousness.

The clamor of the press was less and less revealing to him, for the essential problems could find no place among the insistencies of personal violence and the inventory of inconsequence. Surely survival was the first and overriding concern. As the nations performed their solemn ceremonial dances and assumed accustomed gestures, behind them loomed the white-coated minions—the armorers of world life extinction. Were it not for these unnamed, sepulchral warriors, the dancers could be viewed more tolerantly. They seemed rather like small boys reluctantly involved in conflict, shouting then shoving, the first blow not yet struck which drives out reason. With the noncombatant extinctionists standing behind them, the small boys are transformed and the first blow can set off the holocaust.

It is important to bring these faceless figures into full light. They have made temporary squabbles into the threat of total extinction; they have evolved powers too strong for the nature of the arguments. Who and what are they? Did they resemble the early astronaut—a brave, innocent, wondrous tool, but not full man? They are too fearfully reminiscent of children with firecrackers; young soldiers delighted by demolition who have evolved into the full maturity that seeks the excuse of Alaskan ports or Panama canals to exercise their deadly atomic toys.

These adolescents are not fit custodians for all life, the inheritance of all creatures, and all men. If life ends, then let us await the death of the sun. We must know these men and their views. If they are like the first innocent astronaut, then may they yet gain that vital deference for this immense journey.

Survival is the first concern. Let us give it that priority and ensure that our destiny is not in the hands of these archaic men who still retain the vengeful view of man against nature, who can carelessly ignore the fruits of evolution and extinguish all life as the remedy for human contests.

If we can gain the assurance that human arguments cannot be resolved by total extinction of all life, then we can proceed to the next problem: that of radiation. What is the nature of the life forms that will exist? Again we must turn to the anonymous white-coated figure, hidden from view, and ask of the radiation level, the mutation rate. This, we understand, was also subject to natural selection. As this is increased, the products will be a result of inadvertence rather than selection. We introduce more randomness into the system; if we increase the mutation rate too much we can become the agents of evolutionary retrogression. This is, indeed, no fulfillment of the uniquely human role we seek. Those of us who look hard to find evidence to reject the view of man as a planetary disease can find no support from this.

If we can be assured of survival, and avoid the calamity of mutational retrogression, then we may move down the scale to a consideration of the numbers of persons who will survive. The simpler plants and animals produce enormous numbers of spores, seeds and eggs, as a means of survival, but as the life forms evolved, they depended less on numbers and more upon protection and nurture. Witness the evolution of man: the long period of human infancy, and the solicitude it requires, may well be one of the best testaments to man as a high evolutionary form. This splendid adaptation, however, does contain the requirement to cherish and to nurture, as the responsibility for the creation of new life.

Animals in the wild, even the most simple kinds, have developed nonrational mechanisms whereby populations are controlled. It cannot, therefore, be beyond the compass of the uniquely rational animal, man, to accomplish that which the simpler creatures do without thought. Here again we look for that evidence to support the proposition that the brain of man is the highest point in biological evolution—we are undermined by the facts of the case. The factors that have contributed to the increase in population are these same elements which can contribute to human well-being, the nurture of man, improved food, sanitation, shelter and—above all—medicine. These are the very agents for cherishing those who are bequeathed life. The necessary solicitude is linked to numbers—based upon the availability of resources and the capacity to provide that nurture which is essential for the achievement of manhood.

We must conclude that these major retrogressive forces, the atomic holocaust, radiation and runaway population growth, must be resolved for man to develop his potential. Extinction, evolutionary retrogression, either through mutation or cultural impoverishment from excessive numbers, can only be an indictment of man. The task requires that these threats be surmounted as central problems in the task of making the earth more fit, and man more fitting.

As a result of his new-found knowledge of experimental ecology the astronaut has changed profoundly. In the first experiment he was confounded to learn that his survival was contingent upon some microscopic algae, bacteria and fungi; his solicitude for them grew with his knowledge. As the experiment increased in complexity, a larger number of creatures became his familiars, and the umbrella of his knowledge and solicitude expanded. They were, after all, essential to his survival, as he was to theirs. Slowly, algae and diatoms, bacteria and fungi, snails, worms, clams, crustaceans, flies and their larvae, beetles, rotifers, fish and their spawn, birds and their eggs and young became known to him—their appearances, their ways, their roles. With this grew a preoccupation for their well-being, and the preconditions for this. Knowledge and solicitude grew hand in hand in these experiments in mutual dependence.

He finally came to understand, not only intellectually but emotionally, that these co-tenants of the experiment, his fellows, were dear to him in the most literal of senses. They were together united in survival and evolution. They were united, all with their own proclivities and dependencies, intermeshed of necessity, receiving life, growing, reproducing, evolving, aspiring to equilibrium in the system, sustaining one another.

The last experiment in the space buoy was an excellent preparation for entering the world at large. If you remember, it had certain stringent requirements, and in retrospect, our friend observed their corollaries on this planet. The energy source was the sun; the environment had to be on, or part of, a rotating sphere with gravity—the earth. It should have such a rotation and inclination as would produce day, night and changing seasons, as indeed it did. An encompassing envelope was essential; the atmosphere fulfilled this role by protecting us from toxic insolation but permitting the transmission of the necessary spectrum. There must be an atmosphere of the necessary gases in certain proportions and pressure, as indeed there was. The great reservoir is the ocean; the evaporation-distillation-transport-condensation-precipitation process is the hydrologic cycle; its storage and circulation elements—the rivers and streams, lakes and aquifers—operate by gravity. In the experiment, it was critical to design temperature-stabilizing mechanisms. All bodies of water performed this role on earth, as did ice caps, clouds, the atmosphere, soils and, of course, vegetation. This later category has been prematurely introduced in this bill of particulars. Yet, plants above all other things satisfied the next requirement, that of ensuring stability in terrestrial processes. In strict order, the next requirement was for a mechanism to transmute the energy of the sun into a food base for all life. The chloroplast performed this, our astronaut had learned. Finally, there was required a biota of creatures, arranged in trophic layers, interacting with each other, both horizontally and vertically, transmitting energy through the system and recycling matter in such a way as to ensure dynamic equilibrium. This, too, was a fair description of the biota in the world at large. There was also required a mechanism for adaptation by which creatures could change in number, form and relationships to exploit the opportunities afforded by a changing environment. The mutation, that essential imperfection of the genetic transmission, satisfied this requirement—moreover, its incidence was itself based upon natural selection.

As the astronaut brought together these two dissociated sections of his mind—the construction of a simplification of the world, and that world as he had come to know it—he shared with us that vast relief that we are not required to be the architects of God, and assemble this vast and complex creation. He came to realize that the world was an evolutionary process that had developed over unimaginable eons of time—changing, adapting, revealing tentative new forms, some of which persisted while others failed. Yet out of this trial had indeed evolved this complex, elaborate and magnificent world which man had so recently entered, the latest dominant species—planetary disease or prospective steward.

The astronaut learned that he had lived in a capsule that was a poor simulation of the earth, but that the world was, indeed, a capsule. The price for survival, persistence and evolution was understanding and intelligent intervention. When he reached that conclusion, a wise world would have decided that he was too precious to send off into space; he and those like him were essential on earth. He had learned in the capsule the first lesson needed for life here: that the earth is a creative process, that man has a unique creative role, that all physical and living processes are arresting energy on its path to entropy and, in so doing, are creating a self-perpetuating and evolving system. Man shares this process; it contains his history. He is here now in this phenomenal universe with his indispensable partners in survival and creation. This is the central lesson of the workman's code in the manual of the good steward.

Processes as Values

During a period when many values have depreciated, the celebrated 5-cent fare on the Staten Island ferry has long persisted. We can savor this as we proceed to the next case study—Staten Island, the Borough of Richmond. But let us see this area within its region, the hinterland of New York City. It is clear from even the most superficial examination that Manhattan and its surround offered a magnificent site for a city. Values are abundant, the crystalline rocks of Manhattan on or near the surface offer magnificent foundations, a splendid deep river and natural harbor, two bays at Jamaica and Newark, the noble Hudson draining a rich and beautiful hinterland, (the paradisiacal river of the Indians which flowed in both directions), the ocean and beaches, marshes and meadows, palisades, ridges and not least, a number of islands, among them Staten Island.

Given the powers of hindsight, it is clear that it would have been most advantageous if an evaluation of these resources had been made some hundreds of years ago and this had been incorporated into a plan. In such a setting a great termitary could be built upon Manhattan whose inhabitants could roam to ocean and river, beach and bay, marshes and meadow and to the many islands.

The ideal is seldom a choice of either/or, but rather the combination of both or all. One dreams of the museum and cabaret, concert hall and ball park within stone's throw, but it would be as splendid if the mountains, the ocean and the primeval forest were at the doorstep, the eagle perched on the penthouse. Save for the mountains, this could easily have been in Manhattan.

The daily trip from suburb to city and back is a retracing of history; the inward trip from country to city symbolizes the evolution from land-based life to the emergence of communities, and the return goes back through time to a hint of the earliest relation of man with the land. It is a deeply felt need and its most powerful testimony is the flight to the suburbs, the greatest population migration in history. The company of men, the power of institution, the competition, stimulus, diversity and opportunity that the city represents are of great value indeed, but the ancient memory insists upon a return to the land, as contrast, into the world of non-human creatures and things. This alternation is both necessary and good. We can think of the city as a great zoo to which the gregarious animals voluntarily make their daily way by familiar trails to enter their cages, rather like the starlings whose penchant for bridge trusses is uncomfortably similar. The instinct of the caged animal to return to the wild seems to persist in that most domesticated of all animals—man. The original setting of Manhattan offered great opportunities for this alternation between city and country, from the greatest concentration of man to the wildest of nature. If the analogy of city as zoo is offensive, does it make a difference if we reverse the figure and assume that the city is the habitat of civilized man and nature is the zoo? There could then be many zoos for terrestrial and aquatic creatures, in oceans and bays, rivers and marshes, forests and meadows—a wonderful choice of zoological gardens where the domesticated animals could visit the wild ones. But the question of who is behind the bars is not easy to resolve, as anyone knows who has watched a contemplative gorilla in a cage.

Whatever position we take it is clear that the hinterland of Manhattan offered the greatest range of environments that could be enjoyed by its inhabitants, and an evaluation would have shown this to be so. But it was not to be, and inexorable growth spread a smear of low-grade urban tissue expunging this great richness and value.

Had our hindsight been applied, Staten Island would have ranked high among the splendid resources for the city population. It is a special place—its geological history has made it so. Silurian schists form the spine of the island, but the great Wisconsin glacier of

103

Pleistocene time left its mark, for there lies the evidence of the terminal moraine. There are glacial lakes, ocean beaches, rivers, marshes, forests, old sand dunes and even satellite islands. Among its treasures were beds of oysters and clams so extensive that the earliest inhabitants could not conceive that they could ever be consumed. Nor were they—like many other resources, they were rendered useless by pollution. Staten Island retained its quality as a bucolic haven rather longer than any other area as near to Manhattan, but in the postwar period the speculative builders made it the testimony to their shortsightedness and greed. Yet, all is not lost; even though the Verazzano Bridge has opened the floodgates to urban development, some splendid residues still remain— the Greenbelt and much of the southern part of the island. Happily too, much of this land is owned by the City of New York and is administered by the Department of Parks. This client asked that a study be made of the island to discern its intrinsic suitabilities from which conclusions would be made upon the use and disposition of the land.

This is then a problem of evaluation: which lands are intrinsically suitable for conservation, for active and for passive recreation, which are most suitable for commerce and industry, and which for residential land use?

Staten Island was and remains a unique resource in New York City, but its value is fast disappearing. The last assault, precipitated by the Verazzano Bridge, could well lead to its demise. Hope for this island refuge lies almost entirely in the fact that the City of New York owns most of the remaining vacant land. It thus falls within the power of the City to determine the destiny of the Borough of Richmond.

What should be the destiny of this land? It could be voraciously consumed by the market for housing. In so doing, the last of the public values for New Yorkers which Staten Island represents will join the oblivion of other New York environs. Can it be otherwise? This study was an attempt to reveal the alternatives for the future destiny of the beleaguered island.

The basic proposition employed is that any place is the sum of historical, physical and biological processes, that these are dynamic, that they constitute social values, that each area has an intrinsic suitability for certain land uses and finally, that certain areas lend themselves to multiple coexisting land uses.

The serpentine ridge and the diabase dyke of Staten Island can only be comprehended in terms of historical geology. The superficial expression of the island is a consequence of Pleistocene glaciation. The climatic processes over time have modified the geological formations, which account for current physiography, drainage and distribution of soils. Various associations of plant species occupy the place, making it possible for a myriad of animal species to exist. Human occupation modifies the natural processes by its own contribution.

The island has come to be as a result of the dynamism that is inherent in all natural process. It is a mute record of mountain building, submergence into ancient, long-extinct seas and lava flows. Ice sheets have advanced over it and retreated. But cycles of seasons and tides, the hydrological cycle and the recycling of vital nutrients are still going on. Hills are eroded and the sediments follow gravitational paths. Dunes form and create bays that fill over time. Hurricanes sweep up over the oceans and bring tidal inundation. It is important to recognize the dynamism of physical and biological processes and, more important, to recognize that these affect man and are affected by his intervention.

Land, air and water resources are indispensable to life and thus constitute social values. The bayshores have a high value for recreational and residential development but also represent a negative value because of their susceptibility to tidal inundation. The surface waters are a resource for water supply, recreation and disposal of effluents, but their positive value is easily abused by pollution. Water management, prevention of erosion, provision of habitat for wildlife and a retreat for study and delight are several of the social values represented by forest land and then lost when a forest is allowed to succumb to advancing development.

A recognition of these social values, inherent in natural processes, must precede prescription for the utilization of natural resources.

Once it has been accepted that the place is a sum of natural processes and that these processes constitute social values, inferences can be drawn regarding utilization to ensure optimum use and enhancement of social values. This is its intrinsic suitability. For example, flat land with good surface and soil drainage is intrinsically the most suitable land for intensive recreation, while areas of diverse topography represent a higher value for passive recreation.

The social values represented by the natural processes more often than not are inherently suitable for a multiplicity of human uses. Flat well-drained land is as suitable for intensive recreation as it is for commercial-industrial development. Areas of diversity and high scenic interest have a high social value for conservation and passive recreation, at the same time being highly desirable locations for residential development. These apparent conflicts can be resolved in a number of ways. Because of their scarcity and vulnerability, certain resources may represent such high value for conservation that other uses should be excluded. Multiple uses of some areas may be permitted if it is assured that intrinsic values are not compromised. Yet in other cases where two uses are coequally suitable, it remains with society to make the choice.

The proposition has been employed and in the following pages can be seen each of the intrinsic suitabilities and the resulting synthesis. We can review it now. The first point to be made is that it is not a plan. A plan includes the entire question of demand and the resolution of demand relative to supply, incorporating the capacity of the society or institution to realize its objectives. The Staten Island Study merely indicates those areas where certain land uses, both single and multiple, can occur with the least costs and the greatest savings and benefits. In order to make a plan, it is necessary to calculate demand for the constituent land uses and the locational and formal requirement of these, and to recognize the instruments available to society in both the public and private domain. The study awaits this information for completion.

But even at this stage it has innovative virtues that justify examination. The first of these is that it employs rational method: the evidence is derived, in the main, from exact sciences. The statements made on the major data subjects—geology, hydrology, soils, plant ecology and wildlife—are collected from substantial sources and are unlikely to contain major errors. This holds true for the interpretations of zones of atmospheric pollution, tidal inundation, rocks in terms of compressive strength, soil drainage and the rest.

In addition to being rational, the method is explicit. Any other person, accepting the method and the evidence, is likely to reach the same conclusions as those demonstrated in the study. This is in direct contrast to the bulk of planning, where the criteria are often obscure and covert. Moreover, this method permits a most important improvement in planning method—that is, that the community can employ its own value system. Those areas, places, buildings or spaces that it cherishes can be so identified and incorporated into the value system of the method. Today many planning processes, notably highway planning, are unable to incorporate the value system of the community to be transected. At best, the planner supplies his own distant judgment.

BEDROCK GEOLOGY

SURFICIAL GEOLOGY

HYDROLOGY

SOIL DRAINAGE ENVIRONMENTS

How does one proceed with this task? Well, we will begin with the original proposition, for it has served us well: nature is process and value, exhibiting both opportunities and limitations to human use. Therefore, we must identify the major physical and biological processes that caused Staten Island to be and that operate there now. We will not, in this case study, describe the content of the data. Many of these will be illustrated but the exposition will be limited to a description of the method alone. The previous studies have been much simpler than this problem—survival by the sea, a highway alignment and the place of nature in the metropolis. In this instance we are required

to identify the entire area for its intrinsic suitability for all prospective land uses. As in the highway problem, all basic data were compiled and mapped—climate, historical geology, surficial geology, physiography, hydrology, soils, plant ecology, wildlife habitats and land use. These data are of little use until they are interpreted and evaluated. For instance, general data on climate are of little significance, but those on hurricanes and the resultant inundation are vital, for with them we can identify gradients of susceptibility to inundation. The basic data are thus interpreted and reconstituted within a value system. In the earlier highway study it was observed that interstate highways generally

105

EXISTING LAND USE

HISTORICAL LANDMARKS

PHYSIOGRAPHIC FEATURES

TIDAL INUNDATION

GEOLOGIC FEATURES

GEOLOGIC SECTIONS

do not exceed a three per cent slope. Thus any existing slopes in excess of this constitute a penalty; slopes of three per cent or less are a saving. Further, it costs more to excavate rock than it does sand or gravel. Moreover, the presence of these latter materials may well be a saving, as they can be utilized in highway construction.

From each of the major data categories a number of factors are selected and evaluated. From geology we identify features of geologic, scientific and educational value and grade them from unique to abundant; rocks are evaluated for their compressive strength and ranked as foundation conditions, and so on, for every category. For certain land uses the maximum condition will be preferable, for others it will be the minimum that has the highest value. The least tidal inundation is to be preferred, but the highest scenic quality is the greatest value.

For each prospective land use there will be certain factors of greatest importance and these can be selected. Moreover, there will be a ranking of importance and so the factors can be arranged in a hierarchy. In addition, in certain cases some factors will be conducive to specific land uses while others are restrictive. In the selection of areas intrinsically suitable for conservation, the factors selected were: features of historic

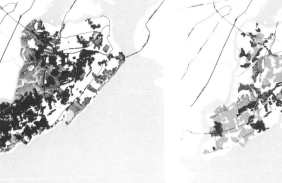
EXISTING VEGETATION

FOREST:ECOLOGICAL ASSOCIATIONS

EXISTING WILDLIFE HABITATS

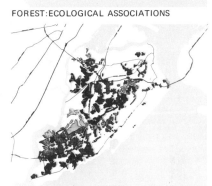
FOREST:EXISTING QUALITY

SLOPE

SOIL LIMITATIONS:FOUNDATION

SOIL LIMITATIONS:WATER-TABLE

107

value, high quality forests and marshes, bay beaches, streams, water-associated wildlife habitats, intertidal wildlife habitats, unique geological and physiographic features, scenic land and water features and scarce ecological associations. As an example of conducive and restrictive factors, selection of the most suitable areas for residential land use would include attractive surroundings, and so scenic land features, locations near water and the presence of historic sites and buildings will be positive factors, while excessive slopes, poor drainage and susceptibility to flooding will be negative factors.

The application of this concept can be seen in the adjacent charts. Over thirty factors were considered. Those considered were subdivided in the categories of climate, geology, physiography, hydrology, soils, vegetation, wildlife habitats and land use. Within each of these categories data were collected on factors of importance to all prospective land use. From the original sources—climate, geology, etc., the factors of greatest importance were selected. In the general subject of climate the matter of air pollution was deemed important as was tidal inundation from hurricanes. Within the category of geology features of unique scientific value were identified and the major surface rock types were classed for compressive strength. Following the identification of the most important factors, each one was evaluated in a gradient of five values. For instance, serpentine and diabase constitute class one foundation conditions while marsh and swamp occupy the lowest rank on the scale. All factors were so evaluated. The relevance of the factors considered to specific land uses was next indicated. Further, the direction of the value system was shown. A blue dot indicates rank order from left to right. A black dot indicates the reverse order. Moreover the importance of the factor must also be evaluated. Factors of highest importance are shown with full black and blue dots; lower values decrease in color and tonal intensity.

ECOLOGICAL FACTOR	RANKING CRITERIA	PHENOMENA RANK I	II	III	IV	V	VALUE FOR LAND USE (C P A R I)
CLIMATE							
AIR POLLUTION	INCIDENCE MAX ► MIN	High	Medium	Low		Lowest	
TIDAL INUNDATION	INCIDENCE MAX ► MIN	Highest Recorded	Highest Projected			Above Flood-Line	
GEOLOGY							
FEATURES OF UNIQUE, SCIENTIFIC AND EDUCATIONAL VALUE	SCARCITY MAX ► MIN	1 Ancient Lakebeds 2 Drainage Outlets	1 Terminal Moraine 2 Limit of Glaciation 3 Boulder Trail	Serpentine Hill	Palisades Outlier	1 Beach 2 Buried Valleys 3 Clay Pits 4 Gravel Pits	
FOUNDATION CONDITIONS	COMPRESSIVE STRENGTH MAX ► MIN	1 Serpentine 2 Diabase	Shale	Cretaceous Sediments	Filled Marsh	Marsh and Swamp	
PHYSIOGRAPHY							
FEATURES OF UNIQUE, SCIENTIFIC AND EDUCATIONAL VALUE	SCARCITY MAX ► MIN	Hummocks and kettleholes within the Terminal Moraine	Palisades Outlier	Moraine Scarps and lakes along the Bay Shore	Breaks in Serpentine Ridge		
LAND FEATURES OF SCENIC VALUE	DISTINCTIVE MOST ► LEAST	Serpentine Ridge and Promontories	Beach	1 Escarpments 2 Enclosed Valleys	1 Berms 2 Promontories 3 Hummocks	Undifferentiated	
WATER FEATURES OF SCENIC VALUE	DISTINCTIVE MOST ► LEAST	Bay	Lake	1 Pond 2 Streams	Marsh	1 The Narrows 2 Kill Van Kull 3 Arthur Kill	
RIPARIAN LANDS OF WATER FEATURES	VULNERABILITY MOST ► LEAST	Marsh	1 Stream 2 Ponds	Lake	Bay	1 The Narrows 2 Kill Van Kull 3 Arthur Kill	
BEACHES ALONG THE BAY	VULNERABILITY MOST ► LEAST	Moraine Scarps	Coves	Sand Beach			
SURFACE DRAINAGE	PROPORTION OF SURFACE WATER TO LAND AREA MOST ► LEAST	Marsh and swamp	Areas of constricted drainage	Dense stream/swale network	Intermediate stream/swale network	Sparse stream/swale network	
SLOPE	GRADIENT HIGH ► LOW	Over 25%	25–10%	10–5%	5–2½%	2½–0%	
HYDROLOGY							
MARINE Commercial Craft	NAVIGABLE CHANNELS DEEPEST ► SHALLOWEST	The Narrows	Kill Van Kull	Arthur Kill	Fresh Kill	Raritan Bay	
Pleasure Craft	FREE EXPANSE OF WATER LARGEST ► SMALLEST	Raritan Bay	Fresh Kill	The Narrows	Arthur Kill	Kill Van Kull	
FRESH WATER Active recreation (swimming, paddling, model-boat sailing, etc.)	EXPANSE OF WATER LARGEST ► SMALLEST	Silver Lake	1 Clove Lake 2 Grassmere Lake 3 Ohrbach Lake 4 Arbutus Lake 5 Wolfes Pond	Other ponds	Streams		
Stream-side recreation (fishing, trails, etc.)	SCENIC MOST ► LEAST	Nonurbanized perennial streams	Nonurbanized intermittent streams	Semiurbanized streams	Urbanized streams		
WATERSHEDS FOR STREAM QUALITY PROTECTION	SCENIC STREAMS MOST ► LEAST	Nonurbanized perennial streams	Nonurbanized intermittent streams	Semiurbanized streams	Urbanized streams		
AQUIFERS	YIELD HIGHEST ► LOWEST	Buried valleys		Cretaceous Sediments		Crystalline rocks	
AQUIFER RECHARGE ZONES	IMPORTANT AQUIFERS MOST ► LEAST	Buried valleys		Cretaceous Sediments		Crystalline rocks	

C CONSERVATION; P PASSIVE RECREATION; A ACTIVE RECREATION; R RESIDENTIAL DEVELOPMENT; I COMMERCIAL & INDUSTRIAL DEVELOPMENT

ECOLOGICAL FACTOR	RANKING CRITERIA	PHENOMENA RANK					VALUE FOR LAND USE				
		I	II	III	IV	V	C	P	A	R	I

PEDOLOGY

ECOLOGICAL FACTOR	RANKING CRITERIA	I	II	III	IV	V	C	P	A	R	I
SOIL DRAINAGE	PERMEABILITY AS INDICATED BY THE HEIGHT OF WATER TABLE MOST ► LEAST	Excellent-good	Good-fair	Fair-poor	Poor	Nil	●		●	●	●
FOUNDATION CONDITIONS	COMPRESSIVE STRENGTH AND STABILITY MOST ► LEAST	Gravelly to stony, sandy loams	Gravelly sand or silt loams	Gravelly sandy to fine sandy loam	1 Sandy loam 2 Gravel 3 Beach sands	1 Alluvium 2 Swamp Muck 3 Tidal marshlands 4 Made land				●	●
EROSION	SUSCEPTIBILITY MOST ► LEAST	Steep slopes over 10%	Any slope on gravelly sandy to fine sandy loam	Moderate slopes (2%-10%) on 1 Gravelly sand or silt loams 2 Gravelly to stony sandy loams	Slopes (0-2%) on gravelly sand or silt loams	Other soils	●		●	●	●

VEGETATION

		I	II	III	IV	V	C	P	A	R	I
EXISTING FOREST	QUALITY BEST ► POOREST	Excellent	Good	Poor	Disturbed	None	●	●	●	●	●
FOREST TYPE	SCARCITY MOST ► LEAST	1 Lowland 2 Upland dry	Marsh	Upland	Upland moist	Absence	●	●	●	●	
EXISTING MARSHES	QUALITY BEST ► POOREST	Good	Fair	Poor (filled)	None		●	●	●	●	●

WILDLIFE

		I	II	III	IV	V	C	P	A	R	I
EXISTING HABITATS	SCARCITY MOST ► LEAST	Intertidal	Water-related	Field and forest	Urban	Marine	●	●	●		
INTERTIDAL SPECIES	ENVIRONMENTAL QUALITY BASED ON INTENSITY OF SHORE ACTIVITY LEAST ACTIVITY ► MOST ACTIVITY	1	2	3	4	5	●	●			
WATER-ASSOCIATED SPECIES	ENVIRONMENTAL QUALITY BASED ON THE DEGREE OF URBANIZATION NON URBANIZED ► FULLY URBANIZED	1	2	3	4	5	●	●	●		
FIELD AND FOREST SPECIES	FOREST QUALITY BEST ► POOREST	1	2		3		●	●	●	●	
URBAN-RELATED SPECIES	PRESENCE OF TREES ABUNDANT ► ABSENT	1		2		3	●				

LAND USE

		I	II	III	IV	V	C	P	A	R	I
FEATURES OF UNIQUE, EDUCATIONAL, AND HISTORICAL VALUE	IMPORTANCE MOST ► LEAST	Richmond Town	1 Amboy Road 2 Tottenville Conference	Area with abundance of landmarks	Area with sparseness of landmarks	Area with absence of landmarks	●	●		●	
FEATURES OF SCENIC VALUE	DISTINCTIVE MOST ► LEAST	The Verazzano Bridge	Ocean Liner Channel	Manhattan Ferry	1 The Goethals Bridge 2 The Outerbridge crossing 3 The Bayonne Bridge	Absence	●	●	●	●	●
EXISTING AND POTENTIAL RECREATION RESOURCES	AVAILABILITY MOST ► LEAST	1 Existing public open space 2 Existing Institutions	Potential nonurbanized recreation areas	Potential urbanized recreation areas	Vacant land (with low recreation potential)	Urbanized areas	●	●	●	●	

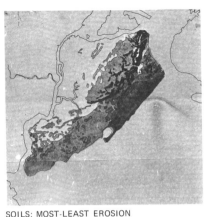

SOILS; MOST-LEAST EROSION

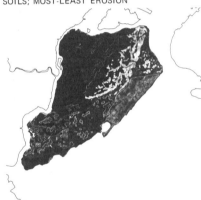

SOILS; LEAST-MOST EROSION

Each factor was mapped in tones of gray from most to least, and this same information was reversed to be employed in inverted order when necessary. All of the maps were made as transparencies. The group of relevant factors for each prospective land use was assembled and photographed. The results were then value gradients that incorporated all the appropriate factors. These maps showed the maximum concurrence of all the positive factors and the least restrictions. Processes, reconstituted as values, indicated the areas intrinsically suitable for each of the land uses considered—recreation, conservation and both the residential and industrial-commercial aspects of urbanization.

C CONSERVATION, P PASSIVE RECREATION, A ACTIVE RECREATION, R RESIDENTIAL DEVELOPMENT; I COMMERCIAL & INDUSTRIAL DEVELOPMENT

As an example of the application of the method, the constituent values employed to reveal areas most suitable for conservation are illustrated. The salient factors selected for this search included:

features of historic value	intertidal wildlife habitats
high-quality forests	unique geological features
high-quality marshes	unique physiographic features
bay beaches	scenic land features
streams	scenic water features
water-associated wildlife habitats	scarce ecological associations

Each of the constituent maps is an evaluation within the appropriate category, represented in five divisions, with the darkest tone representing the highest value and the lowest value shown as blank. All twelve maps were made into transparent negatives, which were superimposed and photographed. The resulting photograph represented the summation of all of the values employed and was therefore indicative of the areas most to least intrinsically suitable for conservation. This photograph was reconstituted into a single map, with the values for conservation indicated in five values. Thus the darker the tone the greater the intrinsic suitability for conservation.

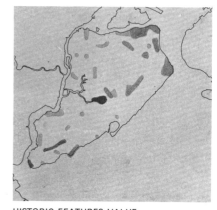

HISTORIC FEATURES VALUE

EXISTING FOREST QUALITY

CONSERVATION AREAS

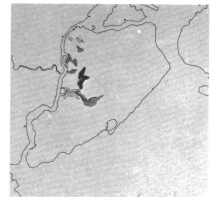

MARSH QUALITY

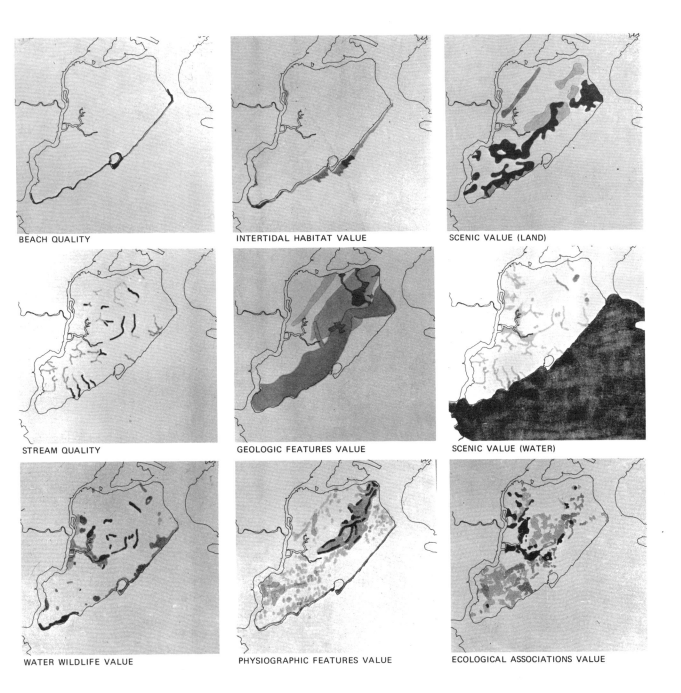

BEACH QUALITY

INTERTIDAL HABITAT VALUE

SCENIC VALUE (LAND)

STREAM QUALITY

GEOLOGIC FEATURES VALUE

SCENIC VALUE (WATER)

WATER WILDLIFE VALUE

PHYSIOGRAPHIC FEATURES VALUE

ECOLOGICAL ASSOCIATIONS VALUE

111

Areas most suited for recreation are determined separately for the two kinds of recreational activity—passive and active. These two are then combined to arrive at the composite suitability for recreation shown on this page. The salient factors selected for determining recreation areas are:

PASSIVE
unique physiographic features
scenic water features, streams
features of historic value
high-quality forests
high-quality marshes
scenic land features
scenic cultural features
unique geologic features
scarce ecological associations
water-associated wildlife habitats
field and forest wildlife habitats

ACTIVE
bay beaches
expanse of water for pleasure craft
fresh water areas
riparian lands
flat land
existing and potential recreation areas

ACTIVE RECREATION SUITABILITY

PASSIVE RECREATION SUITABILITY

Landscape Architects: COPE, LINDER AND WALMSLEY

RECREATION AREAS

112

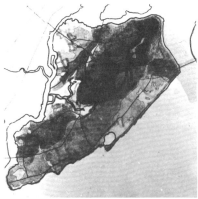

RESIDENTIAL SUITABILITY

UNSUITABILITY FOR URBANIZATION

Areas most suited for urbanization are determined separately for the two major components of urbanization: residential and commercial-industrial developments. For each of these the most permissive factors are identified. These are:

RESIDENTIAL
scenic land features
riparian lands
scenic cultural features
good bedrock foundations
good soil foundations

COMMERCIAL-INDUSTRIAL
good soil foundations
good bedrock foundations
navigable channels

The most restrictive factors which are common to these developments are also identified:

slopes
forested areas
poor surface drainage
poor soil drainage
areas susceptible to erosion
areas subject to flooding

The composite suitability for urbanization is arrived at by combining these and is shown on this page.

URBANIZATION AREAS

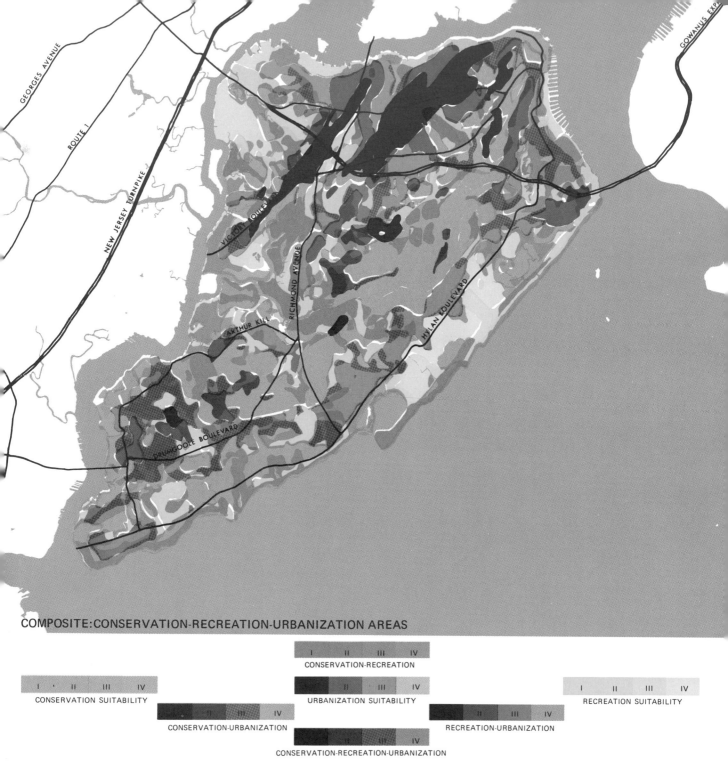

COMPOSITE:CONSERVATION-RECREATION-URBANIZATION AREAS

I   II   III   IV
CONSERVATION-RECREATION

I   •   II   III   IV
CONSERVATION SUITABILITY

I   II   III   IV
URBANIZATION SUITABILITY

I   II   III   IV
RECREATION SUITABILITY

I   II   III   IV
CONSERVATION-URBANIZATION

I   II   III   IV
RECREATION-URBANIZATION

I   II   III   IV
CONSERVATION-RECREATION-URBANIZATION

There are now maps of intrinsic suitability for residential land use, commerce-industry, conservation, passive and active recreation. These have an existence in their own right, but we seek to find not only intrinsic single uses, but also compatible coexisting ones and areas of competition. We can then take complementary pairs and reduce them to single maps. Commerce-industry and residential use can be incorporated into a single map of urban suitability. Active and passive recreation can be combined into a single one of recreational suitability. We then have a residuum of three maps—Conservation, Recreation and Urbanization—which we are required to resolve. While the single suitabilities could be represented using tones of gray on transparent maps, this technique cannot avail us now. It is necessary to employ color. Let us allocate yellow to conservation and reconstitute the tones of gray into a range of brightness. We will map recreation in grades of blue and urbanization in gray. Where a land use has no conflict, nor is it complementary, we can map the area in its appropriate color and in a scale of brightness appropriate to its value. Where there are complementarities, such as recreation and conservation, the combination of blue and yellow will produce green and the brightness will reflect the degree of value. The combination of gray and blue—urbanization and recreation—will show in the blue-gray range while a coequal suitability for all three categories will result in the combination of gray, blue and yellow producing a range of gray-greens. In the preparation of the final map it is impossible to resolve the suitabilities, compatibilities and conflicts by superimposition and photography and so the preemptive method was used. This consisted of locating all primary suitabilities not in competition with any other primary values and mapping them, thus preempting the appropriate areas. This is continued with secondary and tertiary values until the summary map shows all unitary, complementary and competing intrinsic land uses. Those shown as coequally suitable for more than one use may either compete or coexist.

By abandoning absolute economic values that cover only a small range of price values, and employing a relative system of most to least, it is possible to include all of the important factors that defy pricing by economists. While this denies an illusory precision of cost-benefit economics, it does show the relative concurrence of positive factors and their relative absence. Although we are unable to fix precise money values on these, it is safe to assume that, in the absence of any supervening value, the concurrence of the majority of positive factors in any one location does indicate its intrinsic suitability for the land use in question.

Another value is that the information so compiled and interpreted constitutes the base data required to subject any planning proposal to the test of least cost-maximum benefit. The values of the area in question for the major land uses have been identified, and the degree to which any proposal will destroy or enhance these can be demonstrated. Moreover, these same data simplify the quest for least-social-cost locations. By making explicit the factors employed, it is possible for society at large and for individuals to insist that the development process, both public and private, respond to these values. It would serve a most useful purpose if maps of the value of an area, and the intrinsic suitabilities, were made public so that developers could know where they planned to tread and, more positively, could be led to areas intrinsically suitable for their energies. Perhaps one of the most valuable innovations of the method is the conception of complementary land uses, the search for areas that can support more than one use. This tends to be in conflict with the principle of zoning, which enforces segregation of land uses. The recognition that certain areas are intrinsically suitable for several land uses can be seen either as a conflict or as the opportunity to combine uses in a way that is socially desirable. In many of the older European cities that are so extravagantly admired, there is a perfectly acceptable combination of residence and shopping

and even certain manufacturing. It is possible to combine land uses but this requires some discretion and even art.

Normally land use maps, and even planning proposals, show broad categories of uses. The maps in this study are more like mosaics than posters—for good reason. They result from asking the land to display discrete attributes which, when superimposed, reveal great complexity. But this is the real complexity of opportunity and constraint. Yet it may appear anarchic, but only because we have become accustomed to the dreary consistency of zoning, because we are unused to perceiving the real variabilities in the environment, and responding to this in our plans.

Certain technical problems are inherent in the method. The first of these is the ensurance of parity of factors. The results will be qualified if the factors are of disproportionate weights. Too, there are limits to the photographic resolution of many factors and this study reached that threshold. The mechanical problem of transforming tones of gray into color of equal value is a difficult one, as is their combination. It may be that the computer will resolve this problem although the state of the art is not yet at this level of competence.

Such is the Staten Island Study. It is one of the most elaborate that the author has undertaken, it has moved forward some distance from the earlier studies, it does offer some hope for a planning process that is rational, explicit, replicable and can employ the values of the community in its development.

The study of Staten Island was commissioned by The New York Department of Parks and produced by Wallace, McHarg, Roberts and Todd, under the direction of the author and performed by Mr. Narendra Juneja assisted by Messers. Meyers, Sutphin, Drummond, Ragan, Bhan and Mrs. Curry.

The ecological field studies were done by Dr. Archibald Reid and Mr. Charles Meyers. Soils maps were prepared by Dr. Howard M. Higbee.

The Naturalists

In an enterprise such as this quest, there is the ever-present temptation to resolve the problem by creating a Utopia wherein live all those admirable people whose views correspond with one's own. Yet, this must be avoided, because if Utopias vary greatly for one man, how much more for many men. There are occasions when a sprig of cherry blossom is utopian and other times when survival itself is the single yearning. But a more modest objective may be achieved—not the philosophy for a Utopia, but only the simplest, most basic views, which can ensure survival and life and which may produce a rational basis for human affairs. This will not inhibit the great flights of courage or love, the unpredictable perceptions or creations. These can be left to their own devices, unaffected by the rut of men and simple rational laws. We can collect the evidence that has been presented fragmentarily and assemble it into some coherent sequence. But, rather than presenting this as a narrative description of natural law, it might be more palatable if invested in a people. They would look much like ourselves but would differ in their attitudes to nature and to man, their ethics and ethos, planning, management and art. These would be entirely based upon the natural sciences, ecology and the ecological view.

These Naturalists, for this is an appropriate name for them, have concluded that evolution has proceeded as much from cooperation as competition; conquest has no primacy in their lexicon, while the quest to understand nature, which is also to say man, dominates their preoccupations. This view, being the basis for the successful evolution of the species, pervades the entire population instead of reposing, as it does with us, in a small number of rather recent and retiring scientists and a few poets. It is, of course, accepted by the Naturalists that the earth and its denizens are involved in a totally creative process and that there is a unique and important role for man. It is agreed that evolution is directional, that it has recognizable attributes and that man is involved in its orderings.

Their cosmography is much different from ours—less encompassing, less certain, less romantic, more modest, and not at all man-centered. They disclaim all knowledge of the origins of the universe, although they seek to learn all that they can of this great genesis. Their knowledge begins with that time after the beginning when there was hydrogen. From this followed the evolution of the elements—helium, lithium, and the rest forged in cosmic cauldrons. This line of evolution terminated when the heaviest elements proved insubstantial and impermanent. The evolution of compounds followed, permitting combination after combination, increasing in complexity until, with the amino acids, evolution stood on the threshold of a new type of organization—life. Their understanding of the evolution of life forms corresponds closely with ours, although their sense of this journey is more immediate and vivid.

Every cosmography contains a creation story and the Naturalists are no different in this respect, save in the nature of the evidence employed. The unknown is the threshold of their minds; wonder is a common companion, but mysticism is not conspicuous. In support of their concept of creation they employ, not mysticism, but replicable experiment—indeed, an experiment which can be conducted by the least of them. This involves simply a glass cubicle enclosing a sterile environment. It is observed that the sunlight falls upon this and that the heat lost equals the heat falling upon the surface. In the companion experiment, a plant, some nutrients, and decomposers in a water medium are introduced into the cubicle. It is observed that the heat lost is less than that gained. Some of the sunlight is utilized by the plant which grows and proliferates. It is observed that the sunlight has been transmuted, with matter, from a lesser to a higher order. Some of the sunlight that otherwise would have been lost is now an ingredient of

117

the plant. Some of the sun's energy had been entrapped on its path to entropy. This is defined as creation—the raising of matter from lower to higher order, negentropy.

Now this is perhaps the most modest creation myth ever advanced, but, as you consider it, it is seen to accommodate all physical and biological evolution. Is it as satisfactory in accounting for cultural evolution and for art? Is the symphony more ordered than random noise, the painting more ordered than the pigments in tubes and the waiting canvas, the poem a higher order than static? One must answer yes, but while this distinction is accurate, it is clearly not sufficient. Yet, this is a modest cosmography; it is enough that its claims are correct even though they are incomplete.

The conception of creation as movement from lower to higher order has its antithesis in destruction, the reduction from higher to lower levels. Evolution is then seen as a creative process, retrogression as reductive.

Creation and reduction, evolution and retrogression, are thought to have attributes. The replicable experiments demonstrating this involve two environments, both equal in area: the first, a sand dune, and the second, a primeval forest covering an ancient sand dune. In the first case, only a few decades have elapsed since the emergence of the dune from the sea; it is sparsely populated by some grasses and herbs; it supports some bacteria and insects, but no mammals. In contrast, the forest has existed undisturbed for millennia, so one could expect it to represent the highest evolutionary expression that the long time period and available denizens could support. The young dune is on the same path, but has not yet attained the creativity of the older example.

What are the attributes of these two systems, the first primitive in an evolutionary scale of which the other is the climax? The dune is simple, dominated by a few physical processes; it consists of a few physical constit-

uents, mainly sand; it contains a few inhabitants and the relations between these can also be described as simple. When the forest is examined in these terms, it is seen to be inordinately complex. The physical processes that occurred, the numbers of species, the variety of habitats and niches (which is to say the roles which were performed), could only be encompassed within the term complex.

If you multiply simplicities, the result is uniformity; the product of complexities is diversity, and so it is found in examining the respective environments. The dune is the result of the uniform behavior of sand par-

ticles, their angle of repose and the action of wind; the conspicuous organisms are the grasses, bent to the wind, reflecting the sunlight, a constancy of uniformity. The forest is completely otherwise—uniformities are nowhere to be found. Although there is a structure of creatures occupying different trophic layers and different levels of stratification, the variation present is a permutation of the large numbers of species, environments, roles and pathways which are, indeed, multiplications of complexities.

The next attribute to be examined is relative instability and stability. The dune is, of course, unstable, subject to the vicissitudes

of wind and ocean, tempered only by the anchoring vegetation. The forest has transformed the dune that was its origin; its own internal climate, microclimate and water regimen are all products of the evolution of the forest. The processes themselves are the basis of stability and the measure of this is not only the implacable, unmoving aspect which it portrays, but the age of its creatures.

For each of those environments, equal in area, the incident energy is the same. In the case of the dune, most of the sunlight that falls is reflected by the sand and only a small proportion is utilized by the few grasses. In the forest, the incident sunlight powers the

119

entire ecosystem; the light reflected is from the leaves of the canopy; the variation in light down to the shadowed floor is utilized by existing creatures. Clearly, in the dune entropy is high, in the forest it is low. If we consider entropy as a measure of greater randomness, disorder and uniformity, then it is apparent that the dune better qualifies for this description than the forest. Indeed, the forest can be described by Lawrence K. Frank's term "organized complexity" while the dune is, in comparison, a less organized simplicity. If high entropy reveals low order, than the dune is low, the forest an expression of high order, of negentropy.

A further measure of creation is the number of species. It is a proposition that species survive only insofar as they can perform a role. Where two species perform identical roles in the same place and time, one will surely succumb. Therefore, the number of species present is an indication of the number of roles being performed. In the dune there are obviously few species, in the forest these are legion. In the dune, with few species, but relatively large populations, interactions will be preponderantly intraspecies. The forest with many species would exhibit interspecies, as well as intraspecies interaction. These relationships might be described, from the point of view of species interaction, as exhibiting independence in the case of the dune, and interdependence in the forest.

Evolution $\longrightarrow$

primitive state	advanced state
simplicity	complexity
uniformity	diversity
instability	stability
	(steady state)
low number of species	high number of species
low number of symbioses	high number of symbioses
high entropy	low entropy

Retrogression $\longleftarrow$

The cosmography has now linked creation with the increase in order in a system, and demonstrated that this is the path of evolution, that the antithesis is destruction, the path of retrogression consisting in the reduction of order from higher to lower levels. Both creation and destruction are seen to have distinctive, descriptive attributes:

Does this hold true outside, in the world at large? Apparently evolution has proceeded from simple to complex, whether we consider elements, compounds, life forms or communities. It seems clear that if you multiply simplicities, then uniformities will result; complexities similarly treated will produce diversity. Observe the difference between an algal bloom and a forest. It then follows that simple, uniform systems will tend to be unstable as a function of these characteristics. They are inordinately vulnerable to epidemic disease in that they provide large, uniform populations for any parasite. In contrast, complex and diverse systems are unlikely to provide large populations of single organisms which are so vulnerable. Moreover, the larger the number of species, the larger the genetic pool capable of adapting to any exigency. On all counts, the complex environment will be more stable. If it is true that simple and uniform systems by definition cannot occupy all available niches, then energy available to the system will not be as fully utilized as in the complex diverse system. Thus, entropy will be high, order low in the simple uniform system, high order and low entropy will characterize the complex diverse ecosystem. Complexity and diversity are describable in terms of numbers of species—therefore, the higher the order, the more the species; and finally, where the environment consists of a community of many species, the interactions are likely to be interspecies, whereas the alternative—large populations of few species—will emphasize intraspecies interaction.

The evidence is available to us whether we examine the regeneration of an abandoned field on its way to becoming a forest, or if we look at the healing scab of ailanthus, sumac and ragweed clothing the railroad embankment. It appears that creation, viewed in thermodynamic terms, does have attributes. This offers a considerable utility both for diagnosis and prescription. The Naturalists could conclude on the state of any system on an evolutionary scale and, moreover, could decide whether it was evolving or retrogressing.

The Naturalists employ both conceptions of fitness, that propounded by Henderson and that by Darwin. Thus the environment is fit for life, for the forms which had preexisted, those which do now exist and those of the future. In addition, the surviving organism or ecosystem is fit for the environment. The process of achieving a fitting between the organism and the environment is a continuous and dynamic one—physical processes are dynamic, but even more the presence of organisms composing environments, themselves changing, is the major component of change. Where fitness is reflected in equilibrium, this is a dynamic equilibrium. Evolution then consists of a tendency towards increasing fitness whereby the organism adapts the environment to make it more fitting and, through mutation and natural selection, adapts itself towards the same end. As the process of fitting exhibits the direction from simplicity to complexity, uniformity to complexity, instability to stability, low to high number of species, low to high number of symbioses and thus high to low entropy, it corresponds to the most basic creative processes in the earth. Fitting and the movement towards fitness were thus creative. The failure to accomplish a fitting, the misfit, is not creative. Processes whereby the system reverts from complexity to simplicity and so on are therefore entropic and destructive. There are two polar conditions, the first creative fitting and the other a destructive unfitting. The measure of fitness and fitting is evolutionary survival, success of the species or ecosystem, and, in the short run, health.

This conception is not modified in any essential way when man is considered nor even when socio-cultural factors are introduced. There would be an environment fit for a man, and a man fit for the environment; the creative process requires that the environment be made more fit, that the man adapt the environment and himself. Tools of culture are fundamentally no different than mutation and natural selection although they can accomplish change at a much greater rate. The creative test is to accomplish a creative fitting. This involves identifying those environments intrinsically fit for an organism or process, identifying the organism, species or institution fit for the environment and inaugurating the process whereby the organism and the environment is adapted to accomplish a better fitting.

As the Naturalists deny themselves the luxury of mysticism and assume that all meaning and purpose can be inferred from the operation of the biophysical world, it is here that they have searched for an ethic. Being natural scientists, their mode of examination takes them into studies of the relations between creatures, in the expectation that those that are operative before the emergence of man might equally hold for the relations between men and nature, between men and men.

They have noted that no organism can exist independently. As each organism has adapted to certain foods, it will expel certain wastes. The product of such a situation would be the exploitation of all available foodstuffs and the creation of a sea of wastes. Remember that the amoeba recoils from its excrement. So there must be at least two organisms; one of these must be photosynthetic, the other would be, in such a minimum situation, a decomposer. Here, in this example of a theoretical situation, the plant, utilizing sunlight, would produce wastes—leaves and detritus—which would be consumed by the decomposers. Clearly, these two creatures are interdependent: they are related as to numbers; they are cooperating for survival. The decomposer has adapted to utilize the wastes of the plant; the plant to utilize the wastes of decomposers. This is described by the Naturalists as altruism—the concession of some autonomy towards the ends of mutual benefit for the creatures involved.

Now the principles affecting the organisms do not change when the numbers of species increase or energy pyramids enlarge or when the pathways become inordinately complicated. In every case, in these astonishingly complex relations in an elaborate ecosystem, all of the organisms must concede some part of their autonomy, which is to say their freedom, towards the ends of sustaining the system and the other co-tenants of it. This corresponds very closely with the proposition of intercellular altruism which has been advanced for us by Dr. Hans Selye. He had noted that while a man consists of some thirty billion billion cells, the original cells are unspecialized and evolve to occupy specialist niches, as tissue, organs and blood. The organism only exists because these cells assume interdependent roles within the totality of a single integrated organism. When first formed, each unspecialized cell is similar to independent unicellular creatures, with an origin, a metabolism, and the capacity to replicate. Yet, each cell concedes some part of this freedom, inherent in nonspecialization, and assumes a cooperative role in the maintenance of the single organism.

Selye extrapolated from intercellular to interpersonal altruism, but for the Naturalists, the entire biosphere exhibits altruism. Every organism occupies a niche in an ecosystem and engages in cooperative arrangements with the other organisms sustaining the biosphere. In every case this involves a concession of some part of the individual freedom towards the survival and evolution of the biosphere.

Now in the consideration of altruism, it is important to reject sentimentality. While the wolf culls the old and weak caribou or the lion the antelope, there is no doubt about the fear of the prey and ferocity of the predator. Numbers are thus regulated and the fittest survive and reproduce, but it is not a picture of lions sleeping with lambs. Yet, if it does not fulfill dreams of idyllic nature, a world without competition, it nonetheless does provide an understanding of the relationships that demonstrably do exist in the living world. One might wish them different, but it is important to find out what they are.

Now energy in a system can just as well be considered as information. The heat that falls upon a creature can inform that creature of the heat falling upon it. But, the information provided has meaning only if the matter or organism can perceive and respond to it. The direction of evolution, or at least the Naturalist's conception of this, is towards higher order, more negentropy, but it is seen that if energy is reconsidered as information, then the capacity to attribute meaning to this energy is also a measure of evolution. If this is so, then apperception is that capacity by which meaning is perceived.

I am sure you have observed that there seem to be several concurrent value systems operating in this cosmography. The first of these is based upon negentropy, and can be measured in entropy units. Thus, creatures can be seen as the makers of negentropy. In this value scale it is clear that the plants are supreme, that behind them fall the indispensable decomposers and that all other life forms have relatively much lower values. It is also clear that the major work is being performed by the smallest creatures; the marine plants lead by a great margin, the terrestrial plants a poor second, and so, in the animal world, the major function of putting plants into more elaborate orders is accomplished by small marine organisms, the small and pervasive herbivores.

If we consider energy as information and use apperception as a value, then quite different creatures assume ascendency. The evolution of more complex perceiving creatures re-

78

flects this value, and here man ranks very high indeed.

If we examine the second criterion, that of cooperative mechanisms ensuring survival and directing the arrow of evolution, we confront a more difficult task. We can see in the lichen an early testimony to symbiosis, the alga and the fungus interfused into a single organism; we can identify the indispensable roles of the aminofying, nitrate and nitrite bacteria, of the pollinating insects and flowering plants, termites and cellulose bacteria and many other examples but in man, symbioses are more highly developed at the involuntary level—as in intercellular altruism—than in social organization. But, apperception is the key to symbiosis, and man is the most perceptive of creatures. This then is his potential: by perceiving and understanding nature, he can contribute to its operation, manage the biosphere, and in so doing, enhance his apperception, which with symbiosis, appears to be the arrow of evolution.

Now, the Naturalists believe less than we do in the divisibility of man from the rest of the biosphere; they think of man in nature rather than against nature. They have a vivid sense of the other creatures in the earth as being of themselves. They know that the beginnings were accomplished by the simplest creatures and that they had not been superseded by subsequent life forms, but only augmented. They know well that most of the world's work is still performed by these early forms. They were his ancestors, they were his history, he had been there in times past, his past is still here. They know that their lineage is still in the sea and upon the land. They know of evolutionary successes in distant time that took their kin into the shallow bays and marshes, to the dry earth, elaborating as they colonized the land, reaching into more and more hostile environments, simplifying again as they reached these extreme environments, until only the most simple pioneers existed at the fringes of life in the arctic and antarctic, the summits of mountains and the oceanic depths. Every man could extend himself through this lineage out to its hostile limits and his. This is no metaphor; it is true and known to be true. So, the value system was not demeaning to ancient and simple forms, they were no more simple than his own unspecialized cells and as indispensable to the biosphere as the emergent simple cells of his marrow were to himself.

But, the search for man's role was not to be found in a thermodynamic role—this other creatures could do much better; it was essential that he was not destructive in these terms. Apperception was surely the key to man's role, he was the uniquely perceptive and conscious animal, he who had developed language and symbols, and this was clearly his opportunity. What of his role? Surely it was as a cooperative mechanism sustaining the biosphere, and this was the great value of apperception, the key to man's role as steward, the agent of symbioses.

Believing, as natural scientists, that meaning could be found in earth, and its processes, both physical and biological, they continuously examined the phenomenal world for that evidence necessary to permit them to conduct that intelligent stewardship which they assume to be their responsibility. In examining all things over long periods of time, they have reached a startling conclusion. They observe that while creatures exhibited many similarities, sufficient to place them in discrete groups, minute examination discloses that neither two sand grains nor any two creatures are in fact identical. Some small reflection confirms that this might, indeed, be anticipated. Similarities increase as the species recedes into simple forms although identical pairs can never be found. As the creatures examined become more complex, the degree of their distinction increases, not only as a function of antecedents and over time (births not simultaneous), but also in the subsequent life experience. This study has led the Naturalists to con-

clude that every thing is its unique self, never having preexisted, never to be succeeded by an identical form. That is, the matter of the creature is absolutely, not metaphorically, unique. It is the single pathway that is itself and will exist only once.

Thus, uniqueness is the basis of their attitude to all things and all life forms; it is upon this that deference and consideration is based. However, uniqueness has the unusual attribute of being singular, but also of being ubiquitous. It, therefore, concedes neither superiority nor inferiority, but simply uniqueness. How much better a claim this is than equality, which is insupportable in fact and a mere claim in comparison.

In this preoccupation with the development of an ethic, no subject has received more attention than that of freedom. The attribution of uniqueness is the basis for the individual's claim for consideration and deference; it is also the basis for his freedom. Clearly each individual has a responsibility for the entire biosphere and is required to engage in creative, cooperative activities. Freedom is thought to be inherent in uniqueness and in the infinite opportunities afforded by the environment, that is, modes of existence and expression are unlimited and the unique individual has these inherent opportunities. Anarchy is rejected because it replaces creation with randomness. Tyranny is rejected because it suppresses the uniqueness of the individual and his freedom. Poised between these two extremes is the concept of creation, linked to uniqueness, freedom, and the responsibility wherein the organism might perform any role that is creative and enhances the biosphere and the evolution of apperception and symbioses.

We know very well that the same evidence can be differently interpreted, and while the Naturalists are familiar with Darwin, they have chosen to emphasize the importance of cooperation, or rather altruism, in the evolution of the biosphere, rather than com-

petition. That is, they see the elaboration of creatures as evidence of increase in creativity, as an increase in apperception, and, most important of all, as an increase in altruism.

The relations between predator and prey cause them no trouble. The creatures so related are mutually beneficial. The wolf culls the aged, infirm and unfit caribou, and, thus, serves their evolutionary development; the caribou feed the wolf—both regulate the numbers of both. This offers no difficulty in the cosmography; nor do parasite-host relationships. This was surely only an early point in the evolution of a mutually beneficial arrangement. It behooved the host to learn to derive benefit from the parasite which the latter had so clearly accomplished. The relationship would in time become mutually beneficial or when the hosts succumbed it would no longer persist.

A great importance is given to roles. As you might expect, their language reflects this. We once called men Weaver and Carpenter, Smith and Wheelwright, Thatcher and Farmer, Potter and Tailor, but the language of the Naturalists encompasses mountains and mosses as well as men. The sun is known as the first giver; mountains have many attributes, among them those which brought this or that from the ancient seas, the bringers of rain. The snowcaps and icesheets are known as those that hold water in reserve, the source of the cool winds. Rivers and streams are mainly known as those that bring water to us. The oceans are the second givers, home of ancient life; the chloroplast and the plant are the third givers, while the essential decomposers are the fourth-order givers, those that return all things.

All creatures are seen in terms of succession. The simplest creatures are known simply as the pioneers, those of the first wave who brought simple order to places of little order. The second wave followed the pioneers and raised the level of order. In this company are not only plants, but animals and the simplest men. Each successive group has assumed a role in the increase of order until the final group consists of the climaxes, those communities of creatures that represented the zenith capable of accomplishment by those beings that existed.

As we have seen, there is nothing pejorative in these descriptions; the conception of uniqueness and the sense of unity that embrace all of the biosphere allowed distinction to be made without allocating either superiority or inferiority. The general cell in the self is neither superior nor inferior to the specialized cell. Having said this, it is nevertheless true that the decomposers are especially regarded, for they alone can ensure the recycling in the system. Volcanoes and lightning are treasured, as are the sea birds that bring phosphorous back to the land, and the spawning fish that bring rich nutrients back from the sea to deposit them high in mountain streams before they die, bringing nourishment to the forests. The bacteria in the soil are seen as a great resource, and these were cultured in soils and considered to be among the highest accomplishments of all creation.

There are also the creatures of the special functions, the pollinating animals, those creatures that aerate the soils, the nitrogen bacteria, and then there are the indicators of successional stages or of retrogression. There are also the communities of the highest expression—those that express most vividly the glory of birth that is the spring, the glory of the working summer, the glory of death that is the autumn, and, of course, the glory of introspection and preparation that is the winter.

If one can view the biosphere as a single superorganism, then the Naturalist considers that man is an enzyme capable of its regulation, and conscious of it. He is of the system and entirely dependent upon it, but has the responsibility for management, derived from his apperception. This is his role—steward of the biosphere and its consciousness.

Now the Naturalists turn to the zoologists and physical anthropologists among them to reveal the nature of man. It is well understood that he has a common ancestry with the apes and that he is a raised ape rather than a fallen angel. They are convinced, as apparently we are not, that his evolutionary success results from exploitation of weapons and a capacity to kill: he was a successful predator. Observation of animals in the wild has convinced them that dominance is a reality, that rank orders are true for all creatures and thus for man. The defense of territory was observed in animals much simpler than man and holds true for him. Among all of the evidence used to discern the historic attitudes that are our traditional response to the fellow and the stranger, the most convincing is the response of the organism to a graft: no matter how beneficial such surgery might be, the body continuously rejects this foreign intrusion. This confirms the observation of the basic hostility of the organism to the unfamiliar. Altruism within the community is the rule, hostility to the stranger is as strongly instilled. As the community enlarges then so must the umbrella of altruism, but it is well to recognize the primitive origins of parochial hostility.

The Naturalists, of course, believe that man is natural, and therefore there are no divisions between the natural and the social sciences. Indeed, if there is a realm of knowledge concerned with the affairs of man it need be no less scientific than any other. They recognized that there are some special problems in dealing with man. While it is easy to relegate an alga or flatworm to species and abstraction, this detachment is more difficult with the evident personality of the individual human. Nonetheless some things are known. They believe that the foetus is influenced by anxiety experienced by the mother and so pay inordinate attention to the conditions attending her and the child she carries. They too have observed orphans and waifs revert to moronity without affection and have concluded that love and cherishing are indispensable to the

growth of children. They know too that trauma from early experience is difficult, if not impossible, to eradicate and so they ensure that the conditions attending the life of the infant and young child are the most felicitous that can be arranged. They have observed the assuaging power of grief and see in this a great capacity for healing. Their devotion to the conception of uniqueness among all things is employed in dealings with man. Thus the environment, both physical and social, must offer the maximum opportunity for the elaboration of each unique personality. Diversity is seen as an important component of this quest—the provision of the maximum number of opportunities and pathways. As reality consists only in the response to those stimuli impinging upon the individual, then the greater the number and diversity of these, the greater the choice. Sensory deprivation produces an impoverished environment and can induce hallucination. Diversity offers the maximum opportunity for the emergence of the unique individual. But it is important to distinguish noise from information.

Their hierarchy of requirements for man runs the gamut from survival to fulfillment. Beyond survival is mere existence, found simply in the satisfaction of physiological needs. The next level is identified by the presence of dignity; here existence is transcended. The last stage is fulfillment and is known to be unrealizable although it is the omnipresent quest and involves healthy men who not only solve problems but who seek them. In this evolution from survival to fulfillment is a corresponding hierarchy of symbioses. The least of these are the cooperative mechanisms necessary for survival, which ascend in number and complexity and reach their highest state in these symbioses which are altruistic and can be better described as love.

Cooperative relationships are as essential for survival as for fulfillment, but their nature has changed in this evolution from a mutuality of interest essential to survival to the transcendent form of love.

Now the attitudes the Naturalists bring to the roles of men are no different than those they bring to the remainder of the biosphere. Men are assumed to be as natural as other creatures—neither apperception nor consciousness suspend natural laws, but only reflect them. Every man, just as every creature, is required to be creative; destructiveness is intolerable. As there were pioneers among plants, so are there among men. The simplest societies are hunting and gathering communities, another type of predator in the forest or the seas, surviving in numbers related to the prey, cautioned to be neither depletive nor destructive, serving in the maintenance of the system while the other creatures performed the major works of creation—as the forest developed in complexity, the soils deepened and the community elaborated, or in the seas where the biota evolved, filling more and more ordering niches.

The next are societies of itinerant farmers. By burning and cultivating, they act as another decomposer and recycler. They perform a slightly creative role, but the major work is still being performed by the forest and the creatures within it. The fixed farmers assume a potentially more creative role but are required to elaborate the biota in order to compensate for the simplifications that monocultures produce. Nonetheless, successful agriculture involves the farmer in a creative role not accomplished in the simpler societies. The terracers are a special group of fixed farmers who arrest nutrients and soils on their path to the sea and in so doing accomplish valuable conservation.

If, as do the Naturalists, you attribute uniqueness to all things and all creatures, and, further, you agree that that which is being considered is that single pathway, itself, which can never be replicated, and can thus never recur, then you have assumed a position vis-à-vis the phenomenal world. This

Naturalist view is much more encompassing than the reverence for some life that Schweitzer proposed; it does not end with those creatures having a utility to man, but encompasses all matter and all creatures. That which is, is justified by being; it is unique, it needs no other justification.

The consequence of these views is the ensurance that the Naturalists will not change preexisting conditions unless they can demonstrate that such changes are creative. Of course, they recognize that change is inevitable—change is accomplished by simply being. They also rightly assume that their existence permits them to claim that which is necessary to sustain them, but these claims are always subject to the necessity of showing an increase of negentropy or an increase in apperception of the system, resulting from such change.

Now the observed fact that life persists because life eats life is not seen as any contradiction of their propositions, nor, indeed, is death any problem to their cosmography. The operation of the biological world requires that the substances of living creatures and their wastes be consumed by other creatures in the creative process of the world. Man too subscribes to this, knowing that his wastes in life, and his substance after death, will be consumed by other creatures in a creative process. Death is seen in a like way, an indispensable part of a creative process. It is only when death is examined out of context that it appears as a reduction from higher to lower levels of order. As the basis for evolution, itself moving to higher orders, it is creative.

The Naturalists have turned to the world at large in order to find laws and forms of government that might work satisfactorily. They have observed that the world is an ordered place and infer that the creatures respond to physical and biological laws that are intrinsic and self-enforcing. Survival is contingent upon operation of "the way of things." This is the basis for the laws: does

this or that correspond to "the way of things?" This way has no central authority, although it does have overweening laws; it has relative hierarchies but no absolute scales; the individual is the basic unit of law and of government, the overwhelming presumption is "in favor of the natural."* But then, there is no unnatural; there are the unknowns and those actions, which, while natural, do not correspond with "the way of things."

When one attempts to create people in whom repose such wisdom and rationality, there is a real danger that there is engendered, not admiration, but annoyance. How sanctimonious they appear to be. Yet that is simply because we have not looked closely enough to see their warts and squints, to see that many of them are ill-formed, bald and fat, that they reveal pettiness, bitterness and jealousy, superciliousness, and even stupidity for, of course, they are thoroughly human. Indeed, as we do look more closely, they appear to be much too human and contentious to be the appropriate repositories for such vital knowledge. The microbiologists are the aristocrats, frightfully superior yet largely ignorant of the visible world; the geologists know too little of the living; botanists too little zoology; and it is not only the taxonomists who are guilty of an ignorance of ecology. Moreover, as a group, their great sin is not that they are human, but that they have a certain professional myopia, they tend to be rather disinterested in human problems, and bring perhaps too clinical a view to art. One of the most serious of criticisms is that they are thoroughly irresolute in the absence of impeccable evidence, and this is a profound weakness in a world which is finally unknowable.

Yet, two things return them to our concern: they are committed to the acquisition of knowledge and in them is encapsulated a great realm of human understanding. In addition, they have in their company not only scientists but humanists who have espoused the ecological view.

125

*Clarence Morris, "The Rights and Duties of Beasts and Trees: A Law Teacher's Essay for Landscape Architects," *Journal of Legal Education,* Vol. 17, 1964, pp. 185-192.

The River Basin

A professional landscape architect or city planner is limited in the projects he undertakes to problems presented by his clients. A professor, in contrast, suffers no such constraints and is enabled to undertake projects he deems worthy of study. When I was appointed as a member of the American Institute of Architects Task Force on the Potomac by Secretary Stewart Udall, that force had no staff and was lacking elementary information on the river basin. This being so, it seemed propitious to present this problem to graduate students in Landscape Architecture, and make the results of their investigation available to the Task Force.

In this case there was no problem of defining the case to be studied—it was the Potomac River Basin. Thus, we were spared the agonies that rack the socio-economic planners whose regions are ephemeral and transitory. At least the river basin is describable—it is united by water; and it is permanent. Yet, it is clear that, while the river basin is a hydrologic unit, it is not a physiographic one; and, if one seeks a more finite division of land, the physiographic region offers this character to an unequaled degree. Here the boundaries are clear, either a half billion years of time reflected in the interfaces of regions, seen in the conjunction of Piedmont and Coastal Plain, or the dramatic confrontation of the Allegheny Front or the Blue Ridge. Whether planners do or do not know it, physiographic regions vary dramatically. They are discrete.

In earlier applications of the ecological planning method, the problems all contained certain limitations. Preoccupations with survival narrowed the study of the New Jersey Shore, concentration on open space alone reduced the scope of the Philadelphia metropolitan study, a highway is only a single function, while the study of the Valleys existed in only a part of a metropolitan and physiographic region. In the Potomac River Basin there is a single hydrologic unit that transects a number of physiographic regions in which the preoccupation is with all prospective land uses. This is a fitting test for the ecological planning method. As the book has proceeded, the reader has acquired some knowledge of physical and biological processes and accepts that this knowledge is essential to understand nature, to propose use or change. The basic theme can then be restated, as for every problem, that it is necessary to understand nature as an interacting process that represents a relative value system, and that can be interpreted as proffering opportunities for human use—but also revealing constraints, and even prohibitions to certain of these.

The method can now be developed more fully than before. It is our intention to understand the Potomac River Basin as an interacting process, to interpret this as a value system and to designate appropriate land uses. Now this is not a plan—a plan is a determination to achieve certain social goals, related to the power of society to accomplish these. No: this exercise seeks only to reveal nature as a working storehouse, with implications for land use and management. This information is an indispensable ingredient to a plan, but is not the plan itself.

The first considerations are historical geology and climate which, in conjunction, have interacted upon the river basin, for they have created the basic form. When this is understood, the various physiographic regions become clearly evident. The current morphology, with climate and lithology, can be invoked to explain the pattern of rivers and streams, the distribution of groundwater, relative quantities and physical properties. The pursuit of this information on the movements of sediments, some by fluvial processes, other from deposition, will reveal the pattern, distribution and properties of soils. When climate, topography, the water regimen and soils are known, the incidence of plants as individuals and as communities becomes clearer. As animals are all either directly or indirectly plant-related—whether in terrestrial or aquatic environments—

127

knowledge of the plant communities, their age and condition, will tend to explain the distribution of animals. We have seen that coal, iron, limestone and rich, productive soils occur where they do for reasons that derive from physical and biological processes deep in geological history. They are where they are . . . because. So too with the Fall Line on the major rivers, where the watercourses cut deep trenches through the gravels of the Coastal Plain after leaving the Piedmont crystalline rocks. Here is the break-of-bulk point where cities were located. There are transportation routes, but these are likely to follow river courses and passes; there are fitting places for cities, level, well-drained sites adjacent to abundant water and surrounded by productive soils, and so the same method can be used to follow land use over time and to see the march and growth of men upon the land. Indeed, even battles can be better understood if the facts of physiography are known. From this same method, the presence of unique sites, limestone caves or garnet beaches—home of oyster and clam, trout and bass—can be found.

An examination of this sort will reveal the most productive soils, the presence of coal and limestone deposits, the relative abundance of water in rivers and aquifers, the great forests, oyster banks, areas of wilderness or relative accessibility, historic forts or areas of great natural beauty. As the regions vary from one another because of their geological history, there will be regional variation in all the resources that are considered. There will also be a relative consistency within each region. So, having acquired this information, it is not difficult to interpret it in terms of the dominant, intrinsic resource or resources. After all, coal exists in only one region, limestone is extensive in only one; the great agricultural soils are concentrated in a single region. From this view can be seen the dominant prospective land use for each region, and this is the first overview. Where is the major recreational opportunity in the basin? Where the agricultural

heartland? Where are the best forest locations? Where the best sites for urbanization? This preliminary investigation can answer such questions, deriving the information from the place itself. So now when we know something of the inventory of the storehouse, we can turn and ask, "what do you want?" The questions can vary. "Where can I find 15,000 acres of land of less than five per cent average slope for a new city, within one hour's travel distance from Washington?" "Where is there coal to be stripped with an overburden of less than 12 to 1?" "Where in West Virginia can I drill and find 600 gallons of water a minute?" "Where can I find a large wilderness area or a wild river, a trout stream or a ski slope?" These questions can be answered.

We have become accustomed to think of single-function land use and the concept of zoning has done much to confirm this—a one-acre residential zone, a commercial or industrial zone—but this is clearly a most limiting concept. If we examine a forest, we know that there are many species—and, thus, that many cooperative roles coexist. In the forest there are likely to be dominant tree species, subdominants and a hierarchy of species descending to the final soil microorganisms. The same concept can apply to the management of resources—that there be dominant or codominant land uses, coexisting with subordinate, but compatible ones.

It takes only a moment of reflection to realize that a single area of forest may be managed either for timber or pulp; it may be simultaneously managed for water, flood, drought, erosion control, wildlife and recreation; it may also absorb villages and hamlets, recreational communities and second homes.

Now we have a program; we seek to find the highest and best uses of all the land in the basin, but in every case we will try to identify the maximum conjunction of these. This, then, is the image of nature as an interacting and living storehouse—a value system.

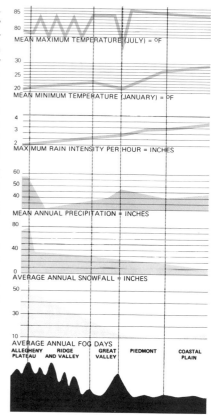

Climate

The most notable factor in considering climate in the basin is the marked correlation with physiography. The Appalachian Mountains affect the Allegheny Plateau and result in a "rain shadow" in the east of this region. Summer and autumn fogs and cloudy conditions are found here. The adjacent Ridge and Valley has great temperature variations and frequent valley fogs. Intense storms and a short growing season mark this province. Piedmont and Coastal Plain share a similar climate, save for the proclivity of the latter to hurricanes. Summers are warm to hot, humidity is high, winters mild, and the growing season longest in the basin. There is then, a marked regional climatic variability.

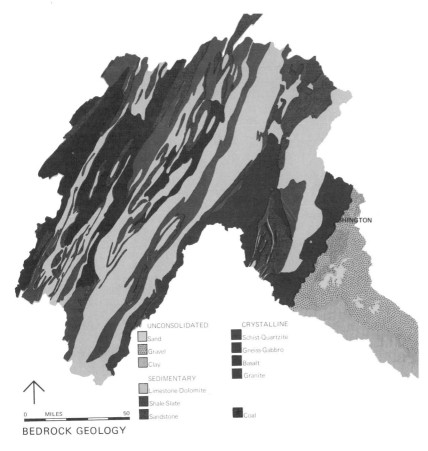

UNCONSOLIDATED

☐ Sand
▨ Gravel
▦ Clay

SEDIMENTARY

☐ Limestone-Dolomite
■ Shale-Slate
■ Sandstone

CRYSTALLINE

■ Schist-Quartzite
■ Gneiss-Gabbro
■ Basalt
■ Granite

■ Coal

0   MILES   50

BEDROCK GEOLOGY

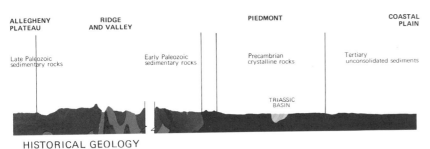

ALLEGHENY PLATEAU	RIDGE AND VALLEY	PIEDMONT	COASTAL PLAIN
Late Paleozoic sedimentary rocks	Early Paleozoic sedimentary rocks	Precambrian crystalline rocks	Tertiary unconsolidated sediments

TRIASSIC BASIN

HISTORICAL GEOLOGY

Geology

The Potomac basin is a subregion of the Atlantic and Gulf Coast system and results from geological activity since Precambrian time, some half billion years ago. Then, thrusts from the southeast determined the conspicuous southwest-northeast trend of the Appalachian Mountain system, and, east of this, the sedimentary margin in the Coastal Plain.

Geologically, the region consists of three major zones: first, the area of very old crystalline rocks in the Piedmont Plateau; and, second, the Allegheny Plateau, which is of more recent sedimentary origin; and, finally, on the east, the very recent series of generally unconsolidated sedimentary strata of the Coastal Plain.

In the Piedmont is the remainder of the very ancient mountain system. It consists of crystalline rocks in strata that are tilted and folded, but the surface has been base-leveled and is now dissected into a mature plateau.

Erosion from these ancient mountains was deposited in Cambrian and Permian times in the inland sea west of the mountains and formed a broad syncline. In the upper layers of this were laid down the coal measures. The Blue Ridge was raised in Permian time, two hundred million years ago when the great southeasterly thrust of the Appalachian Revolution compressed the strata of the geosyncline into a series of parallel folds, oriented southwest-northeast. Erosion, uplift, and further erosion have produced the present condition revealed in the long, narrow, sharply crested parallel mountain ridges that alternate with the equally long, narrow, and steep valleys composing the Ridge and Valley Province.

The sedimentary terraces of the Coastal Plain were laid on an igneous base, beginning in Cretaceous times. These, derived from Appalachian erosion and marine deposition, now dip to the southeast.

129

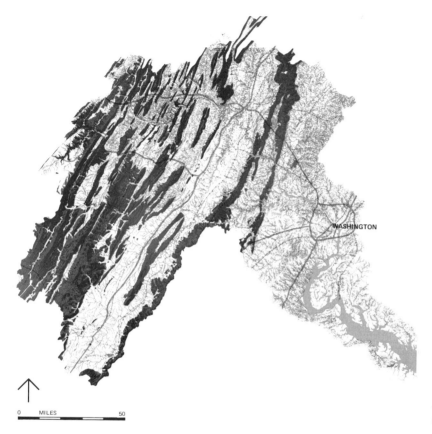

WASHINGTON

↑

0   MILES   50

ALLEGHENY PLATEAU

Although a mountain feature today, the Allegheny Plateau can be better understood as an ancient sea, which from the Paleozoic period to the Carboniferous, was being filled by sediments. From these depositions resulted the limestones, green and red sandstones, more limestone, then shale. In the later Carboniferous the sea became a marsh and in successions of marshes the horsetail forests grew, which, later compressed, resulted in the coal seams. Sandstones were interlayered with coal during this period. At its end, it was in freshwater marshes that the most recent coal measures were formed. This plateau is a great syncline with regular beds. Its edge is revealed in the Appalachian front, which rises 1500 feet from the valley floor.

THE RIDGE AND VALLEY PROVINCE

This region is about fifty miles wide in the basin and extends east from the Allegheny Front. Unlike the Blue Ridge, which was subjected to violent deformation in Cambrian and Permian times, the ridges and valleys are the result of compression into a number of folds. The resistant sandstone persisted in ridges while the softer limestones and shales were eroded to form the valleys. The configuration is unique in the region, with series of parallel ridges and valleys that rise from elevations of 500 feet to 2500 feet. These symmetrical ridges and valleys, broken only occasionally by wind and water gaps, are the most conspicuous physiographic feature of the entire basin.

THE GREAT VALLEY

This great, broad valley, twenty miles wide, extends across the entire basin with its eastern boundary the Blue Ridge. It is generally developed on steeply inclined limestones, but there are three major subdivisions—the hilly area to the west composed of sandstone, shale, limestone and quartzite; the valley proper composed of limestones and dolomites; and the three- to six-mile-wide

Physiography

From source to ocean, the Potomac transects six physiographic regions from the Allegheny Plateau to the Ridge and Valley Province, thence to the Great Valley, Blue Ridge and Piedmont, and, finally, to its estuary in the Coastal Plain.

The divisions are perfectly clear. The Allegheny Front reveals the interface of the first two provinces. The parallel narrow valleys and ridges continue until meeting the Great Valley, and this province terminates dramatically with the Blue Ridge. On the east begins the Piedmont, which terminates at

the Fall Line, where the crystalline rocks are replaced by the sediments and characteristic physiography of the Coastal Plain.

The materials of these regions are consequently quite different. In the Allegheny Plateau one finds a geosyncline where coal measures lie in bands with shale and sandstone; the Ridge and Valley reveals sandstone ridges and limestone valleys; the Great Valley is formed mostly on limestone. The Blue Ridge is composed of gneisses and schists whose layers stand on end or are overturned; the Piedmont consists of crystalline granites, schists, gneisses and gabbros, while the Coastal Plain reveals sands, gravels and marls.

ALLEGHENY PLATEAU

BLUE RIDGE

RIDGE AND VALLEY

PIEDMONT

GREAT VALLEY

COASTAL PLAIN

strip of Martinsburg shale, which bisects the valley.

While this is a generally rolling landscape, there are variations. The greatest topographic change occurs in the western hills, the limestone valley discloses a continuously rolling landscape with little dissection, while it is the shale areas that provide the flattest land.

THE BLUE RIDGE

This most conspicuous of features, rising 2000 feet above the Piedmont, is a complex, highly squeezed and metamorphosed series of slow-weathering gneisses and schists. It ranges in width from 1 to 5 miles. This is the eastern escarpment of the western mountain system. In the narrower portions in Pennsylvania, it is a single ridge; but it is usually more complex, with many attendant spurs.

THE PIEDMONT

This province varies from 30 to 50 miles in width in the basin; it slopes generally eastward from about 500 feet at the western edge, to 300 feet at the east. It is, as has been observed, the residue of the ancient mountain system that has been base-leveled and subsequently eroded into the present plateau. In the crystalline rock areas, variations in altitude of 400 feet can be found, but in the important subprovince of Triassic time, on less resistant rocks, relief is only half as much. Along the western boundary of the province is a narrow belt of monadnocks, outliers of the Blue Ridge, introducing the Appalachian mountain system.

COASTAL PLAIN

The most recent geologic activity in the basin has been the appearance of the Coastal Plain—a series of sediments of fluvial and marine origin, still largely unconsolidated and raised to their present level through a series of upheavals and subsidences. These consist of sand, gravel, clays and marls.

131

Hydrology

The Potomac drains a basin of almost 15,000 square miles; its major tributaries are the North and South Branches, the great Shenandoah, the Cacapon, Conococheague Creek and the Monocacy. Stream characteristics vary enormously through the hundreds of miles, from the smallest mountain tributaries, the meandering Shenandoah, to the great wide estuary of the lower Potomac.

In the Allegheny Plateau there is the greatest precipitation, almost 60 inches of rainfall, 80 inches of snow—and this, of course, affects hydrology. This area is drained by the North Branch and Wills Creek, and owing to the high precipitation and very steep gradients, the discharge rates are high.

Because of the rainshed, the Ridge and Valley Province has the lowest precipitation in the entire basin. Yet, it is an area with high variability, experiencing both droughts and intense storms and with periodic flash flooding. Here stream gradients are still high and discharge rates high for streams of any order, with the result that the buildup of flood waters is greater here than in any other province. Paradoxically, there are areas of permeable rock where mountain streams have no flow, save storm runoff.

The Great Valley is drained by the Shenandoah south of the Potomac, and the Conococheague and Antietam Creeks to the north. These are now meandering streams with low gradients. Here rivers cross a limestone valley and there is considerable percolation, with the result that streams are quite small.

In the Piedmont, drainage dissection is mature, and the streams make indirect ways to the Potomac. They have cut broad, shallow valleys in their headwater sections through which they flow in a succession of pools and rapids as harder and softer formations are crossed. The middle and lower courses are often gorge-like. While the form

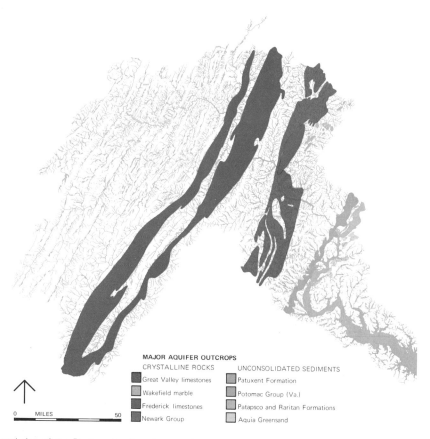

MAJOR AQUIFER OUTCROPS

CRYSTALLINE ROCKS
- Great Valley limestones
- Wakefield marble
- Frederick limestones
- Newark Group

UNCONSOLIDATED SEDIMENTS
- Patuxent Formation
- Potomac Group (Va.)
- Patapsco and Raritan Formations
- Aquia Greensand

0   MILES   50

and size of the Piedmont valleys have a relation to geologic structure, the stream courses, on the whole, have not been strongly influenced by bedrock. This region, with the Coastal Plain, suffers the most intense storms—as much as 4 inches in an hour—and these often produce high water and damaging floods.

The hydrology of the Coastal Plain is dominated by the estuary; the tributary streams are characteristically short, draining directly into the Potomac. These streams seem to coincide with the boundaries of sedimentary terraces, and they have accomplished considerable dissection in the area

south of the river. The gradients are low in this generally flat region, as are the discharges.

The estuary is in reality a drowned valley, caused by subsidence, and reaches back to the Fall Line, where, at the Great Falls, the interface between the two regions is dramatically revealed. Floods here are caused by intense precipitation from tropical storms, when a normal month's precipitation may fall within 48 hours. High tides, a full estuary, and intense precipitation combined with east or northeast winds, constitute the elements that contribute to flooding of the estuary.

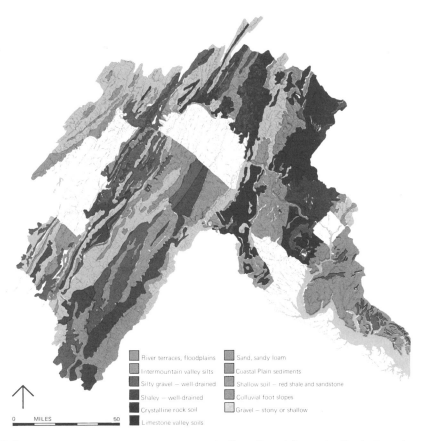

River terraces, floodplains
Intermountain valley silts
Silty gravel — well-drained
Shaley — well-drained
Crystalline rock soil
Limestone valley soils
Sand, sandy loam
Coastal Plain sediments
Shallow soil — red shale and sandstone
Colluvial foot slopes
Gravel — stony or shallow

0   MILES   50

Groundwater

Groundwater has not been extensively studied, but it is known that very large resources of groundwater are to be found in the Allegheny Plateau, notably in sandstone, limestone and shale formations. In the Ridge and Valley, there are local resources of hard water, but the Great Valley is essentially an aquifer throughout. In the Piedmont, it is mainly in the Newark Series of the Triassic period that groundwater resources are to be found. The Coastal Plain, composed entirely of porous material, also contains extensive groundwater resources. Groundwater is highly variable in the region.

Soils

In the Allegheny Plateau, the soils have been derived mainly from sedimentary shale and sandstone and are not inherently productive. The major soil types are stony, gravel, sandy and silt loams. Erosion has been, and still is, severe.

Like those of the Plateau, the soils of the Ridge and Valley are thin, erodible and infertile, except in certain limestone uplands and in the valley bottomlands, which are as fertile as can be found in the entire country. Yet, with the exception of shale formations, the limestone soils of the Great Valley are as fertile as those infrequent valley bottoms in the Ridge and Valley: here is located the great agricultural heartland of the basin.

Like those of the Great Valley, the soils of the Piedmont are mainly residual, except for those on the Newark formation. Marked differences in the character of the rock have given rise to a number of soil types. The most important of these are the "red clay" lands, with red clay subsoils, and gray to red soils, ranging in texture from sands to clays.

For the most part, the soils in the Coastal Plain are excessively drained, owing to the unconsolidated nature of the strata.

133

Plant Associations

In this enormous basin with its range of physiographic expression, it is to be expected that a wide range of vegetation types and communities will be observed and, indeed, this is so. As plants are very specific to environments, the ecologist who knows the presence, pattern and distribution of plants can infer more accurate information about their environments than is generally available from existing information on climate, soils, the water regimen and other factors.

The broadest level of examination reveals the presence of three major divisions of forest associations distributed in broad bands from east to west. The first of these is the oak-pine association; the second, the oak-chestnut; and the third is the legendary mixed mesophytic forest that escaped the Pleistocene ice sheets and whose very center is the Appalachian Mountains.

The oak-pine association extends from southern New Jersey to Georgia, its western boundary in the basin is the Pamlico-Wicomico terrace adjacent to the Fall Line. It is thus the dominant association of the Coastal Plain, its components being the white, willow and pin oak, hickory with sourwood and sweet gum as constant companions. Pines take hold on dry sites and poorer soils. Loblolly and Virginia pine appear in almost pure stands in drained or sloping areas at the southeastern tip of the basin.

In this region are to be found wild rice marshes, magnolia bogs, stands of bald cypress and the impressive black gum.

The oak-chestnut association is now a misnomer, as the chestnut was eliminated by blight in the first quarter of this century, but as no new climax has been discerned, it retains its old name. This great association exists in three of the physiographic regions —the Piedmont, Great Valley, Ridge and

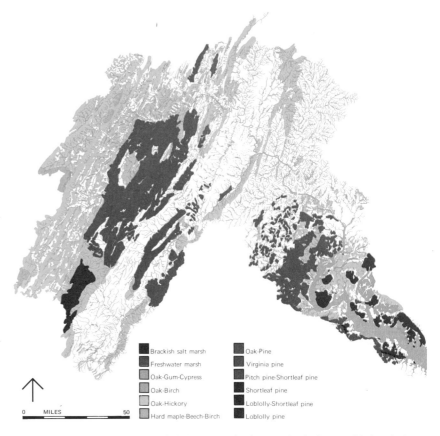

Brackish salt marsh
Freshwater marsh
Oak-Gum-Cypress
Oak-Birch
Oak-Hickory
Hard maple-Beech-Birch

Oak-Pine
Virginia pine
Pitch pine-Shortleaf pine
Shortleaf pine
Loblolly-Shortleaf pine
Loblolly pine

0   MILES   50

Valley—and terminates at the Allegheny Front. Each of these regions shows characteristic variations of this theme.

In the Piedmont there are two divisions of the oak-chestnut forest. The upper Piedmont shows a predominance of oaks—black, red, post, chestnut, and white oaks. In the inner Piedmont, chestnut-oak formed almost pure stands, with red oaks, black gum, tulip poplar and hickory. *Pinus pungens* is found on windswept ridges.

On the highest summit of the Blue Ridge— Hawk's Bill, over 4000 feet high—are spruce and fir, while on lower slopes exists the

mixed mesophytic forest with beech, hemlock, white pine and tulip poplar. The predominant species on the intermediate slopes are red and white oak.

There are other variants in the Great Valley. The rocky slopes of the Great North Mountains are covered with chestnut-oak, but the valley proper is an oak-hickory forest.

The forests of the Ridge and Valley Province are predominantly oak. On intermediate slopes, red and white oak occur on moister and east-facing slopes, chestnut-oak on higher rocky slopes and crests. Valley floors

134

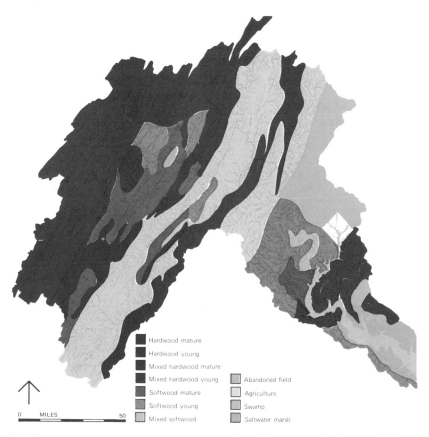

Hardwood mature
Hardwood young
Mixed hardwood mature
Mixed hardwood young
Softwood mature
Softwood young
Mixed softwood

Abandoned field
Agriculture
Swamp
Saltwater marsh

0   MILES   50

in this province are predominantly white and red oak, with hickories and tulip poplars. In certain of these there were once open park landscapes of natural prairie. These were very fertile and have been put to farms.

The great mixed mesophytic forest dominates the Allegheny Plateau. The dominant trees of this forest are the finest hardwoods of the United States—beech, sugar maple, sweet buckeye, red and white oak, tulip poplar and basswood. This great inheritance has been ravaged, cut over several times and burned repeatedly, with the result that it has seriously retrogressed. Seldom does the mixed mesophytic forest return.

Wildlife

It is common knowledge that squirrels eat acorns and robins worms, that starlings, pigeons and mockingbirds associate with man, but that bear, wildcat, and eagles tend to avoid him. Trout like cold water, bass a little warmer, and catfish prefer it warm and muddy. Oysters, clams and mussels each occupy their band of the intertidal zone; creatures are specific to environments.

So if we can discern different environments and know the proclivities of creatures for these, it will be possible to establish the pattern and distribution of wildlife in the

region. Of course, unlike plants, wildlife are mobile—the migratory birds are conspicuously so; all creatures move, although the territories of animals are rather smaller than commonly believed.

In order to identify resources of wildlife, environments were divided into two major categories—terrestrial and aquatic. The former was subdivided into forest types with a distinction as to age—thus, mature hardwood forest, young hardwood forest and so on for softwood and mixed forests. Agricultural land was divided into intensive and abandoned. Aquatic environments were subdivided into salt, brackish and freshwater.

135

Water Problems

Having observed the intense precipitation that occurs in the uplands of the watershed, the susceptibility of the Ridge and Valley Province to flash floods, the fact that tropical storms occur in the Coastal Plain and the Piedmont, we cannot be surprised to learn that the Potomac is a flood-prone river. When we consider that its tributaries and the main stem cross limestone valleys frequently, then we will not be surprised to learn that it is also subject to astonishingly low flows. Indeed, its physiography, the underlying rock, the direction of flow of the major tributaries, and the pattern of precipitation, together with the absence of natural impoundments afforded by glaciation, make the Potomac one of the most variable of rivers on the eastern seaboard.

As coal occurs in the Allegheny Plateau, at the origins of the river, we can expect that acid mine drainage will be a problem and, indeed, orange streams are common. Too, the great Appalachian forest has been mauled and as a result there is a great deal of erosion in this region. This holds true for the Ridge and Valley Province, and as one proceeds down the river, the increase in population and absence of adequate treatment add sewage and sediment to the river. It proceeds to become dirtier by the mile until it

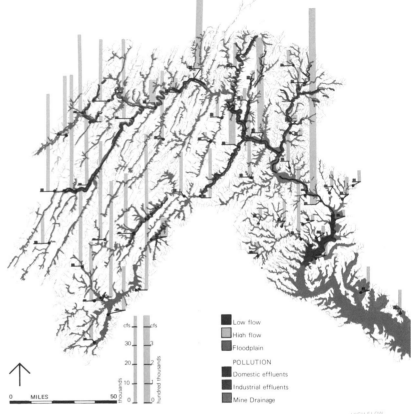

Low flow
High flow
Floodplain

POLLUTION
Domestic effluents
Industrial effluents
Mine Drainage

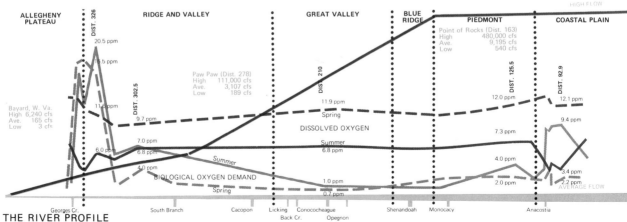

THE RIVER PROFILE

ALLEGHENY PLATEAU RIDGE AND VALLEY GREAT VALLEY BLUE RIDGE PIEDMONT COASTAL PLAIN

DIST. 326
20.5 ppm
16.5 ppm
11.8 ppm
DIST. 302.5
9.7 ppm

Bayard, W. Va.
High 6,240 cfs
Ave.   165 cfs
Low   3 cfs

7.0 ppm
6.8 ppm
6.0 ppm
4.0 ppm

Paw Paw (Dist. 278)
High 111,000 cfs
Ave.   3,107 cfs
Low   189 cfs

DIST. 210
11.9 ppm
Spring

DISSOLVED OXYGEN

Summer
6.8 ppm

Point of Rocks (Dist. 163)
High 480,000 cfs
Ave.   9,195 cfs
Low   540 cfs

DIST. 125.5
12.0 ppm

DIST. 92.9
12.1 ppm
9.4 ppm

7.3 ppm

4.0 ppm

3.4 ppm
2.2 ppm

HIGH FLOW

Summer

BIOLOGICAL OXYGEN DEMAND

Spring

1.0 ppm
0.7 ppm

2.0 ppm

AVERAGE FLOW

Georges Cr.   South Branch   Cacopon   Licking   Conococheague   Shenandoah   Monocacy   Anacostia
Back Cr.   Opequon

UNIQUE—NATURAL

UNIQUE—CULTURAL

Scenic corridors ⌄↵   ⊛ Historic structures

Significant peaks ▲   ▲ Historic battle sites

Sites of geologic interest ⊡

Sites of vegetational interest ■   ⧆ Trout streams

Land-based recreation sites ●   ⊛ Water-oriented recreation sites

0   MILES   50

UNIQUE SITES

reaches the Capital. In the estuary new problems arise where algal blooms absorb oxygen to such a degree that fish are killed extensively, and where pollution has reduced oyster and clam resources.

Interpretation

Given these data, we must now interpret them. We wish to see in the natural processes that have been examined a value system to which man can respond. To that end the data can be analyzed. The first factor to be considered would be uniquenesses or resources that are extremely rare. These may be of popular or personal importance—the

presence of great deposits of coal or the habitat of a rare warbler—but if we wish to understand the region and its resources, this is an important category. It can be divided into natural phenomena and cultural manifestations. Into the former fall garnet beaches and limestone caves, mountain summits and trout streams, areas of geological and ecological importance. In the subcategory of unique or important cultural values, the presence of historic buildings, places and spaces is significant.

In addition to uniqueness, it is important to identify the presence of economic minerals, the presence and abundance of water re-

sources, factors of slope that affect almost every prospective activity, and to consider the subject of accessibility. The earlier considerations of soils, forest types and wildlife constitute an interpretation and, indeed, are themselves value systems.

Given information on these matters, it becomes possible to prescribe the intrinsic dominant land use for each physiographic region and for its various constituent parts. The region, then, must be described as phenomena, seen as process, reconstituted into a value system from which single and multiple, intrinsically suitable land uses can be identified.

137

Mineral Resources

The mineral resources of the basin include coal, limestone, sands and gravels, fuller's earth, but it is the first that is by far the most important. Coal can be understood in terms of seams and their occurrence, and this information can be related to their availability to exploitation with present and prospective technology. Thus, the coal measures can be divided into outcrops that can be removed by normal open cast methods and outcrops covered by overburden. When the ratio of overburden to coal is within the range of 12 to 1 up to a limit of 30 to 1, coal may be removed by stripping.

There are important consequences to coal mining in this region. Outcrops frequently occur on the steep slopes of ridges and the spoil from the mines is simply tipped over the edge, enormously disfiguring the landscape. Stripping despoils large areas of land, leaving Bunyanesque furrows of overburden. This is only occasionally replanted—although when it is, it often results in astonishing tree growth.

Slope

The incidence of various slopes is of importance for a wide variety of factors—where one can ski or find flat sites for cities and

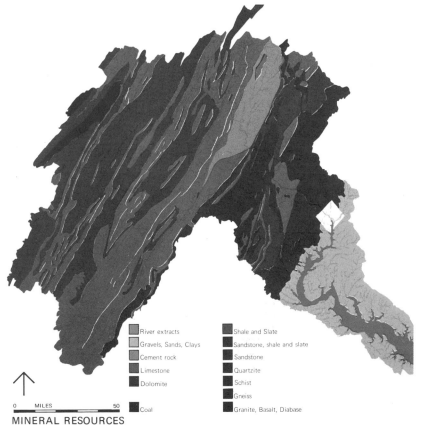

River extracts
Gravels, Sands, Clays
Cement rock
Limestone
Dolomite
Coal

Shale and Slate
Sandstone, shale and slate
Sandstone
Quartzite
Schist
Gneiss
Granite, Basalt, Diabase

0 MILES 50

MINERAL RESOURCES

towns, transportation corridors, or wild rivers. As can be seen, these exhibit a marked regionality, abundant in the Ridge and Valley Province, all but absent in the Coastal Plain, associated with stream dissection in the Piedmont and the Great Valley.

Accessibility

The direction of the prevailing topography, running uniformly northeast-southwest, interposes continuous barriers between Washington and the hinterland. This has the result of diminishing the economic value of much of this land because of the difficulty of travel from Washington. Positively, it has ensured that large areas of land are still remarkably wild, considering their proximity to the National Capital.

Water Resources

Reasonably, the quantity of water available in surface streams and rivers will increase as the system moves to the terminus. It is important to know the available, dependable low flow at every point along the length of the tributaries and the main stem. In addition, it is of some importance to know of available water that can be obtained from aquifers, both as to quantity and physical properties.

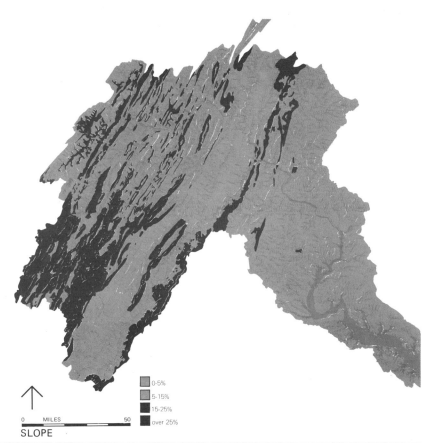

0-5%
5-15%
15-25%
over 25%

0   MILES   50
SLOPE

94

139

Intrinsic Suitabilities

AGRICULTURE

Subsurface geology, climate, soils, slope—and thus drainage—together with exposure, determine the appropriate types of agriculture that should, or can, be practiced in the entire basin.

These factors are variable in the basin but exhibit some consistency within the physiographic regions and subregions, so we can predict suitabilities according to characteristics. Immediately the primacy of the Great Valley is apparent. The Piedmont reveals extensive productive areas; these are sparse in the narrow valleys of the Ridge and Valley Province and all but absent in the Allegheny Plateau. While the soils of the Coastal Plain are poor and infertile, with abundant fertilizer these can be made to produce valuable vegetable crops.

FORESTRY

The locational determinants for commercial forestry are a radius of 25 miles from an existing pulp mill, on a fifth-order stream or larger, with lax or nonexistent zoning restrictions, and with forests on slopes of less than twenty-five per cent.

A second category of commercial forestry, based on softwoods, occurs in the Coastal Plain.

A further category of forestry is operable—noncommercial: the areas that may be logged but will be so devastated that their regeneration is not in the foreseeable future. The final category is nonoperable—as a result of inaccessibility, steep slope, distance from mill or stream, there is no present possibility of economic lumbering. In addition to these categories the two lowest classes of agricultural suitability, associated with steep slopes and erodible soils, are recommended for forest cover.

140

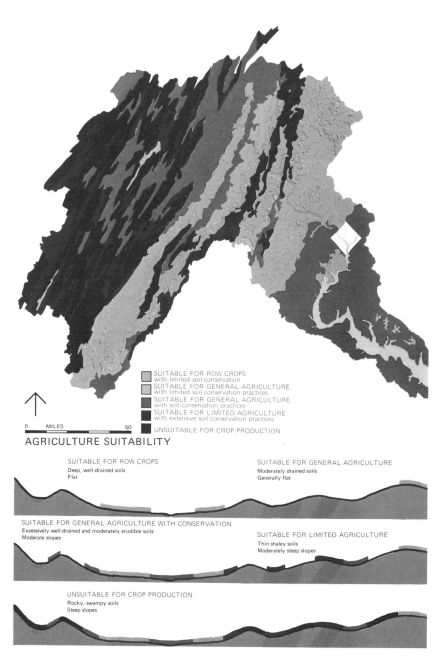

0   MILES   50

AGRICULTURE SUITABILITY

SUITABLE FOR ROW CROPS
with limited soil-conservation
SUITABLE FOR GENERAL AGRICULTURE
with limited soil-conservation practices
SUITABLE FOR GENERAL AGRICULTURE
with soil-conservation practices
SUITABLE FOR LIMITED AGRICULTURE
with extensive soil-conservation practices
UNSUITABLE FOR CROP PRODUCTION

SUITABLE FOR ROW CROPS
Deep, well-drained soils
Flat

SUITABLE FOR GENERAL AGRICULTURE
Moderately drained soils
Generally flat

SUITABLE FOR GENERAL AGRICULTURE WITH CONSERVATION
Excessively well-drained and moderately erodible soils
Moderate slopes

SUITABLE FOR LIMITED AGRICULTURE
Thin shaley soils
Moderately steep slopes

UNSUITABLE FOR CROP PRODUCTION
Rocky, swampy soils
Steep slopes

CROP LAND

PASTURE

FOREST

95

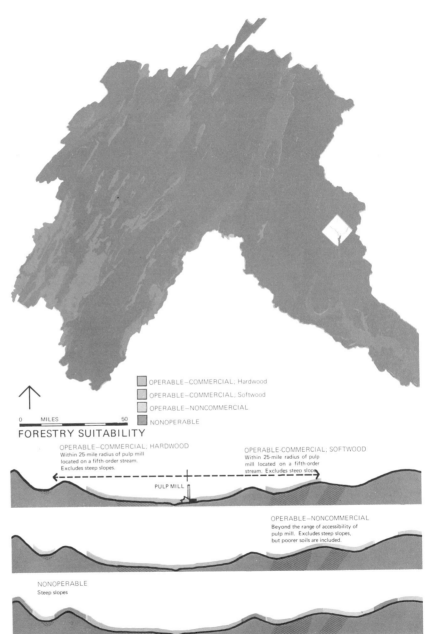

OPERABLE–COMMERCIAL, Hardwood
OPERABLE–COMMERCIAL, Softwood
OPERABLE–NONCOMMERCIAL
NONOPERABLE

0   MILES   50

FORESTRY SUITABILITY

OPERABLE–COMMERCIAL, HARDWOOD
Within 25-mile radius of pulp mill
located on a fifth-order stream.
Excludes steep slopes.

OPERABLE–COMMERCIAL, SOFTWOOD
Within 25-mile radius of pulp
mill located on a fifth-order
stream. Excludes steep slopes.

PULP MILL

OPERABLE–NONCOMMERCIAL
Beyond the range of accessibility of
pulp mill. Excludes steep slopes,
but poorer soils are included.

NONOPERABLE
Steep slopes

141

RECREATION

The data necessary to compile a plan of recreational suitability have already been discussed. From geological information can be discovered the presence of limestone caves, sedimentary deposits on hilltops where shells and fossils may be found. Information on climate can reveal areas suitable for summer recreation or for winter. Physiography reveals summits and ridges, difficult and inaccessible countryside; hydrology shows the pattern of rivers and streams, while from the forest associations a wide body of information can be inferred—not least the presence and abundance of wildlife. From studies of land use the presence of historical artifacts revealing the exploration of the estuary, the Indian forts, exploitation of the Appalachian region and the Civil War are all revealed. Accessibility will determine those areas suitable for wilderness as opposed to those capable of short-term, intensive recreation. Clearly, there are regional resources: the Coastal Plain is the major resource for water-based recreation; the Allegheny Plateau and the Ridge and Valley Province offer the maximum opportunities for terrestrial recreation; the Great Valley and the Piedmont offer little that is unique, while the Blue Ridge does to an exceptional degree. While the Allegheny Plateau intrinsically offers the maximum quality as the site of the great Appalachian forest, it has been so abused with great swaths of open cast mining spoils, mauled forests and acid rivers that this potential is incapable of capture at the present. In the Ridge and Valley Province exists the greatest recreational potential in the basin. The cool summer climate, combined with low rainfall and the lovely and dramatic landscape, offer unrivaled opportunity. In the Great Valley, this is limited to the surrounding hills and the opportunities for exploring caves or driving through a farm landscape. In the Piedmont much of the same experience is possible, but increased by the opportunities to examine the emblems of history.

142

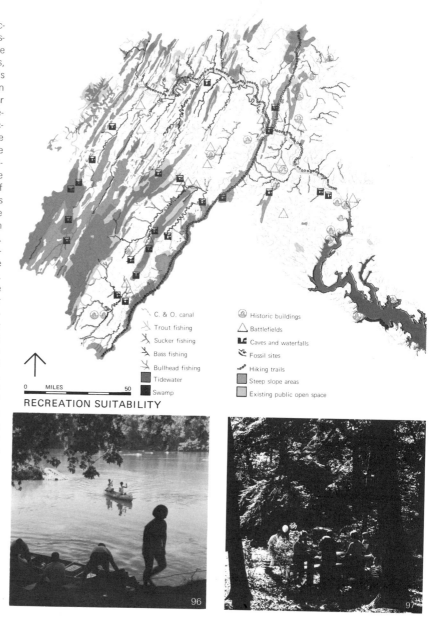

C. & O. canal
Trout fishing
Sucker fishing
Bass fishing
Bullhead fishing
Tidewater
Swamp

Historic buildings
Battlefields
Caves and waterfalls
Fossil sites
Hiking trails
Steep slope areas
Existing public open space

0 MILES 50

RECREATION SUITABILITY

96

97

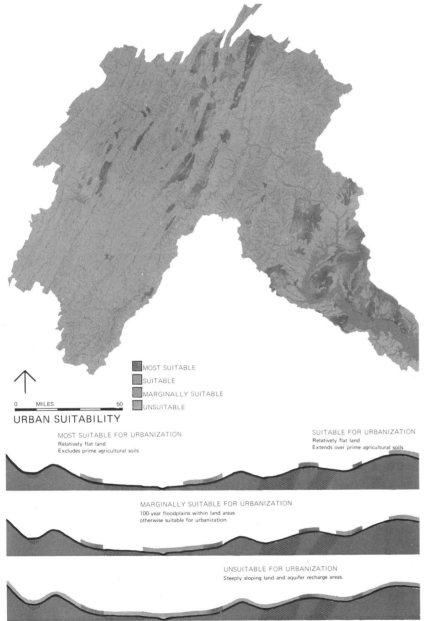

MOST SUITABLE
SUITABLE
MARGINALLY SUITABLE
UNSUITABLE

0   MILES   50

URBAN SUITABILITY

MOST SUITABLE FOR URBANIZATION
Relatively flat land
Excludes prime agricultural soils

SUITABLE FOR URBANIZATION
Relatively flat land
Extends over prime agricultural soils

MARGINALLY SUITABLE FOR URBANIZATION
100-year floodplains within land areas
otherwise suitable for urbanization.

UNSUITABLE FOR URBANIZATION
Steeply sloping land and aquifer recharge areas.

URBAN

In order to determine the sites that qualified as suitable for urbanization, a number of criteria were developed. The land should have slopes of no greater than five per cent incline; it must not be in the 50-year flood-plain, nor in an important aquifer recharge area, nor in fog pockets or high and exposed elevations. Adequate water supplies must be available, and the required highways must not need to be constructed through slopes over fifteen per cent.

As is to be expected, there is again a marked regionality. It is all but impossible to find such sites in the Allegheny Plateau, and where they exist they could support only hamlets or small villages. In the Ridge and Valley Province the sites are attenuated in the valleys, but a number can be found. The Great Valley offers fewer opportunities than might have been expected, as much of the area overlies aquifer recharge. In the Piedmont there is confirmation of the present location of urbanization in the basin: this is the most suitable of the physiographic regions for this function. However, much of the suitable land is also prime farmland.

The Coastal Plain offers opportunities that are restricted by the presence of aquifer recharges, a high water table and the forest's tendency to burn.

The variation in the size of available sites is as striking as their incidence. Only the smallest of sites are available in the Plateau, rather larger ones are discerned in the Ridge and Valleys, still larger in the Great Valley, with opportunities for several new towns revealed in both Piedmont and Coastal Plain.

This study does not suggest that urbanization should occur on the locations shown. It merely reveals which lands meet the criteria for urbanization that have been selected.

143

The matrix (not reproduced in full here) lists the following land use categories along both axes:

- URBAN
- SUBURBAN RESIDENTIAL
- INDUSTRIAL
- INSTITUTIONAL
- MINING: shaft-mined coal, active opencast coal, abandoned coal spoil
- QUARRYING: stone and limestone, sand and gravel
- VACATION SETTLEMENT
- AGRICULTURE: row crops, arable, livestock
- FORESTRY: even-stand softwood, uneven-stand softwood, hardwood
- RECREATION: saltwater oriented, freshwater oriented, wilderness, general recreation, cultural recreation, driving for pleasure
- WATER MANAGEMENT: reservoir, watershed management

Natural determinants columns: SLOPE (0-5%, 15-25%, over 25%); SOILS (gravels, sands, loams, silts); AQUIFER RECHARGE AREAS; WATER SUPPLY DEPENDABILITY; VEHICULAR ACCESSIBILITY; CLIMATE (temperature extremes, fog susceptibility); AIR POLLUTION; WATER POLLUTION.

Consequences columns: SOIL EROSION; FLOOD AND DROUGHT CONTROL; STREAM SEDIMENTATION.

Legend (intercompatibility of land uses):
- ● INCOMPATIBLE
- LOW COMPATIBILITY
- MEDIUM COMPATIBILITY
- FULL COMPATIBILITY

Legend (natural determinants):
- INCOMPATIBLE
- LOW COMPATIBILITY
- MEDIUM COMPATIBILITY
- FULL COMPATIBILITY

Legend (consequences):
- ● BAD
- POOR
- FAIR
- GOOD

DEGREE OF COMPATIBILITY

Optimum Multiple Land Uses

The preceding studies of intrinsic suitabilities for agriculture, forestry, recreation and urbanization reveal the relative values for each region and for the basin within each of the specified land uses. But we seek not to optimize for single, but for multiple compatible land uses. Towards this end a matrix was developed with all prospective land uses on each coordinate. Each land use was then tested against all others to determine compatibility, incompatibility and two intervening degrees.

From this it was possible to reexamine the single optimum and determine the degree of compatibility with other prospective land uses. Thus, for example, an area that had been shown to have a high potential for forestry would also be compatible with recreation, including wildlife management. Within it there might well be opportunities for limited agriculture—pasture in particular —while the whole area could be managed for water objectives. Yet, in another example, an area that proffered an opportunity for agriculture as dominant land use could also support recreation, some urbanization and limited exploitation of minerals.

Adjacent to the matrix on intercompatibility is another that seeks to identify the resources necessary for prospective land uses— productive soils for agriculture, coal and limestone for mining, flat land and water for urban locations, and so on. The final matrix is devoted to the consequences of the operation of these land uses. Where there is coal mining, there will be acid mine drainage; agriculture is associated with sedimentation, urbanization with sewage, industry with atmospheric pollution. The sum of these, in principle, allows one to consider the intercompatibility of land uses, the natural determinants for their occurrence and the consequences of their operation.

When the results of the matrix are applied, the maximum potential conjunction of coexisting and compatible land uses for the basin is revealed. In every case the dominant or codominants are associated with minor compatible land uses.

When the results are examined, it is clear that mining, coal and water-based industry offer the maximum opportunity in the Allegheny Plateau, with forestry and recreation as subordinate uses. In the Ridge and Valley Province, the recreational potential is dominant, with forestry, agriculture and urbanization subordinate. In the Great Valley, agriculture is the overwhelming resource, with recreation and urbanization as lesser land uses. The Blue Ridge exhibits only a recreational potential, but of the highest quality. The Piedmont is primarily suitable for urbanization with attendant agriculture and nondifferentiated recreation. The Coastal Plain exhibits the highest potential for water-based and related recreation and forestry, and a lesser prospect for urbanization and agriculture.

This is a method by which the nature of the place may be learned. It is because . . . and so, it varies. In its variety, it offers different resources. The place must be understood to be used and managed well. This is the ecological planning method.

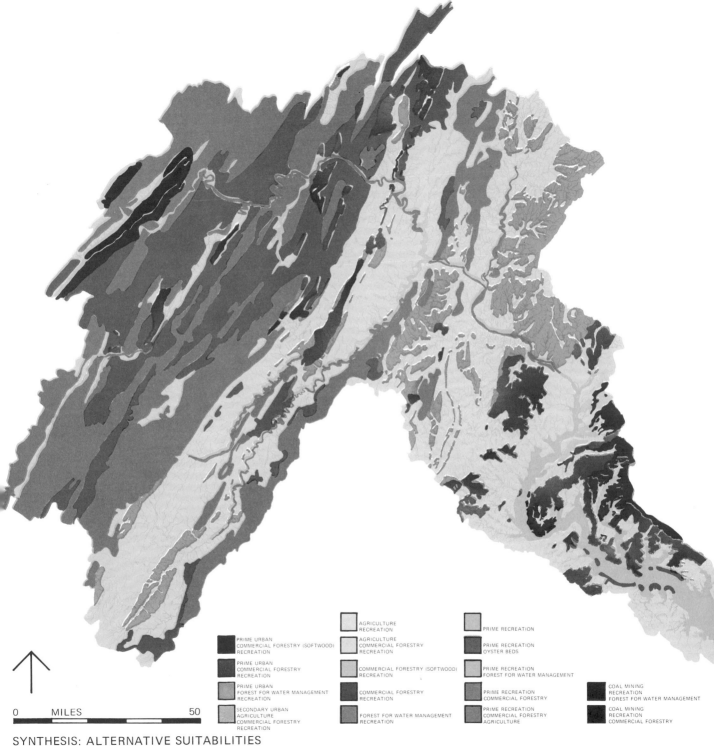

SYNTHESIS: ALTERNATIVE SUITABILITIES

0   MILES   50

PRIME URBAN
COMMERCIAL FORESTRY (SOFTWOOD)
RECREATION

PRIME URBAN
COMMERCIAL FORESTRY
RECREATION

PRIME URBAN
FOREST FOR WATER MANAGEMENT
RECREATION

SECONDARY URBAN
AGRICULTURE
COMMERCIAL FORESTRY
RECREATION

AGRICULTURE
RECREATION

AGRICULTURE
COMMERCIAL FORESTRY
RECREATION

COMMERCIAL FORESTRY (SOFTWOOD)
RECREATION

COMMERCIAL FORESTRY
RECREATION

FOREST FOR WATER MANAGEMENT
RECREATION

PRIME RECREATION

PRIME RECREATION
OYSTER BEDS

PRIME RECREATION
FOREST FOR WATER MANAGEMENT

PRIME RECREATION
COMMERCIAL FORESTRY

PRIME RECREATION
COMMERCIAL FORESTRY
AGRICULTURE

COAL MINING
RECREATION
FOREST FOR WATER MANAGEMENT

COAL MINING
RECREATION
COMMERCIAL FORESTRY

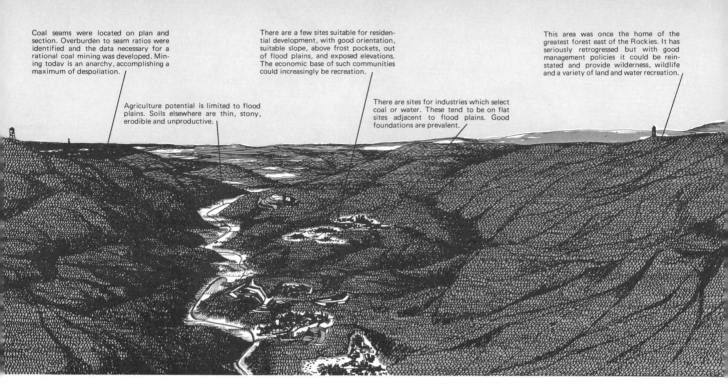

Coal seams were located on plan and section. Overburden to seam ratios were identified and the data necessary for a rational coal mining was developed. Mining today is an anarchy, accomplishing a maximum of despoliation.

Agriculture potential is limited to flood plains. Soils elsewhere are thin, stony, erodible and unproductive.

There are a few sites suitable for residential development, with good orientation, suitable slope, above frost pockets, out of flood plains, and exposed elevations. The economic base of such communities could increasingly be recreation.

There are sites for industries which select coal or water. These tend to be on flat sites adjacent to flood plains. Good foundations are prevalent.

This area was once the home of the greatest forest east of the Rockies. It has seriously retrogressed but with good management policies it could be reinstated and provide wilderness, wildlife and a variety of land and water recreation.

The Physiographic Regions:

The studies of the entire basin were conducted at a scale of 1:250,000, and thus there were many details that escaped attention, and indeed, the causal relations of physiography, soils, climate and vegetation could only be imperfectly discerned. For that reason, areas were selected in each of the physiographic regions for more detailed study where this causality could be seen. These were undertaken at the scale of 1:24,000. Each of the areas selected was thought to be typical of its region.

ALLEGHENY PLATEAU

This great province has been savaged—forests felled and burned, coal carelessly mined, wastes widespread and streams acid. The land was rich but the wealth was removed, a degraded land and impoverished people remain. Yet there are resources still, abundant

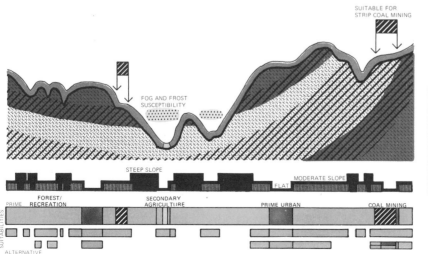

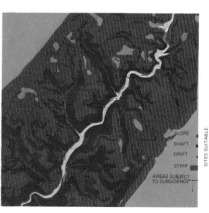

Highly productive agriculture exist on alluvium and limestone soils on wide valley bottoms.

Forests here should be managed for recreation rather than lumbering alone. Fishing, climbing, white water canoeing, hunting are typical recreational pursuits possible here. Urbanization can select good foundations, southeast orientation, medium slope, locations above flood plains and frost pockets, protected from winter winds.

coal, latent forests, a wildlife and recreation potential of the highest value. But to capture this requires a knowledge of resources as revealed here, plans and management policies which reflect this understanding. It will also require time and man to heal this land and its people.

RIDGE AND VALLEY

The absence of coal may explain the lesser depredations in this region. It offers the greatest resource of terrestrial recreation in the Basin. Although valleys are narrow they are remarkably fertile. The forests are not of high commercial value but have great value for recreation—the prime resource of this region. Urbanization has too often been located on flood plains. Better sites on higher ground with medium slopes, good orientation, above frost pockets can be located. Recreation is an important regional resource, constituting a high social value.

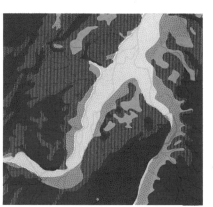

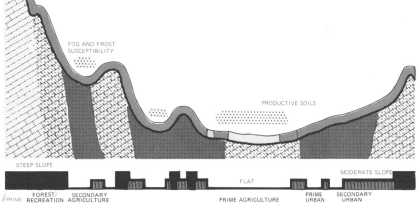

147

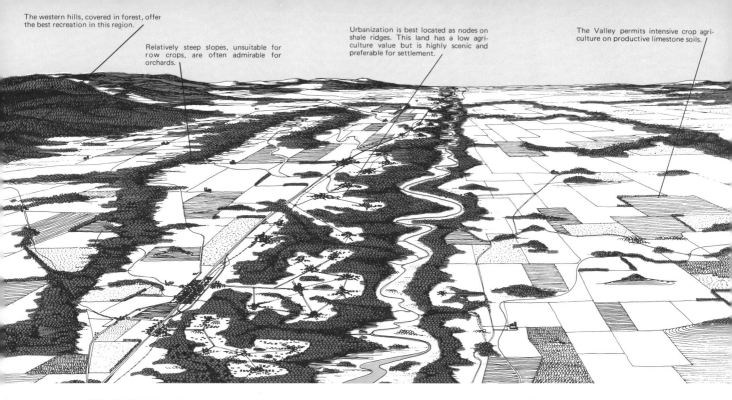

The western hills, covered in forest, offer the best recreation in this region.

Relatively steep slopes, unsuitable for row crops, are often admirable for orchards.

Urbanization is best located as nodes on shale ridges. This land has a low agriculture value but is highly scenic and preferable for settlement.

The Valley permits intensive crop agriculture on productive limestone soils.

THE GREAT VALLEY

The Great Valley is one great agricultural region east of the Rockies—a broad, generally flat valley with predominantly rich limestone soils. There are, however, three subdivisions—the western hills on sandstone, shale, limestone and quartzite, the wide belt of Martinsburg shale and the valley proper of limestone and dolomite. In brief the hills provide the maximum recreational potential, the limestone the agricultural resource, and the shale the best locations for urbanization. This last is important as it ensures that urbanization does not occur over the aquifer.

The resources and their distribution are most felicitous—wooded hills, a fertile valley, a swath of shale suited for urbanization, the latter bordered by a fine river and exhibiting considerable scenic quality.

148

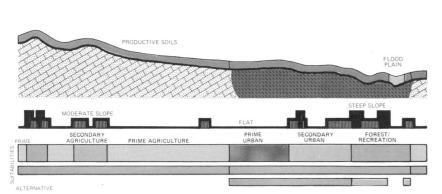

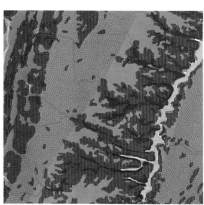

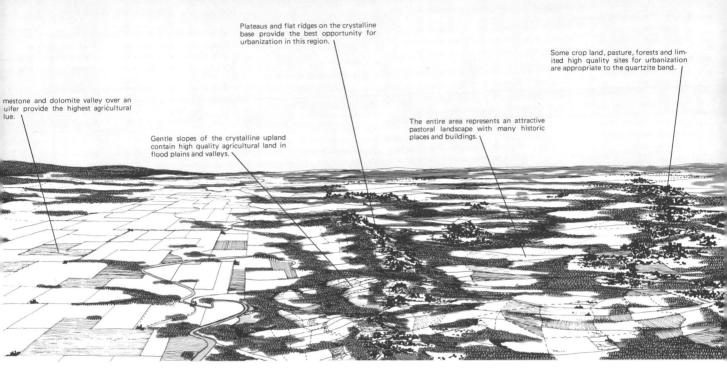

Plateaus and flat ridges on the crystalline base provide the best opportunity for urbanization in this region.

Some crop land, pasture, forests and limited high quality sites for urbanization are appropriate to the quartzite band.

mestone and dolomite valley over an uifer provide the highest agricultural lue.

The entire area represents an attractive pastoral landscape with many historic places and buildings.

Gentle slopes of the crystalline upland contain high quality agricultural land in flood plains and valleys.

THE PIEDMONT

The section of the Piedmont illustrated reveals a great complexity—a limestone and dolomite valley, a preCambrian upland of crystalline rocks fissured with intrusions, a broad band of quartzite, yet another of shales. Intrinsic suitabilities respond to geology and the consequential physiography, hydrology and soils. The limestone and dolomite valley is most suited for agriculture, the shales for pasture and non-commercial forests, some crops, pasture and forests are appropriate to valleys and flood plains in the crystalline area. The most suitable urban sites fall in the crystalline region on flat plateaus and ridges. They are absent on limestone, rare on the shales. This is an area on the edge of urbanization. Opportunities abound but planning must respond to the specific opportunities and constraints afforded by the region.

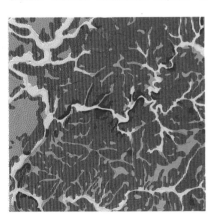

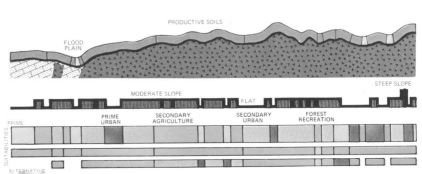

PRODUCTIVE SOILS

FLOOD PLAIN

STEEP SLOPE

MODERATE SLOPE

FLAT

PRIME URBAN

SECONDARY AGRICULTURE

SECONDARY URBAN

FOREST RECREATION

PRIME

SUITABILITIES

ALTERNATIVE

149

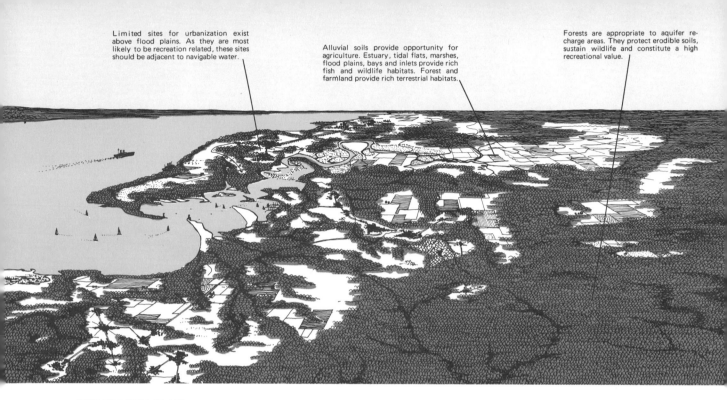

Limited sites for urbanization exist above flood plains. As they are most likely to be recreation related, these sites should be adjacent to navigable water.

Alluvial soils provide opportunity for agriculture. Estuary, tidal flats, marshes, flood plains, bays and inlets provide rich fish and wildlife habitats. Forest and farmland provide rich terrestrial habitats.

Forests are appropriate to aquifer recharge areas. They protect erodible soils, sustain wildlife and constitute a high recreational value.

THE COASTAL PLAIN

The area of the lower Potomac reveals the characteristic physiography of the Coastal Plain—estuary, bays, inlets, meandering streams and marshes. Forests are abundant, the water table is high, soils are mainly quartzite sand. This region offers water based recreational opportunity to a unique degree. Agriculture is limited, as are sites for urbanization. Forestry constitutes a present value as do fisheries.

Water is the major value here and the main determinant of intrinsic suitabilities. Forests are fire prone, ground water can be polluted, the water table is generally too high for urbanization, soils too infertile for widespread agriculture. Yet there are elevated sites suitable for building, alluvial soils suited for agriculture, both land and water wildlife habitats are abundant.

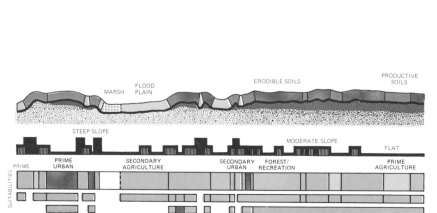

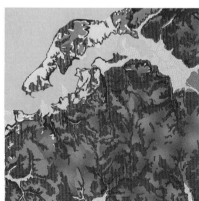

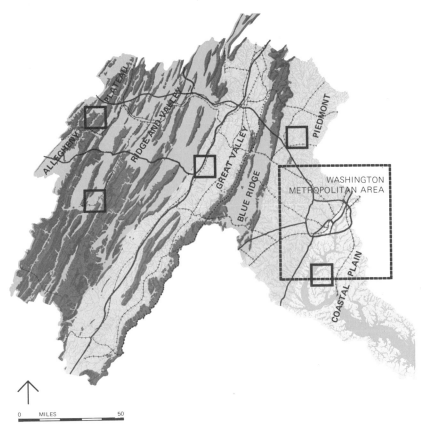

Figure labels on map: ALLEGHENY PLATEAU, RIDGE AND VALLEY, GREAT VALLEY, BLUE RIDGE, PIEDMONT, WASHINGTON METROPOLITAN AREA, COASTAL PLAIN

0 MILES 50

When I first came to Philadelphia, my new friends, on learning that I was a landscape architect, sought my advice for their ailing dogwoods. My knowledge of plants had been good enough for Scotland, but was inadequate for the United States, and so I escaped the role of plant nurse. But even those who are acquainted with landscape architecture are somewhat surprised at the scale of concern epitomized in the Potomac Study; and yet they need not be. In the 18th century a handful of landscape architects made over the whole of England, and in so doing accomplished the greatest transformation of an entire country that has ever been accomplished. I do not apologize for repeating Capability Brown's response on being asked to undertake some work in Ireland. "I am sorry," he is reported to have said, "I have not finished England yet."

There clearly is a desperate need for professionals who are conservationists by instinct, but who care not only to preserve but to create and to manage. These persons cannot be impeccable scientists for such purity would immobilize them. They must be workmen who are instinctively interested in the physical and biological sciences, and who seek this information so that they may obtain the license to interpose their creative skills upon the land. The landscape architect meets these requirements. He has the precedents of the 18th century to give him courage.

Such is the method—a simple sequential examination of the place in order to understand it. This understanding reveals the place as an interacting system, a storehouse and a value system. From this information it is possible to prescribe potential land uses—not as single activities, but as associations of these.

It is not a small claim, it is not a small contribution: but it would appear that the ecological method can be employed to understand and formulate a plan with nature, perhaps design with nature.

During the year of 1965-66 graduate students of landscape architecture and regional planning of the University of Pennsylvania undertook a study of the Potomac River Basin from which this chapter is derived. It engaged eighteen students during the Fall and twelve students during the Spring. This mammoth work produced five hundred maps and several pounds of reports. The compression necessary to reproduce this work within its present confines has resulted in a great simplification and many omissions which diminish the actual quality of both data and interpretation. Yet, it remains a landmark, the first ecological planning study conducted in the United States, and the prototype for planning studies of this kind.

The students who participated in the data collection phase and the interpretations of basin wide scale were: Messrs. Bradford D., Bradford S., Chitty, Christie, Dawson, Felgemaker, Galantowicz, Kao, Leach, Meyers, Murphy, Rosenberg, Sinatra, Terpstra, Tourbier, Westmacott, White and Wolfe.

The interpretations at the scale of physiographic regions were undertaken by the following:
Allegheny Plateau: Messrs. Tourbier and Westmacott
Ridge and Valley: Mesdames Bradford and Terpstra
Great Valley: Dawson
Piedmont: Seddon
Coastal Plain: Felgemaker.

The study was under the direction of the author assisted by Dr. Nicholas Muhlenberg.

Parts of this study were simplified for incorporation in **The Potomac**, the report of the A.I.A. Task Force on the Potomac, by Wallace, McHarg, Roberts and Todd, under the direction of Narendra Juneja. The entire study was made available to, and employed by the A.I.A. Task Force on the Potomac.

151

The Metropolitan Region

A city occupies an area of land and operates a form of government; the metropolitan area also occupies an area of land but constitutes the sum of many levels and forms of government. It is united neither by government, planning nor the expression of these. While the name has been coined to describe the enlargement of the older city, it is appropriate to observe that this is more a convenience for cartographers than a social organism. Yet the coalescence of sepia blotches exists, encircling the city.

The American dream envisioned only the single-family house, the smiling wife and healthy children, the two-car garage, eye-level oven, foundation planting and lawn, the school nearby and the church of your choice. It did not see that a subdivision is not a community, that the sum of subdivisions that make a suburb is not a community, that the sum of suburbs that compose the metropolitan fringe of the city does not constitute community nor does a metropolitan region. It did not see that the nature that awaited the subdivider was vastly different from the pockmarked landscape of ranch and split-level houses.

And so the transformation from city to metropolitan area contains all the thwarted hopes of those who fled the old city in search of clean government, better schools, a more beneficent, healthy and safe environment, those who sought to escape slums, congestion, crime, violence and disease.

There are many problems caused by the form of metropolitan growth—the lack of institution which diminishes the power to effect even local decisions, the trauma that is the journey to work, the increasingly difficult problem of providing community facilities. Perhaps the most serious is the degree to which the subdivision, the suburb and the metropolitan area deny the dream and have failed to provide the smiling image of the advertisements. The hucksters made the dream into a cheap thing, subdivided we fell, and the instinct to find more natural environments became the impulse that destroyed nature, an important ingredient in the social objective of this greatest of all population migrations.

Let us address ourselves to this problem. In earlier studies we saw that certain types of land are of such intrinsic value, or perform work for man best in a natural condition or, finally, contain such hazards to development that they should not be urbanized. Similarly, there are other areas that, for perfectly specific reasons, are intrinsically suitable for urban uses. This method has been applied to the Potomac River Basin, its constituent physiographic regions: there is no good reason why it should not be applicable to the metropolitan region of Washington.

Thus we can state as a proposition that certain lands are unsuitable for urbanization and others are intrinsically suitable. If our hearts are pure and our instincts good, then the lands that best perform work for man in a natural condition will not be those that are most suitable for urbanization. And because we are not necessarily pure or good, but lucky, it transpires, as we have seen before, that if one selects eight natural features, and ranks them in order of value to the operation of natural process, then that group reversed will constitute a gross order of suitability for urbanization. These are: surface water, floodplains, marshes, aquifer recharge areas, aquifers, steep slopes, forests and woodlands, unforested land. As was discussed in the study of metropolitan open space, natural features can absorb degrees of development—ports, harbors, marinas, water-related and water-using industries must be in riparian land and may occupy floodplains. Surface water, floodplains and marshes may be used for recreation, agriculture and forestry. The aquifer recharge areas may absorb development in a way that does not seriously diminish percolation or pollute groundwater resources. Steep slopes, when forested, may absorb housing of not more

WASHINGTON

than one house per three acres, while forests on relatively flat land may support a density of development up to one-acre clusters.

We can expect that there will be regional and subregional variation in intrinsic suitabilities. After all, this region includes parts of the Coastal Plain and the Piedmont; within the latter there is the important Triassic subprovince. Indeed, topographic variation is least in the Triassic area and greatest in the crystalline Piedmont. Stream dissection, and thus steep slopes, are greatest in the Piedmont, followed by deposits of the Lower Cretaceous. Streams are all but absent in the

Triassic area, but abundant in the remainder of the Piedmont—less so in the Coastal Plain. Aquifers are concentrated in the Triassic area and Coastal Plain, but absent in the remaining Piedmont.

This being so, there are revealed areas that are intrinsically unsuitable for urbanization, and these are shown. We can now plot the reverse, and indicate the areas that are suitable for urban uses. Here is the obverse of the first, and what is revealed is the regionality of urban suitability: a broad swath of land running parallel to the Triassic formation is shown to be the most suitable area, with a greater opportunity north of the

NATURAL FEATURES

- SURFACE WATER
- FLOOD PLAIN
- AQUIFER OUTCROP—COASTAL PLAIN
- AQUIFER OUTCROP—PIEDMONT
- STEEP SLOPES
- UNCONSOLIDATED SEDIMENTS
- CRYSTALLINE BEDROCK

URBAN SUITABILITY

- PRIME—No restrictions
- SECONDARY—Forested
- QUALIFIED—Aquifer outcrop
- RESTRICTED—Steep slopes
- UNSUITABLE—Flood plain
- UNAVAILABLE—Institutional lands
- UNAVAILABLE—Public open space

Potomac than south of it. Lesser areas are visible in the Coastal Plain.

When an uncontrolled growth model is projected, it is seen that development bears no relation either to definitions of natural process values or to intrinsic suitability. Indeed, when the Year 2000 Plan developed for Washington, is examined against these factors, it is seen that it is almost as oblivious as is unplanned growth.

It is most disconcerting to conclude that not only does uncontrolled growth fail to recognize intrinsic suitabilities and unsuitabilities for urban growth, but that the formal planning process is almost as culpable.

We require more precise information on which to base our decisions. It is not enough to describe land as unforested: one must examine its agricultural value, factors of foundations, suitability of soils for septic tanks and their susceptibility to erosion and the relative values of groundwater resources. To this end, a sector of the metropolitan region has been examined more specifically. It extends north and west from the Capitol to enclose an area of almost four hundred square miles, reaching out to the rural perimeter, including both Dulles Airport and the new town of Reston.

Maps illustrated in this section were produced for the AIA Task Force on the Potomac by Wallace, McHarg, Roberts and Todd. The work was under the direction of Dr. David A. Wallace, was supervised by Mr. Narendra Juneja and performed by Messrs. Bradford, Bachelor, de Boer and Drummond.

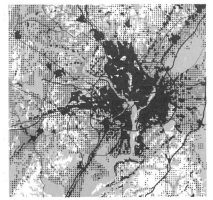

UNCONTROLLED GROWTH TO YEAR 2000
PROJECTED GROWTH CONFLICTS
Green represents areas generally unsuitable for urbanization

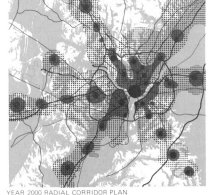

YEAR 2000 RADIAL CORRIDOR PLAN

155

RELIEF

Over 500 feet

500–400 feet

400–300 feet

300–200 feet

200–100 feet

Below 100 feet

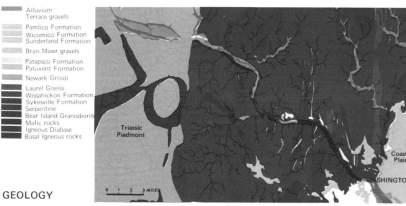

GEOLOGY

Alluvium
Terrace gravels

Pamlico Formation
Wicomico Formation
Sunderland Formation

Bryn Mawr gravels

Patapsco Formation
Patuxent Formation

Newark Group

Laurel Gneiss
Wissahickon Formation
Sykesville Formation
Serpentine
Bear Island Granodiorite
Mafic rocks
Igneous Diabase
Basal Igneous rocks

HYDROLOGY

Surface water

Flood plain

Shallow aquifers—
CRETACEOUS AND
TERTIARY FORMATIONS

Deep aquifers—
TRIASSIC FORMATION

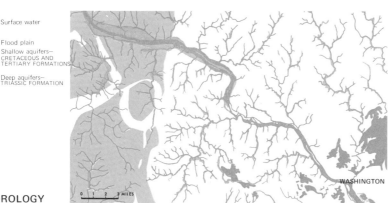

The Quadrant

The method has now been used repeatedly and follows the familiar litany of historical geology, physiography, hydrology, and so on, and thereafter interprets these data to reveal intrinsic suitabilities. In this exercise the major prospective land use is urban; it is this that the method seeks to select. There is also an effort made to relate the density of prospective development, not only to the characteristics of the land, but also to its carrying capacity.

The area under study reveals both its characteristics and its variability when geology, physiography, hydrology, soils and slopes are examined. The major divisions of the Triassic Piedmont, the crystalline Piedmont and the Coastal Plain are immediately evident. In the Triassic formation the area is quite flat, streams are few and show little dissection, floodplains are absent, the substructure is limestone—it is associated with an important deep aquifer—and the soils are rich.

In the crystalline Piedmont there are two subdivisions which are roughly divided by the Potomac. In the southern section the slope map most clearly reveals the fissures of streams and the marked dissection that accompanies them. The study area reveals the greatest topographic variety, which is displayed by the entire Piedmont. The landscape is folded, small in scale, and soils are variable in response to topographic change and conditions of slope and exposure. There is little groundwater.

The Coastal Plain is generally 200 feet lower than the adjacent Piedmont and the change occurs in the Fall zone. The topography of the Coastal Plain is flat, but it is distinguishable from the Triassic formation by the pattern of streams, their floodplains, and the associated dissection. There are several elements unique to this region—escarpments and terraces, the marshes and bays and the estuarine aspect which the Potomac assumes in this region.

156

When this area is considered in terms of the incidence of factors that render it unsuitable for urbanization, it is seen that the major aquifer and the productive soils of the Triassic formation represent an important value and thus a constraint. Dulles Airport now withdraws 1000 gallons per minute from this groundwater. The southern section of the Piedmont is broadly unsuitable because of the abundance of steep slopes and the absence of large areas of relatively flat land. The northern section of this region has the fewest constraints and offers the greatest opportunity for urbanization. The Coastal Plain does contain aquifers, flood-plains and marshes, but also areas of land that impose few constraints.

Existing woodlands persist as residues of earlier and larger forests or as areas of farm-land that have been abandoned and have returned to forest. Because of their value in diminishing runoff, reducing erosion and sedimentation and sustaining wildlife—in addition to their scenic and recreational uses—it was decided that in this study, such woodlands should be considered a value and thus only marginally capable of accepting urbanization.

The presence of Dulles International Airport exerts a significant influence upon land uses in the area—mainly detrimental. The zones of 90 and 80 decibels have been identified—this sound level is equivalent to an average machine shop or the noisiest street corner in New York City. For this reason, the F.H.A. has refused to insure loans on residential construction within these zones. They are, therefore, considered unsuitable for urban development.

In this study it is assumed that given the possibility of choice, prime agricultural land should not be employed for urban land uses on the grounds that this sterilizes an irre-placeable resource, all but irreversibly. For this reason, soils were identified in terms of four grades of agricultural potential pro-duction—row-cropland, cropland, pasture

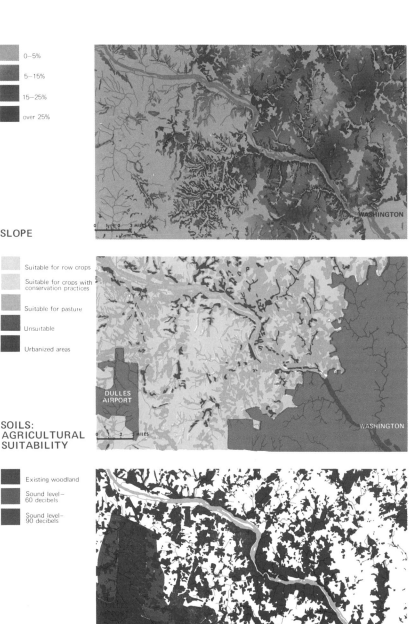

0–5%

5–15%

15–25%

over 25%

SLOPE

Suitable for row crops

Suitable for crops with conservation practices

Suitable for pasture

Unsuitable

Urbanized areas

DULLES AIRPORT

WASHINGTON

SOILS: AGRICULTURAL SUITABILITY

Existing woodland

Sound level— 60 decibels

Sound level— 90 decibels

WASHINGTON

WOODLAND AND SOUND LEVELS

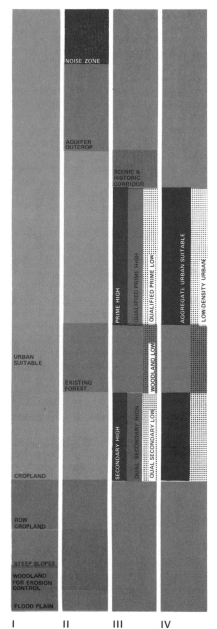

and permanent woodland to diminish erosion on susceptible soils or excessive slope.

From the foregoing information, certain lands were selected as unsuitable for urbanization. These included row-cropland and cropland, floodplains, slopes in excess of fifteen per cent, areas which (for reasons of erosion due to slope or soils) should be in forest cover, major aquifer recharges, forests and noise zones. The areas suitable for urbanization in this initial examination were the least productive agricultural soils—mainly pasture land. Examination quickly revealed that this provided inadequate space for future urban growth and that other lands would have to be utilized.

Clearly some agricultural land will be absorbed by urbanization. It was decided that both cropland and woodland should be investigated for urban suitability, but that this should be based on the characteristics of soils for the provision of foundations and for their usability for septic tanks, and that these qualifications would determine which of the cropland should be designated as suitable for urban development. The same analysis was accorded to forest.

The highest category of suitability in this analysis is noncropland with a capacity to bear foundations of high-density construc-tion. The second category is identical to the first, save that it is cropland. The next category consists of low-bearing-capacity soils that are incapable of supporting septic tanks. These, it was thought, would be suitable for medium-density development, served by sewers. The next category was identical to the preceding, save that it involved the employment of cropland. A further category included poor-bearing-capacity soils that were capable of supporting septic tanks and thus could be used for low-density development. This condition, where cropland is lost, constitutes the next category.

The aggregate of these conclusions is a discrimination system whereby the propensity of the region to support urban land uses is disclosed. It selects surface water and floodplains, steep slopes (over fifteen per cent), major aquifer recharges, noise zones and soils susceptible to erosion from which it is recommended that development be excluded.

Agricultural land is examined in detail, pasture land is identified as the least sacrifice of agricultural land for urban use, cropland is divided into categories of suitability, for foundations and septic tanks. Those forests able to support septic tanks are indicated for low-density development.

As cities are not composed entirely of buildings, and countryside is not entirely without them, the entire area has been examined to find large blocks of land that are preponderantly suitable for urban uses. The study of the enlarged metropolitan region and that of the Quadrant revealed the propensity of the land itself to support urbanization and showed the resulting system of both open space and urban structure that would result if this method were employed. The most arresting fact is the regional variability and the abundance of land available for prospective metropolitan growth. It is clear that many alternative patterns could be employed within any conscious plan.

URBAN SUITABILITY SELECTION PROCESS

PHASE I: Exclusion of flood plains, woodlands for erosion control, steep slopes, row-cropland, cropland.

PHASE II: Exclusion in addition to Phase I of aquifer outcrops, noise zones, existing forest cover.

PHASE III: Exclusion in addition to Phases I and II of scenic and historic corridors. Ranking of urban suitability based upon bearing capacities of soils and suitability for septic tanks.

PHASE IV: Identification of aggregations of urban suitable land.

URBAN SUITABILITY SELECTION PROCESS

SUITABLE FOR
URBANIZATION

CROPLAND

ROW–CROPLAND

STEEP SLOPES

PERMANENT WOODLAND
required for erosion control

FLOOD PLAIN

ASE I

DULLES AIRPORT

0   1   2   3 MILES

WASHINGTON

URBAN SUITABILITY SELECTION PROCESS

SUITABLE FOR
URBANIZATION

CROPLAND

EXISTING FOREST COVER

STEEP SLOPES AND
PERMANENT WOODLAND

FLOOD PLAIN AND
ROW CROPLAND

NOISE ZONES

AQUIFER OUTCROPS

ASE II

DULLES AIRPORT

0   1   2   3 MILES

WASHINGTON

PRIME HIGH
High bearing capacity soils, no v

SECONDARY HIGH
High bearing capacity soils over e

QUALIFIED PRIME HIGH
Poor bearing capacity soils, no v

QUALIFIED SECONDARY
Poor bearing capacity soils suitab
septic tanks

QUALIFIED PRIME LOW
Poor bearing capacity soils suitab
septic tanks over cropland

QUALIFIED SECONDARY
Poor bearing capacity soils over e

WOODLAND LOW
Soils suitable for septic tanks wi
existing forest cover

EXISTING FOREST COVE

SCENIC AND HISTORIC
CORRIDOR

UNSUITABLE
FOR URBANIZATION
From previous suitability selectic

WASHINGTON

PHASE III

URBAN SUITABILITY SELECTION PROCESS

POTENTIAL URBAN ARE
Prime and Secondary suitability
previous selection steps

POTENTIAL LOW-DENSIT
DEVELOPMENT AREAS

EXISTING FOREST COVE

OTHER OPEN SPACE
Areas unsuitable for urbanization
from previous selection steps

URBAN AGGREGATES
IN ACRES

7000

18,000

10,000

8000

DULLES AIRPORT

WASHINGTON

PHASE IV

This, of course, is not a plan. It merely shows the implications that the land and its processes display for prospective development and its form. The plan can be developed only when there is adequate information on the nature of demand, its locational and resource characteristics, the capacities to realize objectives and, indeed, the social goals of the community. It is enough to say here that—whatever the characteristics of demand—the formulation of a plan for the metropolitan region should respond to an understanding of natural processes. It must plan with nature.

Finally, this investigation is concerned with the matter of form. If growth responds to natural processes, it will be clearly visible in the pattern and distribution of development —and, indeed, in its density. But the formal investigation, it must be admitted, is not at a very high level. By responding to nature, one only avoids the allegation of ignorance, stupidity and carelessness. When we can demonstrate this elementary level of intelligence and perception, then we may aspire to more elevated objectives; but that is clearly premature.

At the moment, much of the area is unaffected by planning. Where planning does occur, its single instrument is zoning and by this device political subdivisions are allocated densities irrespective of geology, physiography, hydrology, soils, vegetation, scenery or historic beauty. The adoption of the ecological method would at least produce the negative value of a structure of open space wherein nature performed work for man, or wherein development was dangerous. It would canalize development to areas that were propitious. Positively, it can be employed to find the morphology of man-nature-Washington.

The Quadrant study was a part of the Potomac River Basin Study undertaken by graduate students of Landscape Architecture of the University of Pennsylvania during the 1965-66 academic year. The students responsible for the Quadrant study were Messrs. Bradford, Chitty, Meyers and Sinatra.

THE NORMAL FATE OF THE LAND

Process and Form

If you remember, in the experiment conducted by the Naturalists, which purported to reveal the attributes of creation and destruction, there was involved the comparison of a young sand dune and a climax forest upon an ancient sand dune. The Naturalist cosmology has used this experiment for a further step. Given this primeval forest, they said, let us permit a man to make a small clearing within it. What is the effect of the man? Well, if he accomplishes nothing, he is clearly a destructive force: he has diminished the creation of the forest and provided no substitute. Let us then consider a second man, who, by living in the forest, comes to learn of its operation. In this case, the Naturalists concluded that apperception of the system was potentially an ordering process—negentropic. In this second case there would still be a reduction of creation, but the potential for its increase was latent in the apperception of the forest by the observing man. In the next instance the man, having learned of the operation of the forest, or some part of it, is enabled to intervene in such a way as to increase its thermodynamic creativity. In this case, he is by definition creative. But let us assume in yet one other case that he uses his apperception, not to increase the creativity of the forest, but to write a poem or paint a picture. In this case the Naturalists concluded that no decision could be made in the absence of either the poem or the painting. One might conclude that a poem increases apperception with the potential of increasing creativity and is thus creative, but the decision must depend upon the poem or painting and the apperception and communication which it contained.

Now, this preoccupation with the artist is not inconsequential to the Naturalists. Of all the subjects they pursued in their quest for knowledge, perhaps none was so intriguing as morphology, and this, of course, is the essence of the graphic and plastic arts. They believe, as we have learned, that nature is process, but they also believe that form and process are indivisible aspects of a single phenomenon. That is, that which is seen to be is an important aspect of that which is. It is a valuable mode for understanding and one indispensable for expression.

Elements are described in terms of form, nucleus and the shells of orbiting electrons; compounds are described by a formal schema. The electron micrograph shows the modular geometry of the atoms, the crystalline form of giant molecules; the microscope can reveal the striking forms of snowflake crystals.

The twin helices of DNA are formal, as are the molecular processes of substrate, enzyme and the catalytic enzyme within the cell.

Here too one finds the conception of fitness: "the greatest efficiency. . .is achieved when the greatest number of enzyme and substrate molecules can interlock closely in 'perfect fit'."[*] It is important to recognize the realm of life's essential attribute: change that is reflected in form. This exhibits, not simple multiplication, but relative growth of the parts, better described as rhythm than as mere modular increase.[**]

Yet the rhythm does not deny the atomic or molecular components of form. To this all physical and biological processes subscribe.

In turning to nature to find the basis for form, the Naturalists have concluded with Henderson in favor of fitness. Unlike art, the term we use, fitness is an appropriate criterion both for natural objects and creatures and for artifices, whereas art is only applied to the last. The Naturalists have decided that the earth is fit and can be made more fitting. Of all roles that man can play, those of apperception and communication are thought to be dominant as the basis for creative expression. The manner of expression is of paramount importance to the objective of making the earth more fitting. What is the expression of fitness?

This mode of enquiry differs substantially from ours, particularly because, emanating

---

[*] Robert B. Platt and George K. Rerd, *Bioscience,* Reinhold Publishing Corp., New York, 1967, p. 232.

[**] C. H. Waddington, The Modular Principle and Biological Form, in *Module Proportion Symmetry Rhythm* edited by Gyorgy Kepes, George Braziller, New York, 1966, p. 23.

163

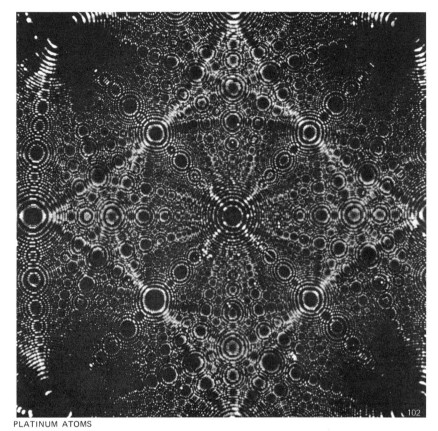

PLATINUM ATOMS

MOLECULES

SNOWFLAKE CRYSTALS

SAND DUNES

from natural scientists, it encompasses all of evolution rather than being preoccupied exclusively with the works of man. Moreover, the word fitness is much less alarming than art, and so the Naturalists do not feel that this is an exclusive preoccupation. With us, art has occult and esoteric pretensions and an intrinsic obscurantism. Fitness is thought to be as much the province of plants and animals as of men, and among men the doctor and the lawyer are as much involved as the poet and the painter. Creativeness, as we have seen, is a universal prerequisite which man shared with all creatures. The divisions that rift our society are absent from theirs. Creative mathematicians, biol-

ogists and economists are thought to be no different from painters, poets and playwrights. No group is ostracized from society because it is exclusively engaged in creativity.

The selection of fitness rather than art, by embracing the natural as well as the artificial, made the preoccupation with creativity one uniting all things. It has one other benefit. The concern with fitness involves meaningful form, and it was seen that evolution has been in this business for a long time and that man is only one of its products. Thus meaningful form is not limited to man and his works, but to all things and all beings.

Consequently the astronomer and geologist, the plant and animal morphologist are just as concerned and competent in the business of meaningful form as the poet and painter, and so too are the mason and carpenter, the machinist and mechanic, the engineer and architect.

Now the fact that things and creatures exist is the evidence that they are fit—they then represent meaningful form. The search for fitness and form must begin with things and with creatures. Wherein lies their fitness and what is its expression? The obvious to them is as apparent to us as the difference between the arctic and the tropics, moun-

106

107

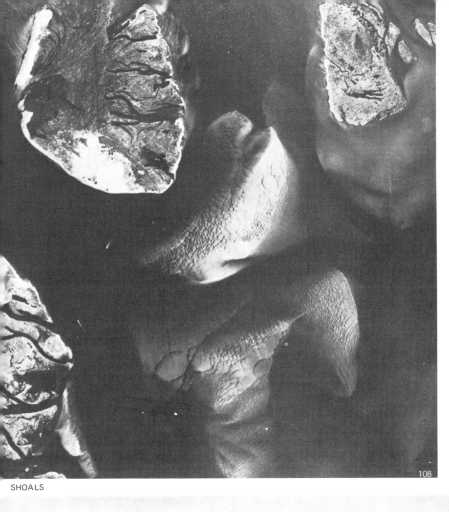

SHOALS

GLACIER   VOLCANIC PLUG

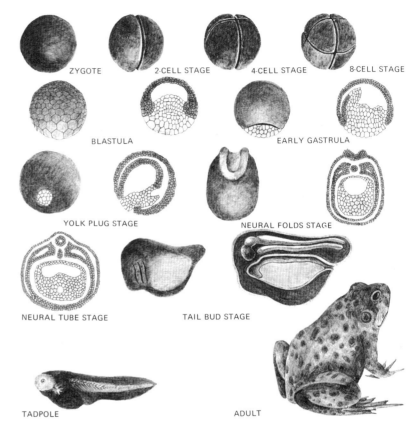

*DNA, DOUBLE HELIX

**DEVELOPMENT OF A FROG

ZYGOTE 2-CELL STAGE 4-CELL STAGE 8-CELL STAGE

BLASTULA EARLY GASTRULA

YOLK PLUG STAGE NEURAL FOLDS STAGE

NEURAL TUBE STAGE TAIL BUD STAGE

TADPOLE ADULT

tains and valleys, minnow and whale, ostrich and owl. They too are able to discern the high craggy young mountains from the lower, soft-rounded residues of erstwhile giants, young rivers from old, piedmont from coastal plain. But many of them can also discern subtle variations within the region--the gentle escarpments revealing the stratification of terraces laid down by Cretaceous seas, the variation in soil color and texture, the adaptations of plants and animals in response to these. They know well of the changes that occur as one rises in elevation on the mountain or moves from sunlit to shadowed face, follows a gradient in rainfall or moves towards the equator.

The world is, for the Naturalists, a great voice of "to whom it may concern" messages, clothed in form—the form of the spiral nebula and the orbits of electrons, the lattices of crystals and of viruses, the phantasmagoria of living things. Now much of this is unseen—it is below the level of vision or hidden within the organisms or consists only of invisible pathways bespeaking the interactions of communities. But much is visible and evident, for instance, the adaptations of birds' feet and bills—the claws of hornbill and woodpecker, osprey, mallard and coot, bittern and ptarmigan, or the bills of finch and toucan, fulmar and spoonbill, avocet and flamingo, kiwi and puffin. In

each of these extremes, the form expresses the process: they are indivisible, and both are explanatory; this is elementary meaningful form at the level of the organ.

So too is there abundant evidence of the expression of process in the organism. The progression of shore birds offered a simple example—the solitary sandpiper, the lesser yellowlegs, the greater yellowlegs and then the willet. The progression continues into the plover, godwit, stilt and avocet, to bittern, egret, heron, ibis, crane, spoonbill and flamingo. In this ascending morphology of adaptations, the length of the legs and the shape of the bill are the most conspicuous

*Arthur Kornberg, The Synthesis of DNA, in *Scientific American,* Vol. 219, No. 4, p. 64, Copyright © 1968 by Scientific American, Inc., all rights reserved.

**After Charles W. Schmidt, *Bioscience,* by Robert B. Platt and George K. Reid, Reinhold Publishing Corp., New York, 1967, Fig. 20-15.

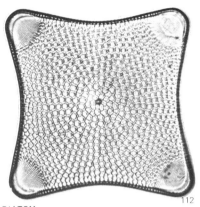

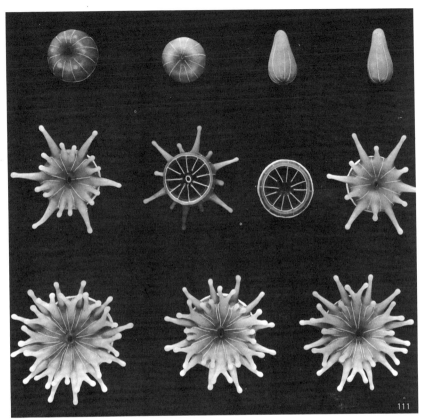

DIATOM

MOTH ANTENNAE

CORAL POLYPS

elements of form. Analogies can be found in fish and reptiles, in amphibians and mammals; and the morphology of adaptation was as clear in the steps reaching towards man.

But form is also communication, revealing creatures of the same species to each other, distinguishing between species, suppressing identity, as in camouflage, or misleading, as in mimicry. Form then is communication, the presentation of meaning.

If apperception is experienced, then communication is involved. Bits of information, questions that can be answered yes or no are the basis of the computer and much of com-

munications theory. But information has one other attribute: meaning. There is an enormous difference in effect if, in a crowded theatre, one shouts, not "hello," but "fire." The bit of information is identical in energy, but the meaning of "fire" results in a totally different response. Energy may heat a body, the same energy may inform the body that it is being heated. So with information, the information may fall upon an unresponsive body or may be perceived as information and meaning.

When the astronaut first took his daily run through the forest, it was merely an undifferentiated shade. As he learned to discern

some of the more striking forms, the information of the forest increased. In a continuous progression he came to learn of the inhabitants, their roles and their evolutionary history, and finally to see the forest as the present stage in a great evolutionary process—ordered, dynamic and indispensable to life. In this progression of learning the forest did not change—only the capacity of the astronaut to read meaning. So too with all form.

If evolutionary success is revealed by the existence of things and creatures, then their creative adaptations will be visible, not only in the organs and the organisms, but in eco-

169

systems as well. If this is so, then the natural communities of plants and animals which the first colonists encountered in aboriginal America were the best expression of environmental adaptation, exploited by available organisms. Where these persist, this will hold true today. Thus not only is there an appropriate community of creatures for any environment, and successional stages towards this climax, but the community is, in fact, expressive of its appropriateness, its fitness.

This is a conclusion of enormous magnitude to those who are concerned with the land and its aspect: that there is a natural association which is most appropriate—indeed, in the absence of man, one which would be inevitable for every place upon the earth— and that that community of creatures is expressive of its fitness. This I would call the identity of the given form.

If this is so, then we can accept that within any generalized area there will be ideal examples, both of fitness and the expression of fitness. In these locations, presumably, there are some special successes that are visible and comprehensible. The ecosystem, the organisms and their organs are not only fit, but are most fitting. This is an important conception because it has a relevance to the man who wishes to design for nature. The man who seeks to create metaphysical symbols is really concerned with idealizing.

We have accepted that the stilt's legs, the eagle's claw, the flamingo's beak and the mouth of the baleen whale are splendid adaptations and visibly so. Then surely it is no leap to see the grace and power of an athlete—the tennis serve, a left hook, a golf swing, the leaping catch—as being in the same realm as the impala's bound, the cormorant's dive, the shark's swerve, the leopard's leap. But the athletic gestures are artificial: must they be judged differently from the tennis racquet, and the golf club, the fielder's glove? Not if fitness is the criterion. The instrument is only an extension of the limb. If this is so, then can we equally

*BIRDS—BILLS AND CLAWS

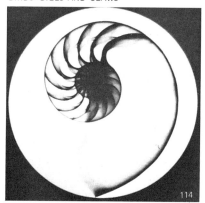

NAUTILUS SHELL

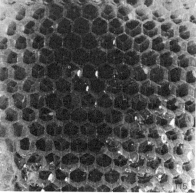

HONEYCOMB

decide if the hammer and saw, the knife, fork and spoon are fit? We can decide that the propeller plane, as it claws its way through the air, is less fit than the tail-powered jet, impelled with assurance.

If we can examine cutlery and tools, then we can also subject chairs and tables to the same test of fitness and proceed to the places where activities occur. Is the dining room fit for dining, the bedroom fit for sleeping or loving? Is the house fit, or the street, the neighborhood or the city? What is unfit? There are dangers here, for we do not know what perfections are represented by the sloth we revile, but we can accept that the

crippled animal whose grace earlier enchanted us is now no longer fit; our language conforms to this notion of the unfit as the unhealthy, crippled, deformed, although there may well be excellences that overcome this. Beethoven transcended deafness. So unfitness would include not only the broken piano, but the defaced painting, the mutilated sculpture, the junked auto in a wild landscape. So too the gawky serve, the cumbrous swing, the grotesqueries of inept movement, and thence their unfit instruments—the warped racquet, the blunt knife, the uncomfortable bed, the smoking fire, the house in shade or the glaring street, the anarchic city; these are all unfit.

170

*After Roger Tory Peterson, *The World of Birds*, by James Fisher and Roger Tory Peterson, Doubleday and Company, Inc., New York, pp. 20-21.

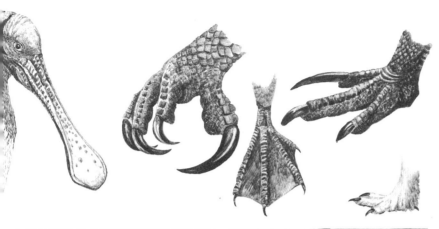

CLIFF SWALLOW NESTS

CAVE DWELLINGS

most fit. Of artifacts we can ask, as we did of the racquet and the club, are they fit? We can discern those which are most fitting. Of the symbol we can ask: what does it express, is it true and, if so, how well is this expressed? In this way it too can be deemed unfit, fit or most fitting.

As we have seen, the Naturalists avoid most of our problems by defining creation in terms both of negentropy and symbiosis, which include all things inert, all things living and all men. There was no single group of creators. They look to the world as the basis for form and for expression, and this is reflected in their language. They make no distinction between science and knowledge, believing them to be indivisible; similarly, they make no distinction between the artist and the non-artist. While they prefer the term artisan, they do employ artist, but reserve it as a judgment for prowess in creation rather than for a profession. Fitness is their measure, and this they use scrupulously; symbols are simply creations having a succinct and heightened expression.

While they look to nature to understand form and to find the basis for expression, a major purpose of this enquiry is to discern the morphology of man-nature and its variation in different environments. After all, if the plants and animals vary from place to place and reveal this variety in their forms, should there not be a variety of man-nature morphologies. So, indeed, there are: the morphology of man-piedmont, man-coastal plain, man-ridge and valley, man-Appalachian Plateau, and so on, for prairies, the Rockies, the Sierras, the deserts.

The forms of new cities are derived in largest part from an understanding and response to natural processes. They believe that land fit for cities can be found, that certain areas are especially felicitous for this purpose. They have concluded that within the city and its immediate hinterland certain natural processes perform work for man and thus constitute a value. They further believe that

Now the symbolic world is not the distant home of the esoteric few but the everyday world we live in. By writing "I am," one makes a symbolic statement that attributes dimension, history, character, and form that may or may not correspond to any reality. This is a symbolic affirmation. When the hieroglyphics that are letters are associated in words and sentences, this is a symbolic statement. Not only the letters but the words, nouns, adjectives and verbs are symbols—indeed, very abstract ones. We are involved with symbolic form and meaning inextricably; this is no unfamiliar realm. Yet, it is true that while many people can assemble letters, words and sentences and be literate, fewer people are as conversant with the language of color, texture, mass, form, and the meanings they reveal. They are like the astronaut as he first confronted the forest. Yet, it is not that they fail to respond to these—only in death can this be avoided— but that the meaning discerned is only a small part of that which is visible. The information is as operative as is the perception of the observer.

As we enter the symbolic world, it is best if we can use the same judgments as before. If the creature exists, it is fit and its expression is likely to reveal some of its fitness. Among these creatures will be one or more that are

TAOS PUEBLO, NEW MEXICO

each area performs some work and has intrinsic value, that the land can be examined to reveal these intrinsic suitabilities and that land uses should respond to this. The converse is just as true: certain areas contain such values, limitations, constraints and, in certain cases, such prohibitions, that urbanization is entirely unsuitable. From this examination of the given form, as process, they have discerned the appropriate morphology of man-city for any location.

As we discuss cities and artifacts an important qualification must be made. Among us it is believed that the most enduring of things are buildings and books, institutions and laws. The Naturalists would find this incredible: surely these are the most recent and ephemeral of creations. It requires a special enlargement of a tiny segment of time to discern man at all, and an even greater magnification to see his works. If one wishes to work creatively with enduring things then the inevitable and central vehicle for passion and preoccupation is life, perhaps even better, consciousness. Save for the atoms themselves, it is life that has longest endured—while continents rise and fall and towering mountain ranges emerge only to erode to inconsequence. Artifacts should be measured in terms of their effect on life, not as independent objects. So the measure of

creation used to value artifacts is the degree of apperception they reveal, their expression of working symbioses and altruism in the form of institution, and the extent to which these are enhancing to life, at the level of the individual, the family, the community and the society. It is life that endures, not artifacts. So, of course, the measure of cities is their culture, but this embraces the visible city as an expression of the given form and as an adaptation to it. This is a visible and manifest expression of the culture—the morphology of man-nature and man-city.

Now this is a rather unromantic and novel approach to form, the view that this pre-

172

119

FALLING WATER

Architect: FRANK LLOYD WRIGHT

occupation is not unique to man but has encompassed all physical and biological processes since the beginning of time. In this sense man is involved in exactly the same type of activity as the chambered nautilus, the bee and the coral, and subject to exactly the same tests of survival and evolution. Form is not the preoccupation of dilettantes but a central and indissoluble concern for all life.

Certainly we can dispose of the old canard, "form follows function." Form follows nothing—it is integral with all processes. Then form is indivisibly meaningful form, but it can reveal ill fit, misfit, unfit, fit and most fitting. There seems to be no good reason to change these criteria for human adaptations. Is the environment fit for man? Is the adaptation that is accomplished fit for the environment? Is the fit expressed in form? There does not seem to be any good reason to change the criteria when considering the symbol. If the purpose of fitness is to ensure survival and evolutionary success for the organism, the species, the community and the biosphere, then adaptations are primarily directed toward enhancing life and evolution. Can we then avoid bringing concern with form into the realm of the enhancement or inhibition to life and evolution? When we link form to life we must retreat to a more basic but united concern with adaptation as creative or destructive. Fitness is then by definition creative and will be revealed in the form of fitness that is life-enhancing.

Indeed, this is not the common view. In our society, we believe that concern for form absorbs only a small section of society, the artists, and that their method requires the rejection of soap, water and normal mores, and the long wait for God or the muse's touch upon the shoulder. I neither reject nor accept this method, but I do recommend the Naturalists' view as being a suitable exercise for the mind during the long waiting periods.

173

The City: Process and Form

As was stated earlier, a professional landscape architect and planner is able to pursue only such problems as his clients proffer him. Not long ago I learned that an intense effort was under way in Washington to enhance the beauty of this grand city and that it was taking the form of planting petunias, zinnias, begonias, (flowers that try hardest to look like colored paper) and, above all, Japanese cherries. Now this is a splendid impulse, and much can be accomplished within its view, but it is clear that there are limits. I was asked if I could discern some principles to guide this signal effort and, predictably, turned to the ecological method for enlightenment.

Clearly, the mandate did not allow any examination of such crucial problems as poverty, slums or congestion; it was directed toward the evolution of a method for undertaking a Comprehensive Landscape Plan for Washington, D.C.*

It has been demonstrated that the ecological method is efficacious in confronting a rural metropolitan region in prospect of urbanization. Can it confront the problem of an existing city? Yet the problem remains that of establishing a value system and responding to it. We require to see the components of the natural identity of the city as a value system, offering opportunities for human

use. However, in addition, it is necessary to submit the creations of men—buildings, places and spaces—to the same type of analysis and evaluation. It is, therefore, essential to understand the city as a form, derived in the first instance from geological and biological evolution, existing as a sum of natural processes and adapted by man. It is also necessary to perceive the historic development of the city as a sequence of cultural adaptations reflected in the plan of the city and its constituent buildings both individually and in groups; some adaptations are successful and endure, others are not. Those that have endured enter the inventory of values; others will succumb as unsuccessful adaptations. This enquiry is described as an investigation into the given form—the natural identity—and the made form—the created city.

The major preoccupation is with form and thus leaves aside the locational factors that explain the sites of cities—tidal limits, fords, bridge crossings, mineral and agricultural resources, propitious climates and the like. It seems to hold that memorable cities have distinctive characteristics. These may derive from the site, from creations of man or from a combination of these. Rio de Janeiro, Naples and San Francisco are immediately associated with dramatic sites. Venice, Amsterdam and Paris are initially identified

with the major artifacts that constitute them. Yet, when cities are built upon beautiful, dramatic or rich sites, their excellence often results from the preservation, exploitation and enhancement, rather than obliteration of this genius of the site. Where this lacks intrinsic drama, excellence can be created by buildings and spaces, as is so amply demonstrated in Amsterdam, Venice and Paris. When a city contains such excellent creations, then these enter the inventory of values, the genius loci. The total city can then be seen as an exploitation of the intrinsic site—the creations of men seen as conscious adaptations to it—that preserve, heighten and enhance its basic qualities. These become values in their own right.

Can one then state, as a proposition, that the basic character of the city derives from the site and that excellence attends those occasions when this intrinsic quality is recognized and enhanced? Can one state, further, that buildings, spaces and places, consonant with the site, add to the genius loci and constitute not only the addition of new resources, but are thus determinants of new form?

If these propositions are true, then we can formulate both the objectives and the method. The former require that the genius of the site be discerned as composed of

175

*Toward A Comprehensive Landscape Plan for Washington, D.C., Wallace, McHarg, Roberts and Todd, U.S. Government Printing Office, Washington, D.C., 1967.

discrete elements, some derived from the natural identity, others from artifacts. These must be evaluated as components of identity, as working processes of value and as containing implications for new formal adaptations.

The method should also undertake to develop principles relative to this value system and, finally, principles should be constructed into policies that will ensure that the resources of the city, site and artifacts, are recognized as values and determinants of form, both in planning and the execution of works. Rio differs from Kansas City, New York from Amsterdam, and Washington from all of them, for good and sufficient reasons. They lie, at base, in the geological history, climate, physiography, soils, plants and animals that constitute the history of the place and the basis of its intrinsic identity.

Washington is because . . . . It is uniquely itself. In order to understand what composes the unique quality of this city, and which elements above all most contribute to this identity, it first becomes necessary to understand its morphology.

If this holds for the natural identity of the city, it is equally true of buildings and places in the city. As perhaps for no other place in the United States, the identity, the form and aspect of Washington are important to the inhabitants of the city, to the nation and the world. The city can be examined as an evolutionary form, reflecting its history in morphology, revealing adaptations successful and otherwise, containing attributes, some of high and others of little value.

The search for identity must begin at the beginning.

This study was commissioned by the National Capital Planning Commission, Washington, D.C., and conducted under the supervision of Ian L. McHarg by Mr. Narendra Juneja, assisted by Messers. Sutphin, Meyers, Robertson and Drummond of Wallace, McHarg, Roberts and Todd. The field survey was conducted by Karen and Charles R. Meyers, Jr.

PIEDMONT
CRYSTALLINE ROCKS

Basic Igneous Rocks

Bear Island Granodiorite

Sykesville Formation

Wissahickon Formation

Kensington Granite Gneiss

Laurel Gneiss

COASTAL PLAIN
UNCONSOLIDATED SEDIMENTS

PLIOCENE – MIOCENE – CRETACEOUS

Patuxent Formation

Patapsco Formation

Monmouth Formation

Chesapeake Group

Bryn Mawr Group

Brandywine Gravel

PLEISTOCENE AND RECENT

Sunderland Formation

Wicomico Formation

Pamlico Formation and Alluvium

Terrace Gravels

0   1/2   1   2   MILES 3

GEOLOGY

In the examination of the Potomac River Basin, the physiographic and metropolitan regions, we have seen, at different scales, the expressions of historical geology. In Washington these selfsame processes are perceptible at a more particular scale.

In the broadest terms, the geology of the District of Columbia reveals a very great variability, reflecting the major divisions of Piedmont and Coastal Plain. It reveals a clearly defined Piedmont, a great crescent of undulating Cretaceous sediments, much eroded, forming the backdrop to a scene of equally well-defined terraces and escarpments composed of recent sediments lying at the confluence of the Potomac and Anacostia Rivers. On these, the formal city of L'Enfant sits. The final region is the much-eroded sediments of the Coastal Plain.

A half billion years of geological history are visible in the District; sediments cover hilltops and speak of ancient seas, while the Flats of the formal city are the most recent of geological expressions.

Variation in geological history will be manifest in physiographic variety, in hills and valleys, plateaus, domes, terraces, escarpments, rivers, streams and marshes. This variety is clearly evident in the National Capital; while the relief is not great, it is certainly consequential.

There are three physiographic divisions that correspond to the geological structure. These are the expression of the Precambrian in the Piedmont, the older Cretaceous sediments and the more recent ones of the Pleistocene. The major dissected plateau, transected by Rock Creek, occupying the west and north, is Precambrian and Lower Cretaceous; the edge of the Coastal Plain, east of the Anacostia, is composed of Upper Cretaceous and early Pleistocene deposits; while the intervening area, mainly the Flats, is of late Pleistocene to recent deposits.

The first of these physiographic regions reveals its character most clearly in the rock formation of the Potomac Palisades, the steep dissection of Rock Creek and the domes upon the plateau, which consists of Lower Cretaceous sediments. The Little Falls reveals the boundary of this region in the Fall Line.

The second region conforms in much of its physiography to the Piedmont although it consists of the oldest sedimentary material. Stream valleys are less dissected than in the Piedmont. Several sedimentary caps of the Lafayette series are evident above the plateau. The unconsolidated sediments of the Coastal Plain have weathered to produce a much more broken topography than is visible elsewhere. Ridges are flatter and more rounded, valleys shallow with attendant bogs. Oxon Run and Piney Branch reveal these characteristics.

The last of the regions in the city was discerned by L'Enfant and described as the Flats, occurring at the confluence of the Potomac and Anacostia Rivers. These consist of two clearly defined terraces, with intervening escarpments. This is the site of the formal city and it was the intervening escarpment that L'Enfant selected as the appropriate seat for the two most important buildings—the Capitol and the White House.

The Potomac enters the District through crystalline rock into which it has cut a deep and narrow channel; it is contained by the Palisades. As it crosses the Little Falls it encounters sedimentary material and cuts this deeply, revealing the exposed rock face. Beyond the Fall Line, it is no longer constrained and expands into the broad aspect of the estuarine river. In this lower Potomac there are wide floodplains and marshes; these are conspicuous in the Anacostia too.

The District reveals a complex physiographic expression and, as a consequence, there will be an equal richness in native plant communities. The Piedmont contains variants of one forest type, the Coastal Plain represents

PIEDMONT

FALL ZONE

COASTAL PLAIN

177

PLANT ASSOCIATIONS—Diagrammatic Section

variation of yet another, but in Washington there occurs that special richness which attends their conjunction.

Indeed, the plant communities found in Washington may well be the richest in the basin. There are, or were, swamp cypress stands, magnolia bogs, wild rice marshes, the mixed mesophytic association of Rock Creek and other major valleys, the pitch pine association of the eastern ridges, the great mixed oaks of the plateau with a number of variants, some emphasizing sassafras, others tulip poplar.

The general divisions of plant associations would conform to the physiographic regions. The north and northwest, consisting of the Piedmont and Lower Cretaceous sediments, support the oak-chestnut forest association with white and black oak as codominants with tulip tree. The ridges in this region are likely to reveal chestnut-oak with pines on particularly well-drained soils. In stream valleys will be found the mixed mesophytic association of beech, basswood and black walnut, with hemlocks on north slopes.

The Anacostia drainage composes the second division, where the ridges are clothed in pines—loblolly, scrub and pitch; oaks occupy the middle slopes, with beech and tulip poplar being dominant in the lower slopes

In the last region, the Flats, we find a floodplain, and sweet gum is the appropriate expression. Meadow soils would support loblolly and scrub pine, on loam soils hickory and black gum would be noticeable.

The given form—the landscape identity—is seen from this provisional and exploratory scrutiny to be highly varied. The landscape reveals on its surface, in rocks, physiography and soils, a half billion years of time; it reveals the two major physiographic regions—Piedmont and Coastal Plain—and the great contrasts these regions manifest. This inter-

BOTTOMLAND

UPLAND MOIST

UPLAND

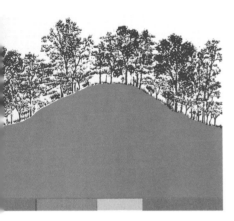

face is dramatized by the Palisades and Little Falls, by the changed aspect of the Potomac in the estuary. It is vivid in the Rock Creek, the surround of hills with their sedimentary caps, the broad valley of the Anacostia and attendant marshes. Not least, there is the precision of the two Pleistocene terraces, the Pamlico and the Wicomico, with their intervening escarpment.

In many cities the given form has been lost irretrievably, buried under undiscerning building, unknown and unexpressed—rivers confined, streams culverted, hills bulldozed, marshes filled, forests felled and escarpments graded into inconsequence. Not so in

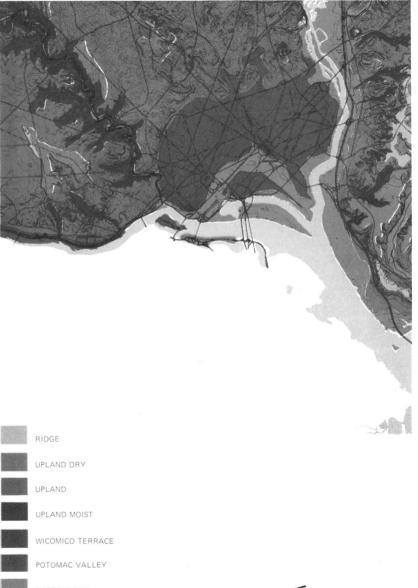

RIDGE

RIDGE

UPLAND DRY

UPLAND

UPLAND MOIST

WICOMICO TERRACE

POTOMAC VALLEY

BOTTOMLAND

MARSH

PLANT ASSOCIATIONS

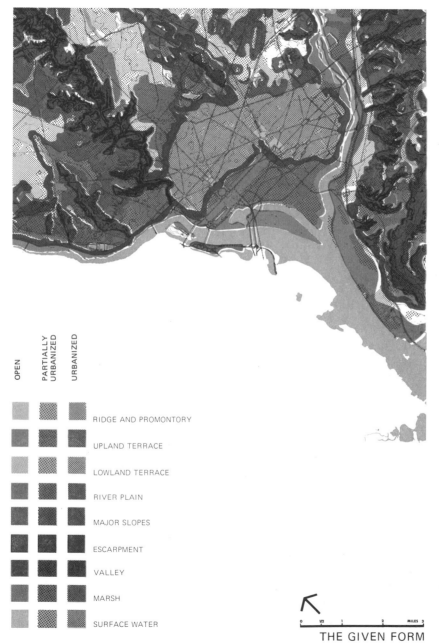

RIDGE AND PROMONTORY

UPLAND TERRACE

LOWLAND TERRACE

RIVER PLAIN

MAJOR SLOPES

ESCARPMENT

VALLEY

MARSH

SURFACE WATER

180

0   ½   1   2   MILES 3

THE GIVEN FORM

Washington, where the major elements still persist, although in various conditions. The surrounding summits are emphasized by Washington Cathedral and the Shrine of the Immaculate Conception. The White House and Capitol achieve their eminence from the escarpment, Rock Creek and Glover Arch-bold unite the Potomac to its hinterland, the ridges that define the Anacostia are clearly evident, while the Potomac reveals its twin identities, above and below the falls. The natural identity is rich and vivid.

The analysis of the constituents of the made form is, like the preceding examination, directed towards the development of a

THE CAPITOL

THE WHITE HOUSE

method rather than the creation of a plan itself. As a result, the study is fragmentary and incomplete. A historical inventory is essential to the discovery of the made form, not merely a compilation of historic buildings, but rather an analysis of the evolution of those adaptations which in sum create the made form. These can be seen as a hierarchy of values.

In the demonstration of the method, attention is directed exclusively to the historic city as this shows a clear relation to the given form and constitutes a single conception of city form.

As reported by William Loughton Smith in 1791, "Major L'Enfant had noted all of the eminences, plains, commanding spots, projects of canals by means of Rock Creek, Eastern Branch and a fine creek called Goose Creek." After surveying the area, L'Enfant was commissioned to prepare a plan for the city. While his vocabulary of civic design was based upon Renaissance concepts, he was acutely aware of the natural characteristics of the site. In parenthesis, however, it might well be said that it was because of his French Renaissance attitudes that he chose to build upon the Flats. Had he been an Italian Renaissance architect, he would surely have located the city on the classic site, the

southeast-facing slopes of the plateau, above.

Following his site analysis, he said that "Nature has done much for it, and with the aid of art it will become the wonder of the world."

It is something of a paradox that the image of the city, most appropriate for the divine right of kings, became the expression for that confederacy which was to become a great democracy. Louis XIV would not have felt strange on the axis of the Mall in the Capital—it was his symbol. The images of Versailles, Tuileries, Place de la Concorde and the Champs Elysées were incorporated into the plan for Washington and united with the existing site. L'Enfant had an overriding concern for the axial arrangement of spaces, their flanking buildings, and for diagonal avenues, but this he coupled with his perceptiveness to the subtleties of land form.

The most prominent position in the Flats was then called Jenkin's Hill, an aspect of the Pamlico-Wicomico escarpment, which L'Enfant described as "a pedestal waiting for a superstructure." This he reserved for the Capitol. The other prominent location, on the same escarpment, he chose for the White House. The limits of his formal plan, defined by Florida Avenue, corresponded to the Wicomico-Sunderland escarpment, the upper limit of the Flats.

Within this, he united the Capitol and the Potomac with the Mall, created a cross axis connecting the latter with the White House, and from these major features, radiated diagonal avenues into the backdrop of hills and summits. This, he advised the President, was intended to contrast with the general regularity and make the real distance appear less, but also to "afford a greater variety of seats with pleasant prospects which can be obtained from the advantageous ground over which these avenues are chiefly directed."

In addition to the Mall, the plan provided

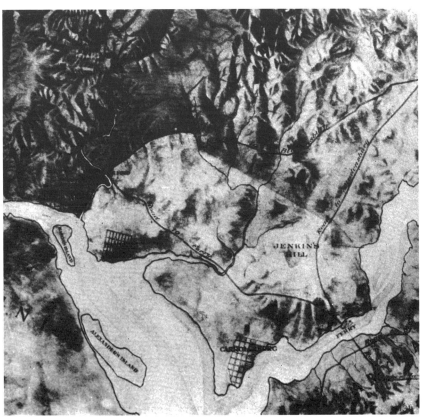

WASHINGTON BEFORE L'ENFANT

for fifteen squares "to be embellished with statues, columns, obelisks and any other ornament." These were carefully sited on advantageous locations.

This plan was a single conception, consistent within the canons of Renaissance city design, but it was adapted to the particularities of the site.

Clearly, the most basic division of Washington is between the formal city and the remainder. It is with the former that this study is concerned. Within this area, bounded by the Potomac, Anacostia and the Wicomico-Sunderland escarpment, there are five major elements—the Mall, the Federal Area, the Formal Avenues, the Interstices and the remaining Open Spaces.

Each of these elements has a distinct identity, and the first three contain the major constituents of the L'Enfant plan. Ecological analysis revealed the given form; we require a method to reveal the identity of the made form. For this we can invoke the intentions of L'Enfant. Renaissance architecture may not be the most appropriate expression of the capital of a great democracy, but it exists and it is irrevocable.

The Mall unites the Potomac, the basic reason for this site, with the most important building, the Capitol: it is the symbolic heart of the Capital and the nation. Clearly, it is the preeminent symbol in the social value system of the city. This above all must be preserved and enhanced.

The symbolic expression of the Federal Government is clearly expressed in the complex of buildings bounding the Mall. They are uniformly neoclassical, heroic in scale and with some consistency of materials, spaces and details. It is clear that this represents a second level in the scale of values, that there is a certain consistency in scale and architecture and that this represents a value and at the same time has implications

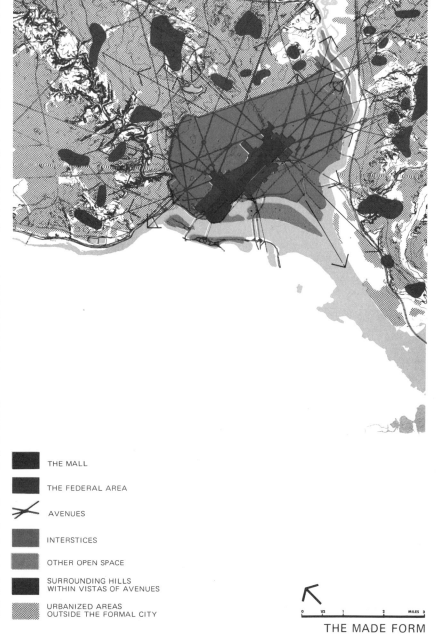

THE MALL

THE FEDERAL AREA

AVENUES

INTERSTICES

OTHER OPEN SPACE

SURROUNDING HILLS WITHIN VISTAS OF AVENUES

URBANIZED AREAS OUTSIDE THE FORMAL CITY

0   1/2   1   2   MILES 3

THE MADE FORM

THE MALL

OTHER OPEN SPACES

AVENUES

for the form of extensions or adaptions. This Federal Area is of historic importance and should be so considered.

The formal avenues are central to L'Enfant's plan—the great avenues, notably the diagonals, unite the entire formal city with its symbolic heart. These avenues are related to distant hills, ridges and rivers. They terminate at Florida Avenue, where the escarpment rises. These are prospective gateways to the formal city and the processional and structural elements that integrate the entire scheme. The Interstices fall between the avenues and contribute to them only on their frontages. L'Enfant presumably ex-

pected these to be filled in with buildings of domestic scale but consonant with federal architecture. These areas have no symbolic importance in the L'Enfant plan.

From Rock Creek, along the Potomac and Anacostia Rivers is a discontinuous system of open spaces. For the most part, they were not a product of the L'Enfant plan and have resulted from filling operations. These areas derive their identity from the rivers and express a major component of the natural identity. In a special sense, the formal city of Washington could exist as a contrived artifice, bounded by hills to the north and rivers to the south. The contrast would be greatest

if these were retained in a natural condition.

This is a most fragmentary examination—and yet the method shows promise. It is possible to examine artifacts in a hierarchy of social values. Recognizing these artifacts and understanding their value will affect policies toward them—their preservation and enhancement.

The authoritarian form of Washington may not be the most appropriate expression for a democratic confederation but is one of the most consistent and identifiable urban forms created since the 18th century. As has been seen, there is a consonance between the given and made forms, the latter exploiting and enhancing the former while creating new values, conspicuously in the Flats, which had little intrinsic drama. The creation of this made form has not resulted in the obliteration of the given form, although much of it has suffered from subsequent city building outside of the formal city.

The image of Washington is of a great city meeting a great river. The Washington Monument is the single most conspicuous element relating the entire city to its symbolic center. Within a fringe of hills and ridges, and edged by the Potomac and Anacostia, the city sits upon the stepped flats. The Mall unites the Potomac with the Capitol, the cross axis unites the White House, the Tidal Basin and the Jefferson Memorial. It is a city of monuments, tree-lined avenues, green open spaces; its buildings are neoclassical and large in scale, the major spaces are heroic.

In the evaluation of the major elements, the Mall, Capitol, White House and Washington Monument, united as a single complex, assume primacy. The governmental buildings within the formal city would assume a secondary position, the skeleton plan of major avenues and streets third, and finally, the major system of open spaces that accompany the rivers.

Clearly, the method could apply at a finer grain and provide the value system for the made form.

In the development of method, the examples employed are likely to reveal only the obvious. Only when the method is fully applied will its benefits be perceived. However, even in the slender application of the method, it is clear that there is a value in pursuing the identities of the given and made form, using the historical method to establish the components of identity and their relative value.

Historic Washington is, in essence, a neoclassical composition set in a half bowl, defined by two confluent rivers and an escarpment, with a backdrop of low hills. The entire city is like an inclined fan with the symbolic city at the base and the ribs revealed in the valleys of the Potomac, Glover Archbold, Rock Creek, Goose Valley and the Anacostia.

This examination allows us to see that Washington is because.... It is not Rio or Amsterdam or Paris. This study has revealed, at least in the broadest outline, why Washington is, as a function of its geological, biological and cultural history. In the adaptations to the site, certain elements have been enhanced, others obliterated, yet entirely new elements of importance introduced. In all of this, a value system has been created, a summation of natural and cultural history. Certain elements are inordinately expressive—hence valuable—others less so. The exercise of an ecological and historical inventory should reveal them.

If it is possible to identify elements and attribute value to them, how then do we respond to this value system? It would be important, in a consideration of the natural identity, to locate and describe the major constituents. We have seen them in brief— the corridors of the Potomac, the Anacostia, Rock Creek, Goose Creek and the Glover Archbold and, in addition, the plateau, vari-

ous summits, ridges and escarpments, the minor valleys and, not least, the Flats: these would be included in the value system of natural identity.

If, indeed, these are the most important elements of the given form, they can be ranked in importance. It would be valuable to see these components in terms of a continuous structure. To what degree are they fully or partially obliterated? Is it important that their continuity be maintained or recovered? How can they be enhanced?

It is clearly possible to select the major physiographic constituents of identity and

EVALUATION:PHYSIOGRAPHIC EXPRESSION
establish the sum of the most important of these as the primary elements of urban structure and value. When these have been evaluated, it is then possible to ensure their preservation and enhancement.

There is another important constituent of the natural identity: that is the expression of plants. As we have seen, there is an enormous variablility in the native plant communities. It would be advisable to prepare a plan of the native plant associations for the entire city and supplement this with information on the changes that occur as a result of adaptations to the environment. This should then become the palette for all

those who are involved in design of projects or the management of land.

Given an ecological inventory and a full description of plant associations—dominant trees, minor trees, shrubs and herbaceous cover, together with descriptions of successions—it becomes possible to establish a palette of plant expression for every site and every project in the National Capital. Given this information, it is possible to select the major elements of expression and ensure representation of the entire dramatic range, not as a dry arboretum, but in a living city— swamp cypress, wild rice swamps, magnolia bogs, the great beech forest that persists in

EVALUATION: ECOLOGICAL EXPRESSION
the Rock Creek Park—each of these dramatic and rich expressions, and many others, could be reintroduced, extended or heightened.

The concept of a palette on the one hand and regulation on the other is just as appropriate for the elements of the made form. There clearly is a palette for the Mall, the Federal Area, the Great Avenues and Streets and for the Open Spaces. These are not as rational as the basis for plant expression, but it is possible to determine rules of consonance and these—rather strangely—derive from the canons of Renaissance city building, architecture and landscape architecture. Strange indeed, but unavoidable.

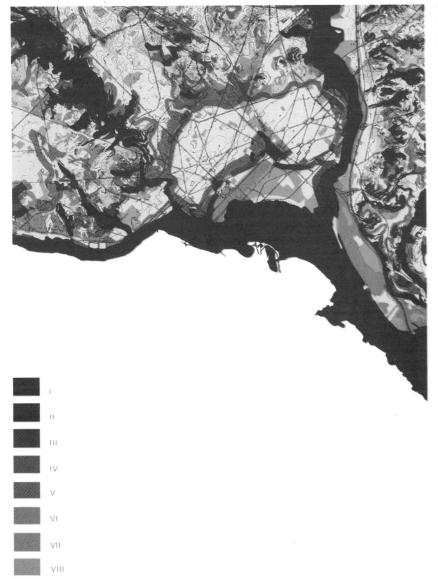

I

II

III

IV

V

VI

VII

VIII

IX

X

PHYSIOGRAPHIC AND ECOLOGICAL COMPONENTS OF THE NATURAL IDENTITY RANKED IN A DESCENDING ORDER OF VALUES FROM I TO X.

0   1/2   1   2   MILES 3

SUMMARY EVALUATION

The establishment of such a value system could be of the utmost utility. It can make public the ascription of value to the component elements of the city, and, it is important to observe, this is quite distinct from the normal measures of land and building value that obtain today. At the moment, parks and historic buildings, attractive places, monuments and rivers, are unlikely to be accorded a value that can arrest their transformation into the most commonplace of economic enterprises. By so evaluating the components of identity of the city, one can better confront the destructive instincts of developer or state highway commission, parking authorities or smaller philistines. Moreover, it is then possible to perceive the role of apparently insignificant sites as part of an important and valuable expression. One further value lies in the provision of a palette for the landscape architect. Instead of the capricious vocabulary of kidney shapes and liver-like begonias, salvias or magenta azaleas, the landscape architect can respond to the major structure of native vegetation appropriate to the site. The completion of a large number of projects within this palette would recreate the major plant components of the natural identity.

By identifying the major components of the given and made forms, and establishing the reason for their importance, it becomes much simpler for art commissions and the like to advise on consonance at least and enhancement at best—not as individual projects, but as contributors to the major elements of identity and value in the city.

Such is the method: the search for the basis of the identity of a city, the selection of those elements—in the natural identity and that of the created city—that are expressive and valuable, that exercise constraints and that proffer opportunities for new development. It is a simple method indeed, but it is an advance over the market mechanism of evaluation—it reveals the basis for form.

The place is because . . . .

185

The City: Health and Pathology

The late G. Scott Williamson was a remarkable man. An English biologist, he was preoccupied with the phenomenon of health. This is, of course, most unusual. There is no generally accepted definition of health, and the medical professions are entirely concerned with disease. But is health only the absence of disease?

One of the most endearing stories of this man concerns a discovery made when he was undertaking a study of the signalmen who maintain lonely vigils while operating the switches on British railroads. The question to be studied was whether these lonely custodians were subject to boredom, which would diminish their dependability. It transpired that lonely or not, underpaid or not, these men had a strong sense of responsibility and were entirely dependable. But this was not the major perception. Williamson learned that every single signalman, from London to Glasgow, could identify infallibly the drivers of the great express trains which flashed past their vision at 100 miles per hour. The drivers were able to express their unique personalities through the unlikely and intractable medium of some thousand tons of moving train, passing in a fraction of a second. The signalmen were perceptive to this momentary expression of the individual, and Williamson perceived the power of the personality.

But Williamson's greatest distinction lay in his certainty that health was as recognizable a phenomenon as disease, and, moreover, that health in the individual was likely to be associated with health of the family and, indeed, of the community. He believed that physical, mental and social health were unified attributes and there were aspects of the physical and social environment that were their corollaries.

In order to test this hypothesis, he created the Peckham Health Center in a working-class neighborhood of London. Unhappily, within a very short period, the Second World War began and the community was disrupted. Nor was it possible to begin the studies after the war, as the Center was nationalized. Williamson died without the proof he sought but certain that the hypothesis was true. Would that it were and that we had the evidence to support it. To the best of my knowledge, this important question is not now being investigated, and those of us who are concerned with the environment do not know whether our actions are beneficial, detrimental or irrelevant to physical, mental and social health.

Now threaded through this narrative, there has been presented a proposition to the effect that creation and destruction are real and, at least hypothetically, measurable. It was stated that creation is the raising of matter to higher levels of order, that destruction is the reduction, that the sum of evolution has been creative, but that there are retrogressive processes which increase entropy. There was an attempt to identify the attributes of creation and destruction. The former was associated with complexity, diversity, stability, a high number of species, symbiosis and low entropy. Reduction and retrogression, in contrast, were associated with simplicity, uniformity, instability, a low number of species, independence and high entropy.

Creativity, we suggested, could assume two forms, the first of these, negentropy, through the physical entrapment of energy, notably in photosynthesis and in the successive orderings accomplished by animals with elevation in the phylogenetic scale, through apperception, and further, through those cooperative mechanisms which are indispensable to increased complexity—and thus evolution—which are symbioses.

Using Darwin and Henderson's definitions of fitness, it appears that the earth is fit for life and all of its manifestations, that the surviving and successful organism, species and community are fit for the environment. If this is so, then the fit creature or community is, by definition, creative; the unfit or misfit, less than fully creative, or reductive. As we have seen, fitness must be revealed in form, and so form then reveals not only fitness but creativity. Form is meaningful, revealing the adaptive capabilities of the organism and the community; it should also reveal, if we could observe this, that these are creative.

It has been earlier suggested that we go one step further. If fitness and unfitness subsume creativity and destructiveness, then can these two terms, in turn, be subsumed under health and disease? Indeed, are not these terms simply different facets of two phenomena that represent polar extremes—the first creativity-fitness-health, the other reduction-unfitness-disease?

Indeed, common usage of the words lends this idea some credibility; creativeness is a better measure of fitness than mere horsepower; the creative are indeed fit, the fit are healthy. Are the destructive unfit and unhealthy?

We can turn to the forest for example. If we find a forest in which the majority of the plants and animals are diseased and dying, there is no doubt that this is an unhealthy forest—it will not be entrapping as much energy as would a healthy one; the creatures will not be raising matter to a higher order than before. This forest will be less than creative, even if it is not destructive; it will not be fit and it will not be healthy. Presumably another forest, consisting of a wide range of species, representing a balanced ecosystem, will be creative, fit and healthy. There will be disease and death in both, but the presence of these in the latter will be an instrument for growth and evolution. Entropy will be high in the former, low in the latter.

If health is indeed a synthesis of the factors of creativity and fitness, then we have at hand a tool of inordinate value for both diagnosis and prescription. We can accept that where stress exists, pathology will occur. The form of the pathology will vary with genetic proclivities and the degree and nature of the stressors, but that need not concern us. We can concentrate attention on the presence of health and disease as indicators of creativity and fitness, destruction and unfitness. By doing so, we can avoid the pitfalls of causality which have handicapped epidemiological studies where it is thought essential to identify the stressor and the resultant pathology. We will rather accept synergesis, the concurrence of stressors and the resultant diseases, which have multiple causes. It is enough for us that certain areas and people will exhibit health, others disease, and these must be responses to the physical and social environment. If we can identify the areas of health and disease, we can then proceed to associate the factors of the social and physical environment that are identified with both. From this information, it may be possible to find the environmental contributors to both health and disease, and move the practice of environmental planning from the abyss of ignorance—the most appropriate description of its present standards of diagnosis and remedy.

Where is the environment of health—physical, mental and social? There is the environment of the creative and the fit. Where is the environment of pathology? There is the environment of the destructive and the misfit, or perhaps better, there is the destructive misfit of social and physical environments.

I once conducted a course euphemistically called "Ecology of the City." This was a modest attempt to bring together the information plant and animal ecologists have developed and apply it to the problems of the city where economic determinism rules unchallenged. It is an extremely difficult venture, because ecologists seek the wildest environments—those least affected by man—and have carefully avoided him as a polluter, not only of the environment, but also of their researches into the behavior of plants and animals. Faced with this poverty of human ecology, and intrigued by Scott Williamson's proposition as to the unity of physical, social and mental health, and their identification with specific social and physical environments, I persuaded a number of students that it might be enlightening to identify the specific environments of pathology—physical, mental and social—for the city of Philadelphia. This, I suggested, could allow future generations of students, and hopefully more skilled researchers, to investigate the correlation between pathology and environment. As planners, landscape architects and architects, our competence lies in manipulating the physical environment, but we are responsive to the idea that social processes are important to the design and planning professions. Physiological adaptation is slow; the environment is more easily manipulated. Social processes provide the instruments for analysis and transformation. Yet we need criteria. If health and pathology are synthetic indicators, then let us employ them.

To this end, it was decided that we would collect all available statistics on these three categories of health and, in addition, that we would compile information on economic parameters, ethnicity, housing quality, air pollution and density.

All data were divided into three categories, highest, intermediate and lowest incidence. All data were mapped on transparencies so that concurrence of factors could be observed. It was believed that the mapping of these data would reveal the environment of pathology and that the absence of this would reveal the areas of relative health—a poor way to discern health, but no other is available.

This type of study has been done before and done better. There is no doubt that skilled statisticians could derive from these data correlations which have not yet been developed. But it is enough for the moment that we can describe the environment of health and pathology. With this we would know where to look for their environmental corollaries.

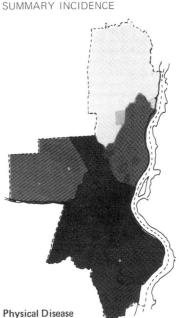

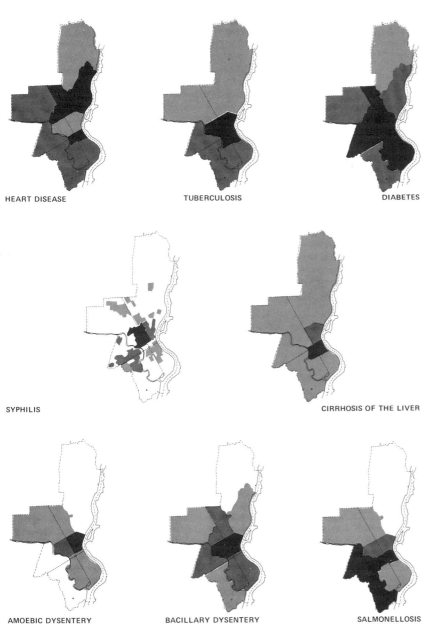

HEART DISEASE

TUBERCULOSIS

DIABETES

SYPHILIS

CIRRHOSIS OF THE LIVER

AMOEBIC DYSENTERY

BACILLARY DYSENTERY

SALMONELLOSIS

SUMMARY INCIDENCE

Physical Disease

Eight factors of physical disease were tabulated and mapped. The data were provided in incidence per 100,000 and these were divided into three equal categories, the highest third being shown in the darkest tone, the next intermediate and the lowest incidence in the lightest tone.

The diseases that were mapped included heart disease, tuberculosis, diabetes, syphilis, cirrhosis of the liver, amoebic dysentery, bacillary dysentery and salmonellosis. The availability of data determined the diseases selected.

It can be seen that the distribution of the highest incidence varies around the center of the city, but that the sum of these is concentrated in the center city and diminishes with distance from it. The rural fringes in Chestnut Hill and the far northeast reveal the lowest incidence of disease—or the highest relative health in terms of physical disease.

189

HOMICIDE

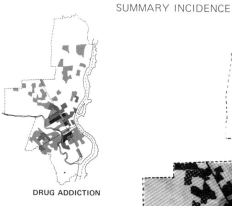

SUICIDE

DRUG ADDICTION

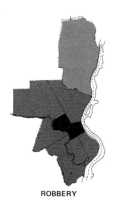

ALCOHOLISM

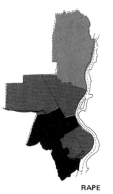

ROBBERY

RAPE

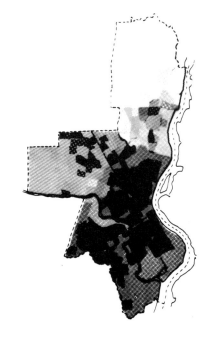

Social Disease

AGGRAVATED ASSAULT

JUVENILE DELINQUENCY

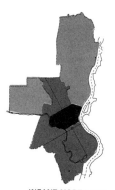

INFANT MORTALITY

The factors of social disease that were collected and mapped included homicide, suicide, drug addiction, alcoholism, robbery, rape, aggravated assault, juvenile delinquency and infant mortality.

These present, in summary, a generally similar pattern to that for physical disease, but the area of the upper third penetrates less far into the northeast and is much more heavily concentrated in the southwest. This too reveals the maximum concentration in the center of the city, with a large central area representing the bulk of social disease and the large peripheral areas conspicuously less represented.

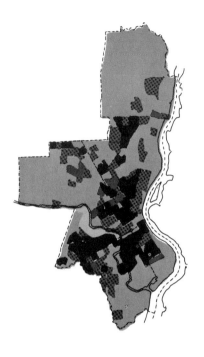

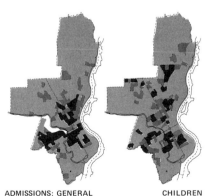

ADMISSIONS: GENERAL   CHILDREN

Mental Disease

The information on mental health is the slenderest of all categories and consists only of information on psychiatric inpatient unduplicated admissions and similar information for children.

These data for mental health show a much more diffuse pattern than for either physical or social disease. While the preponderance remains a central-city phenomenon, the distribution includes almost all of the city, although Chestnut Hill and the northeast and southern part of the city are conspicuously free of identified mental disease.

Pollution

Three factors of air pollution were identified and mapped—suspended dust, settled dust and the sulfate index. As can be seen, factories that accompany the Delaware River and are concentrated in the south of the city coincide with the major concentration of these pollutants, which diminish with distance from these locations. The far northeast and Chestnut Hill are conspicuously free of them.

Ethnicity

The ethnic groups that were tabulated and mapped included Germans, Irish, Italians, Poles, British, Russians and nonwhites.

These groups congregate in regions that together form a jigsaw puzzle. Negroes are concentrated in North and West Philadelphia, Italians in South Philadelphia, the Irish in the southwest, Poles in the east, Germans in the near northeast and near north, Russians in the north and British in the northwest.

SUSPENDED DUST

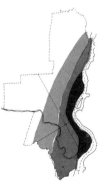

SETTLED DUST

SULFATE INDEX   191

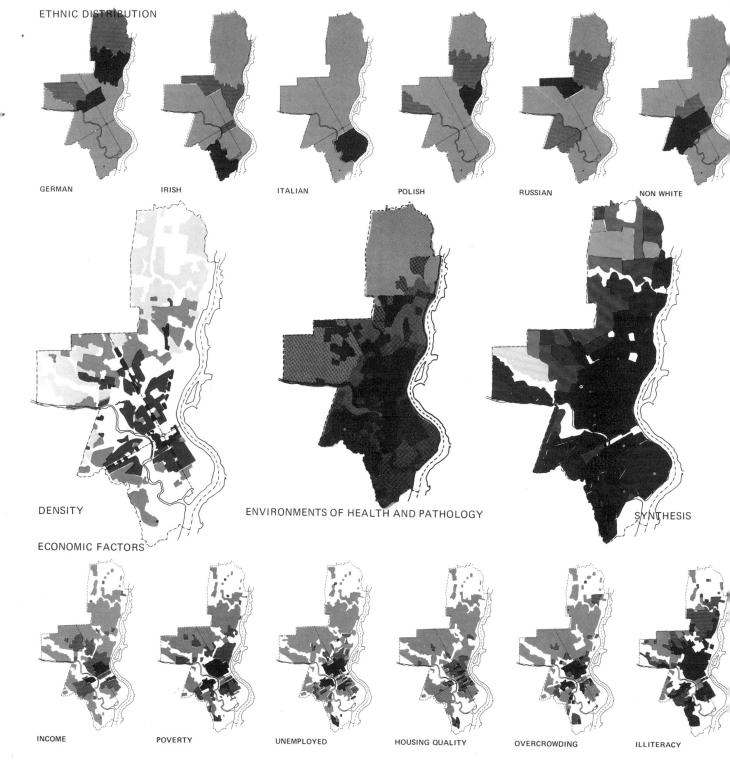

ETHNIC DISTRIBUTION

GERMAN   IRISH   ITALIAN   POLISH   RUSSIAN   NON WHITE

DENSITY

ENVIRONMENTS OF HEALTH AND PATHOLOGY

SYNTHESIS

ECONOMIC FACTORS

INCOME   POVERTY   UNEMPLOYED   HOUSING QUALITY   OVERCROWDING   ILLITERACY

Economic Factors

The factors that were identified and for which data were procured included income, poverty, unemployment, housing quality, overcrowding and the number of persons without high school education.

These factors reveal that the poor and the underprivileged are concentrated in a relatively small area encircling the commercial center. This area is small relative to those occupied by the upper thirds in physical, social and mental disease. While the area of poverty is at the heart of the concentration of diseases, these extend considerably beyond, and we cannot claim that poverty is the explanation for the incidence of physical, social and mental disease. The answer is more complex than this.

The Environments of Health and Pathology

Each of the summary maps of physical, mental and social health have now been presented independently, together with summaries of economic factors, ethnicity and pollution. Each map is presented in three tones, each a one-third division from white to black. By superimposition and photography, it is possible to add the factors concerned and obtain a summation that is as accurate as the components. Each summary was similarly employed to provide the composite map of physical, social and mental disease, entitled The Environments of Health and Pathology for Philadelphia. The three maps show a generally similar pattern, with variations only of degree.

The pattern is very clear—the heart of the city is the heart of pathology and there is a great concentration of all types of pathology encircling it. This persists with only a small diminution to the south, but there is a profound distinction between the incidence in the central and adjacent city and the northwest and northeast.

It is premature to predict correlations. The single obvious one is not poverty, but density—indeed, the adjacent population map bears a remarkable correspondence to the pattern of pathology.

Synthesis

On the assumption that man is a synthesizing creature able to make extremely discriminating judgments of complex situations, the students who were collecting and mapping the data for this study were required to form rotating teams, each of three students, and subject the entire city to their own relative appraisal. In this, there was no counting of death or disease, but rather of blocks and neighborhoods to identify where children laughed or did not, the demeanor of policemen, the presence of garbage in the streets, broken glass or overturned automobiles, street trees, playgrounds, parks, defiant scribblings on walls, care, pride or despair. If there is a distortion in this study, it is because a number of the students were architects who value the visual senses rather highly and who would prefer urban rather than suburban environments, but, although the group was diverse, they reached a consensus without difficulty. The synthetic map was prepared before the individual data had been mapped—it was not affected by the data. This synthetic map contains a finer grain of examination than the health data, but corresponds to a considerable degree with the map of the environments of health and pathology.

It would appear that the perceptive student can perceive environmental variations that correspond to health and disease. It would be of the utmost value if this subjective impression could be reinforced by objective studies so that the elements that were observed and weighed could be identified as the components of the environments that contribute to health and pathology. This would provide the objective basis for the practice of city planning, landscape architecture and architecture—no less than for medicine, social services and government.

Investigations into the subject of urban pathology in the past decade have concentrated on the factor of density, overcrowding and social competition with results that have been described wryly by Dr. John Calhoun as "pathological togetherness." Most of the experiments have been conducted on animals, both in the wild and in laboratories—mice, rats, shrews, voles, lemmings, muskrats and deer. The results have been consistent in most cases. The major experiments have been undertaken with rats by Dr. Calhoun and Dr. Jack Christian—both ecologists.

It was through the chance discovery that a large number of wild muskrats had died inexplicably that Dr. Christian became involved in this field. He found that it was not infectious disease that had caused their death, but stress, as was disclosed by examination of their endocrinal processes. Possibly this was induced by increased numbers and density. Dr. Christian then undertook successive experiments to investigate the relation of pathology and the endocrine system with density as the stressor. For a decade or so he performed experiments in the Philadelphia Zoo with rats. These begin with a small breeding population in an "extensive" environment in which there is a superabundance of food, water and litter. The animals breed and population increases. As it does, however, the size of litters begins to decline, intrauterine resorption is observed, followed by deformed young, failure of the mothers to provide milk, and cannibalism.

When numbers are reached that have been recognized as half of the maximum population, the phenomenon of clustering becomes apparent when subordinate animals form themselves into balls of a dozen or so. Thereafter comes the onset of adult disease. This mainly takes the form of the characteristic diseases of stress—cardiovascular and renal diseases. The mortalities in adults increase, the population curve flattens and then begins an irreversible decline in population.

From these repeated experiments, Dr. Christian has concluded that as density increases, so do social pressures, which manifest themselves in stress diseases; that this affects not only reproductive capacity (ACTH and androgens inhibit the gonadotrophins), but induces heart and kidney disease.

Dr. Calhoun has reported the population-density/disease relationships that Dr. Christian has observed, but his experiments have been more concerned with the social behavior changes that accompany increases in density. The well-known rank order of animals has been defined by Dr. Calhoun for the rats in his experiments as dominant males, probers, homosexuals and withdrawn catatonic animals. The incidence and the types of diseases are reported by Dr. Calhoun to relate to rank order. Thus, the dominant animals have little disease but disease increases in the descending order of social rank. Moreover, in the upper ranks, disease is mainly physical, but social deviation increases with decline in social rank. The probers exhibit deviant behavior, being hypersexual and marginally homosexual; the homosexual rats exhibit more deviance while the catatonic rats are asocial and exhibit extreme mental pathology.

Dr. Calhoun has shown that rank order is also associated with mobility. The dominant animals have the greatest mobility. This is accompanied by a large number of social interactions which tend to be gratifying. As the order declines, encounters provide less gratification, and result in reduced mobility, until, at the bottom of the scale, the catatonic rats are all but immobile. Apparently the encounters experienced by the subordinate animals produce antagonisms that cause them to be deviant, in turn causing more antagonisms and hence more deviance.

When population increases, it does so reasonably by increasing the number of subordinate animals. The stresses which they experience inhibit procreation and it is this that Dr. Christian invokes as the involuntary population control mechanism. Stress inhibits population growth, at least in rats.

Dr. Christian has reported that the primary effects of population increase, and the density and social pressure that result, are the reduction in gonadal activity in subordinate animals, increase in blood sugar and blood pressure, increased mortality in the young, mainly due to failure of lactation and negligence by mothers and, finally, stress disease in subordinate adults.

Both of these investigators are convinced that the effects they have observed in animal societies hold for man. In this, they are confirmed by the similarity of the diseases experienced by the experimental animals and by urban man. Yet, their critics have held that the limitations on movement in the animal experiments, combined with the absence of the capacity to accomplish remedy, invalidate any comparison between animals and man. The fact that children in Harlem have a range of not more than four blocks tends to discount the limitation of movement thesis, but even more persuasive is the statement by P. Leyhausen. "Nearly five years in prisoner-of-war camps taught me that overcrowded human societies reflect the symptoms of overcrowded wolf, cat, goat, mouse, rat and rabbit communities to the last detail and that all differences are mainly species-specific; the basic forces of social interaction and organization are *in principle* identical and there is a true homology between Man and Animal throughout the whole range of vertebrates."*

It is only with the background of the animal studies conducted by Christian and Calhoun, and the insistence that there is a homology between man and animal, that we can examine the most elaborate study of urban disease. This is The Midtown Manhattan Study conducted by the Cornell Medical School.

In this study, the area of New York between

*P. Leyhausen, "The Sane Community—A Density Problem?" *Discovery*, September, 1965.

Park Avenue and the East River, 59th to 96th Streets, was intensively examined and compared with the whole of Manhattan and the boroughs.

The average density of the midtown area is 600 persons per acre, four times that of Manhattan as a whole, ten times that of Bronx-Brooklyn, and 130 times that for Staten Island.

In this area there is a population of 380,000 persons. A probability sample of 1910 persons was selected for interviews on mental health. These lasted over an hour on the average, and were conducted by psychiatrists and social workers. The professional caliber of the interviewers and the duration of the interviews are of great importance, considering the gravity of the conclusions.

The broadest conclusion of the report was that there was a marked increase in disease from the boroughs to Manhattan, Manhattan to midtown, midtown to the East Side.

In a comparison between the boroughs and midtown, the latter was seen to have twice as much suicide, accidental death, tuberculosis and juvenile delinquency, and three times as much alcoholism. Comparison of the Park Avenue band, wherein live some of the richest and most powerful families in the United States, and the third-generation relief recipients of the East Side, revealed that disease was high in both cases, but on the East Side there was three times as much suicide, accidental death, tuberculosis, and infant mortality and ten times as much alcoholism.

If these figures are disturbing, then the disclosures on mental disease are positively frightening. It was found that, in the sample population, twenty per cent were so mentally incapacitated as to be indistinguishable from patients in mental hospitals, a further sixty per cent showed symptoms short of impairment, and only twenty per cent were free of the symptoms of mental disease.

Sadly, this great study excluded the entire subject of the physical environment and little of the nature of institution in the social environment. As a result, many important variables are unknown—pollution and noise levels, families or persons per room as opposed to rooms per person, the physical characteristics of buildings, and much more. In the absence of this vital information, it becomes necessary to speculate on some of the variables that are density-related. Clearly, privacy diminishes as density increases; with high density comes high noise level, an increase in social competition and a reduction in the possibility of escape.

On the subject of noise, Professor Mangeri has written, "any noise above 90 decibels in intensity and 4000 cycles per second in frequency induces a constant generalized arterial spasm, thereby increasing peripheral resistance and subjecting the heart to abnormal strain."* This noise level is frequently reached and exceeded in cities and may well be contributing to pervasive heart disease.

Pollution of the atmosphere now has an enormous literature, and there is general agreement that sulfur dioxide, carbon monoxide, lead, hydrocarbons, nitrous oxides and ozone are indeed dangerous poisons. There is a smaller literature on the subject of atmospheric ionization. This deserves increasing attention as it has not only physiological but also psychological effects. Positive ionization, normally a by-product of all combustive processes, is now believed to be an important stressor.

Normal clean air is negatively ionized; normal urban air is usually positively charged. It appears that positively charged carbon dioxide tends to immobilize the cilia of the bronchus and causes the mucus to become viscous, with the result that it becomes difficult to expel the pollutant particles. The conclusion, then, is not only that atmospheric pollutants are poisonous—and that many are carcinogens—but that the attendant positive ionization reduces the capacity of the organism to deal with these assaults. The immobilized cilia and viscous mucous membrane do not return to normal except in the presence of negatively charged oxygen.

Experiments conducted by the United States Navy have confirmed that positive ionization induces anxiety, tension, eroticism and low morale while negative ionization contributes to a feeling of well-being.

In nature, negative ionization is produced by lightning and thunderstorms, water falling in rain, waterfalls and fountains. It is believed that the oxygen expelled in plant photosynthesis is negatively charged.

Stimuli, either superabundant or infrequent, can be important stressors. When there are very many stimuli, as in city center, and even more importantly, when most of these are meaningless, they act as noise. It becomes necessary to exclude them. When the exclusion is effected or when the majority of stimuli have no meaning, there can occur sensory deprivation. Both are serious stresses. Studies of sensory deprivation have shown it to produce hallucinations. Overload, according to Dr. James Miller, leads to a succession of responses—omission, errors, filtering, queuing, approximation, multiple channeling and, finally, escape. This paradox of sensory overload and deprivation sounds suspiciously like anomie and the lonely crowd.

While urban pathology is one of the most serious of problems, the purported remedy is thoroughly inadequate. Usually, what is described as a slum is obliterated and a new group of buildings rise to replace the old community. The original inhabitants are seldom able to live in the new buildings. In the original community, there is usually an intermeshed fabric of social dependence and a considerable tolerance of ethnic and religious variation. When the slum is destroyed, there is normally a large number of persons who are deprived of the social support of the community and who gravitate to institutions. Welfare and social service increase markedly. There is good evidence that the old community is destroyed. There is little evidence that renewal creates community or that the displaced find new community.

How does one proceed to deal with this most urgent of problems? It would seem important to identify the environments of health and pathology. This has been done for Philadelphia. At least we now know where health and disease live. It is possible to begin to investigate the factors of the social and physical environment that are identified with these polarities and with the intervening stages. At the moment, it seems clear that crowding, social pressure and pathology do correlate sufficiently to justify more serious investigation. In this vein, it is reasonable to ask why the poor should live on the most expensive of central urban land, which requires the highest density.

At the beginning of this chapter was presented the proposition of G. Scott Williamson that the health of the individual was linked with that of the family and the community, that physical, mental and social disease were unitary manifestations. The central proposition of this book has been that creativity and destruction are real phenomena, that both have attributes, that fitness and unfitness—in the evolutionary sense—are expressions of these, as are health and disease.

We need to know where are the environments of health for there the environment is fit, the adaptations are creative. There is a creative-fit-healthy environment. What are its components? All this we must know to create the humane city.

Data for this study were collected and mapped in 1966 by graduate students in Landscape Architecture and City Planning at the University of Pennsylvania. Credit is given to Messrs. Bradford D. and S., Bragdon, Chitty, Christie, Davis, Feldman, Felgemaker, Kao, Meyers, Murphy, Rosenberg, Seddon, Sinatra, Sutphin, Terpstra, Tourbier, Westmacott, Wolf and Zeigler.

*Salvatore Mangeri, *Medical Tribune*, March 29, 1965.

Prospect

The astronaut was only an author's device, his persuasion helps no one; the Naturalists are a fiction and their imagined Utopia cannot be found. We remain ourselves, unchanged; the problems we confront have heightened imperceptibly during the reading. We are still like Thurber's moth, insisting that we invented the flame; nature is our creation and we shall dominate and subjugate it, for that is our divine destiny. We relinquished integration when we found consciousness and in rejection we move to disintegration. But the prospect offers us several choices—the quickest is annihilation as anthropocentric man produces the holocaust; population explosion is slower. Starvation is real and prevalent; it will become worse, but starving cries can be unheard from far around the world. The erosion of the rights of man will strike others first, and our losses will be imperceptible; children will be born who did not know life otherwise. The land will be raped and creatures extirpated because the insistencies will be so loud; who can plan for the long term when survival is today? The cities will grow as they have, enlarging the pathology of their hearts, growing into necropoles. What other prospect can you see?

This book offers one prospect. It consists of evidence gathered from wiser men—small patches from the brilliant vestments of their minds, collected in a ragbag of memories and notes and now assembled in a single patchwork quilt. When, a year or so ago, I first embarked on this adventure, I had neither the courage nor the ambition for the work that has ensued. But the evidence, as it was collected and pieced together, made larger claims than I had anticipated. It was rather like an exercise in simple arithmetic when the sum of one column must be added to the next, inexorably increasing in number, power and significance. The quilt has lost much of the brilliance of its parts in this assembly. There are incongruities, the seams are imperfect, but finally, although the product is only a patchwork quilt, is it not one piece of cloth?

Does the process of creation involve the employment of energy and matter in raising levels of order? Matter is not destroyed but order can be reduced; is then destruction better termed reduction—anticreation? Is it accurate and useful to consider the earth as a single superorganism, the oceans and the atmosphere as organic? Do the processes of creation and reduction each exhibit characteristics and can these be subsumed under negentropy and entropy? Are fitness and fitting measures of creation in ecosystems? If form and process are merely aspects of the single phenomenon of being, can there be a conception of intrinsic form? And finally, are health and pathology the most synoptic criteria for creation and reduction, fitting and unfitting? If so, we have a model. Moreover, we have criteria. The first is negentropy, the increase in levels of order. The second is apperception, the capacity to transmute energy into information and thence to meaning—and to respond to this. The third is symbiosis, the cooperative arrangement that permits increase in levels of order and requires apperception. The fourth is fitness and fitting—the selection of a fit environment and the adaptation of that environment, and of the organism, to accomplish a better fitting. The final criterion is the presence of health or pathology—the evidence of creative fitting, requiring negentropy, apperception and symbiosis.

This model contains the possibility of an inventory of all ecosystems to determine their relative creativity in the biosphere. This same conception can be applied to human processes. Agriculture and forestry merely exploit the negentropic product of photosynthesis; hydroelectric power utilizes the negentropy provided by the hydrologic cycle, but certain manufacturing—the transmutation of iron ore, limestone and coal into computers—constitutes an increase in the levels of order and can thus be considered negentropic. All living processes require perception, but education in general and art and science in particular are the most developed human expressions of this. Commerce, politics, law and government are mainly symbiotic while architecture, landscape architecture, engineering and construction are adaptive processes engaged in fitting of organisms and environment.

This suggests an ecological value system in which the currency is energy. There is an inventory of matter, life forms, apperceptive powers, roles, fitness, adaptations, symbioses and genetic potential. Consumption optimally involves the employment of energy in the raising of levels of matter. Matter is not consumed but merely cycled. When not employed in the cycle, it assumes the role of a reserve. Given a uniform source of energy, the period of entrapment is essential for the increase in creativity—coal represents long-term entrapment, fresh vegetables only short-term. Moreover, the entrapped energy must be transferred through successive levels of organisms, each level sustaining higher levels. The biosphere does not consist of a pyramid of organisms but of ecosystems in which many different creatures coexist in interdependence, each with its own process, apperception, roles, fitness, adaptations and symbioses. This system has an energy source as its currency, an inventory of matter, life forms and ecosystems, and reserves in the inventory—the cycles of matter, genetic and cultural potential. Energy is degraded but is replaced; some energy is arrested on its path to entropy and this increases the inventory and enhances the creative capacity of the biosphere.

The application of this model requires elaborate ecological inventories. Happily, recent technological advances facilitate these. Earth satellites with remote scanning devices with high-level air photography and ground-level identification can provide rich data and time series information on the dynamism of many natural processes. When such inventories are completed they can be constituted into a value system. They can also be identified not only in degrees of value but of tolerance and intolerance. These data, together with the conception of fitness, constitute the greatest immediate utility of the ecological model. Ecosystems can be viewed as fit for certain prospective land uses in a hierarchy. It is then possible to identify environments as fit for ecosystems, organisms and land uses. The more intrinsically an environment is fit for any of these, the less work of adaptation is necessary. Such fitting is creative. It is then a maximum-benefit/minimum-cost solution.

These inventories would then constitute a description of the world, continent or ecosystem under study as phenomena, as interacting process, as a value system, as a range of environments exhibiting degrees of fitness for organisms, men and land uses. It would exhibit intrinsic form. It could be seen to exhibit degrees of health and pathology. The inventories would include human artifacts as well as natural processes.

Certainly the most valuable application of such inventories is to determine locations for land uses and most particularly for urbanization. Urban growth in the United States today consists of emptying the continent toward its seaboard conurbations, which expand by accretion and coalesce. This offers the majority of future necropolitans the choice between the environments of Bedford Stuyvesant and Levittown. There must be other alternatives. Let us ask the land where are the best sites. Let us establish criteria for many different types of excellence responding to a wide range of choice. We seek not only the maximum range of differing excellences *between* city locations, but the maximum range of choice *within* each one.

Consider a time when ecological inventories have been completed. A sample survey of the population is made. Those interviewed are asked to enumerate the ideal characteristics of climate, scenery, recreation, employment, residence that constitute their utopian preferences. The results are searched for concurrences from which emerges a social program for a new urban America. The ecological inventory is searched for sites that conform to the aspirations of those interviewed. The match reveals the urban Utopia of choice. John Kenneth Galbraith has released us from the strictures of economic determinism; our present urban pattern is the product of bondage to toil. What is the pattern of an urban America based upon choice, freed from economic determinism? We can find out and we could create it—a more worthy objective than the conquest of space.

The benefits of the ecological view seem patent to me, but equally clear are the profound changes which espousal of this view will effect. The Judeo-Christian creation story must be seen as an allegory; dominion and subjugation must be expunged as the biblical injunction of man's relation to nature. In values it is a great advance from "I-it" to "I-Thou," but "we" seems a more appropriate description for ecological relationships. The economic value system must be expanded into a relative system encompassing all biophysical processes and human aspirations. Law must reflect that death or injury through flood, drought, avalanche, mudslide or earthquake can result from human negligence or malice and thus should fall within the jurisdiction of the courts. Medicine must be more concerned with creating the environment of health than with therapy alone. Industry and commerce must expand their accounting to include all costs and benefits. But it is in education that the greatest benefits lie. Here separatism rules, yet integration is the quest. This ecology offers: the science of the relations of organism and the environment, integrative of the sciences, humanities and the arts—a context for studies of man and the environment.

In the quest for survival, success and fulfillment, the ecological view offers an invaluable insight. It shows the way for the man who would be the enzyme of the biosphere—its steward, enhancing the creative fit of man-environment, realizing man's design with nature.

Photo Credits

1	Glasgow Herald
2	Glasgow Herald
3	Meyers
4	Meyers
5	Meyers
6	Meyers
7	Meyers
8	Meyers
9	Meyers
10	Meyers
11	Meyers
12	Meyers
13	McHarg
14	McHarg
15	Meyers
16	Meyers
17	Meyers
18	Meyers
19	Aero Service Division, Litton Industries
20	The Evening Bulletin
21	Ayre Dvir
22	Ayre Dvir
23	American Red Cross
24	Aero Service Division, Litton Industries
25	Eileen Christelow Ahrenholtz
26	Eileen Christelow Ahrenholtz
27	Peter Blake
28	Aero Service Division, Litton Industries
29	Aero Service Division, Litton Industries
30	United States Department of Housing and Urban Development
31	Elliott Erwitt, Magnum Photos
32	Grant Heilman
33	unknown
34	Walter Hege
35	United States Department of Housing and Urban Development
36	Aero Service Division, Litton Industries
37	Aero Service Division, Litton Industries
38	United States Department of Agriculture Forest Service Photo
39	NASA
40	J. Dixon, United States Department of the Interior, National Park Service Photo
41	ESSA
42	Courtesy of the American Museum of Natural History
43	NASA
44	Grant Heilman
45	Eileen Christelow Ahrenholtz
46	Grant Heilman
47	Arthur F. Fawcett, United States Department of the Interior, National Park Service Photo
48	Aero Service Division, Litton Industries
49	Grant Heilman
50	Grant Heilman
51	Grant Heilman
52	Aero Service Division, Litton Industries
53	New Mexico State Tourist Bureau
54	California Anti-Litter League
55	Grant Heilman
56	unknown
57	unknown
58	Alwin Seifert
59	unknown
60	Historic Urban Plans, Ithaca
61	McHarg
62	British Travel & Holiday Association
63	J. Clarence Davis Collection, Museum of the City of New York
64	McHarg
65	NASA
66	Green Spring & Worthington Valley Planning Council
67	Green Spring & Worthington Valley Planning Council
68	Green Spring & Worthington Valley Planning Council
69	NASA
70	United States Department of the Interior National Park Service Photo
71	Aero Service Division, Litton Industries
72	Aero Service Division, Litton Industries
73	Cope, Linder and Walmsley
74	Peter Winants for THE ROUSE COMPANY The Village of Cross Keys, Baltimore County, Maryland
75	Richard Erdoes
76	Grant Heilman
77	United States Department of the Interior National Park Service Photo
78	Aero Service Division, Litton Industries
79	United States Department of the Interior National Park Service Photo
80	United States Department of the Interior National Park Service Photo
81	Grant Heilman
82	United States Department of the Interior National Park Service Photo
83	United States Department of the Interior National Park Service Photo
84	United States Department of the Interior National Park Service Photo
85	United States Department of the Interior National Park Service Photo
86	United States Department of the Interior National Park Service Photo
87	United States Department of the Interior National Park Service Photo
88	United States Department of the Interior National Park Service Photo
89	United States Department of the Interior National Park Service Photo
90	United States Department of the Interior National Park Service Photo
91	United States Department of the Interior National Park Service Photo
92	United States Department of the Interior National Park Service Photo
93	Aero Service Division, Litton Industries
94	United States Department of the Interior National Park Service Photo
95	Grant Heilman
96	United States Department of the Interior National Park Service Photo
97	United States Department of the Interior National Park Service Photo
98	Aero Service Division, Litton Industries
99	M. Woodbridge Williams, United States Department of the Interior, National Park Service Photo
100	Skyviews
101	Aero Service Division, Litton Industries
102	Professor Erwin W. Muller
103	Dr. Ralph Wyckoff
104	Courtesy of the American Museum of Natural History
105	United States Department of the Interior National Park Service Photo
106	United States Department of the Interior National Park Service Photo
107	United States Department of the Interior National Park Service Photo
108	Aero Service Division, Litton Industries
109	Alva Blackerby, United States Department of Agriculture
110	United States Department of the Interior National Park Service Photo
111	Courtesy of the American Museum of Natural History
112	unknown
113	Richard L. Cassel
114	unknown
115	American Honey Institute
116	United States Department of the Interior Fish and Wildlife Service
117	Gunda Holzmeister
118	New Mexico State Tourist Bureau
119	Paul Mayer
120	Aero Service Division, Litton Industries
121	National Capital Planning Commission
122	M. Woodbridge Williams, United States Department of the Interior, National Park Service Photo
123	M. Woodbridge Williams, United States Department of the Interior, National Park Service Photo
124	M. Woodbridge Williams, United States Department of the Interior, National Park Service Photo
125	Meyers
126	United States Department of Agriculture, Forest Service Photo
127	Robert Winters, United States Department of Agriculture
128	Meyers
129	National Capital Planning Commission
130	National Capital Planning Commission
131	National Capital Planning Commission
132	National Capital Planning Commission
133	National Capital Planning Commission
134	National Capital Planning Commission
135	Eileen Christelow Ahrenholtz
136	Andreas Feininger